BASEBALL'S FABULOUS MONTREAL

Royals

The minor league team that made major league history

by William Brown

with a foreword by Ken Singleton

Cataloguing in Publication Data (Canada)

Brown, William, 1959-

The fabulous Montreal Royals : the minor league team that made major league history.

Includes bibliographical references and index.

ISBN 1-895854-64-4

1. Montreal Royals (Baseball team) - History. 2. Baseball teams - Quebec (Province) - Montréal - History. 3. Baseball - Quebec (Province) - Montréal - History. 4. Minor league baseball - Quebec (Province) - Montréal - History. 5. Baseball players - Quebec (Province) - Montréal - Biography. I. Scott, Terry. II. Title.

GV875.M66B76 1996   796.357'64'0971428   C96-941116-2

You can find our complete and ever-evolving
catalogue on the Internet at:

http://www.rdppub.com

BASEBALL'S FABULOUS MONTREAL

Royals

The minor league team that made major league history

by William Brown

edited by Terry Scott

with a foreword by Ken Singleton

ROBERT DAVIES PUBLISHING
MONTREAL 1996

Copyright © 1996, William Brown
ISBN 1-895854-64-4

Edited by Terry Scott
Book Design and production by Mary Hughson
Cover illustration: Jackie Robinson, interpreted by Mark Cavanagh
Cartoons by Aislin and John Collins
Photographs from the archives of *The Montreal Gazette* except where indicated.
Archives nationales du Québec photos : P48P1158, P48P2097, P48P12823, P48P12829.

ROBERT DAVIES PUBLISHING,
311-4999 Saint-Catherine Street, Westmount, Quebec, Canada H3Z 1T3
☎1-800-481-2440 / ☎ 1-514-481-2440 📠 1-888-RDAVIES

Distributed in Canada by General Distribution Services
☎1-800-387-0141 / ☎1-800-387-0172 📠 1-416-445-5967;

in the U.S.A., from General Distribution Services,
Suite 202, 85 River Rock Drive, Buffalo, NY 14287
☎ 1-800-805-1083

For all other countries, please order from publisher.

e-mail: rdppub@vir.com
Visit our Internet website: http://rdppub.com

The publisher takes this opportunity to thank the Canada Council
and the Ministère de la Culture du Québec (Sodec)
for their continuing support of publishing.

Dedication

This book is dedicated to my father,
who took me to the ballpark when I was a boy;
and to my mother,
who took me to the library.

Cartoon by, Aislin

Table of Contents

Foreword

In one of life's curious coincidences, Jackie Robinson broke big-league baseball's color barrier and reached the majors in 1947, the year I was born. Jackie died in 1972, the same year I was traded by the New York Mets to Montreal, the city in which Branch Rickey's "great experiment" was launched.

Indirectly, the Montreal Royals are a part of my boyhood baseball memories. My father was a staunch supporter of the Brooklyn Dodgers, whose major Triple A affiliate was the Royals. When I first got interested in televised baseball games, I would sit with my Dad in the living room of our New York home and watch performers such as Jackie Robinson, Roy Campanella, Don Newcombe, Dan Bankhead and Junior Gilliam. All of them had, at some point, served an apprenticeship in Montreal before joining the Dodgers.

In retrospect, one is struck by the immensity of the talent that passed through Montreal during the Royals' affiliation with the Dodgers. Brooklyn was renowned for having one of the finest farm systems in major-league baseball and Montreal fans truly had a unique opportunity to admire a galaxy of rising stars.

I don't know if watching Jackie and some of the other former Royals on a TV screen with my father inspired me to become a baseball player. I do know that I am indebted to Robinson and the men who followed in his footsteps for integrating major-league baseball.

Montreal played an integral role in that integration. In fact, Branch Rickey's "great experiment" was so successful it changed baseball and society forever. I think Montreal should be proud of the role it played in such an historical development.

Jackie Robinson made a tremendous impact in his one minor-league season in Montreal. But the Royals left their mark on minor-league baseball for a half-century, as this book well chronicles.

When I joined the Expos in 1972, I knew only that Montreal had enjoyed a great minor-league history. I also knew that there had been a lengthy gap between the demise of the Royals and the birth of the Expos.

As someone who played Triple A ball before reaching the majors with the New York Mets, I can relate to the special bond that exists between a minor-league club and its community. When the franchise is as successful and high-profile as the Royals were over the years, there are memories that last a lifetime.

This book is bound to rekindle some memories as it traces the evolution of baseball in Montreal.

— Ken Singleton

Ken Singleton in Expos uniform.

Delorimier Stadium, home to the Montreal Royals from 1928 to 1960.

Introduction

There Used to be a Ballpark Here

On a September evening in 1960, players from the Montreal Royals gathered at the top of Delorimier Stadium's dugout steps for a photograph. Dutifully, they arranged themselves shoulder-to-shoulder, kneeling on one knee, with an elbow or forearm set on the other. The players wore their white home uniforms with the blue piping around the collar and down the front of the shirt, where the word "Royals" appeared, as if hand-written, across the chest. Underneath blue caps, bearing the letter "M" in white, were a collection of faces, about to be frozen in time. Behind the players was a scattering of fans, vastly outnumbered by a backdrop of empty seats. The photo appeared in a Montreal newspaper the next morning with the caption: "END OF AN ERA?"

At the time of the snapshot the Royals were in last place and in the last days of the franchise's worst season in 33 years. For most of those years the club had been the top farm team of the Brooklyn Dodgers, the fabled, talented, hard-luck boys of the National League. Some of the best major leaguers of the 1940s and '50s had played for the Royals on their way to the Dodgers, and the Royals were usually the team to beat in the International League. But when the parent team left Brooklyn for the West Coast following the 1957 season, the Royals' days were numbered. The Los Angeles Dodgers established a Triple-A farm team in Spokane, Washington, which meant the Royals were no longer the organization's No. 1 affiliate.

In the past the Royals had boasted such future Dodgers' stars as Jackie Robinson, Carl Furillo, Roy Campanella, Duke Snider, Don Newcombe, Carl Erskine, Junior Gilliam and Don Drysdale. By the late 1950s, things had changed. The Royals were mainly stocked with veterans such as Sandy Amoros, Sparky Anderson and Tommy Lasorda - good minor league players who, in the case of Amoros and Lasorda, had some big-league experience but who were no longer considered to be major-league material. The Dodgers' future stars were now in Spokane, not Montreal.

The Dodgers sold Delorimier Stadium in 1956, after owning it for more than a decade, and were now merely tenants at the park, the Royals' home since 1928. By their last home game of 1960, the Dodgers still hadn't renewed their lease for the 1961 season, leaving the Royals' front office worried. The team's general manager, Fernand Dubois, spoke of an "ominous silence" on the part of the Dodgers. There was talk the Dodgers would sever ties with the Montreal team after the season ended the following week. The Royals lost the final home game to the Buffalo Bisons 7-4 in front of a measly 1,000 spectators, scattered throughout a stadium with a seating capacity of more than 20,000.

The Royals finished the season by losing three games in Rochester, including an 11-inning loss in the final game, on September 11, 1960. They finished the season with 62

Jackie Robinson and Branch Rickey embark on baseball's "Noble Experiment."

Two legendary Dodger managers. Walter Alston (left) took Tommy Lasorda under his wing when the two were Montreal Royals. Courtesy La Presse.

wins and 92 losses, almost 40 games out of first place. A few days later, the Dodgers announced they would not continue operating a team in Montreal. The organization said the Royals had been losing too much money over the last few seasons. Attendance had fallen sharply. In 1960 only 130,000 fans turned out at Delorimier Stadium. That was far short of the team's glory years in the '40s and '50s, when it often had the league's highest attendance figures. In 1949, the team drew more than 600,000 fans, one of the best-ever turnouts in the minor leagues. The arrival of televised baseball was cited as a reason for the Royals' demise. Others attributed it to boredom because the Royals had slipped competitively. And many thought it was time the city received a major-league franchise.

In the weeks that followed, there was some talk about local businessmen buying the Royals and possibly using the team as a springboard for a major-league club. The Dodgers were willing to sell the team and International League president Frank Shaughnessy approved of the idea but it never happened, and after 55 seasons the Royals expired. They left behind more than a newspaper photograph which signified the end of an era. They left a collage of memories that are the product of the hopes, joys and disappointments of 55 baseball seasons, each with a life and rhythm of its own. There were plenty of triumphs amid the trials and tribulations. The Royals won nine pennants, seven league championships and three Junior World Series' titles.

Until their death the Royals, who got their name from Mount Royal, the mountain in the middle of Montreal, were one of the cornerstones of the International League, baseball's oldest continually operating minor league. For anyone who actually remembers seeing Jackie Robinson carried around Delorimier Stadium following the Junior World Series championship in 1946 or

Jimmy Ripple make a diving, somersaulting catch in centre field, the legacy of the Royals is easy to define. It is a collection of memories that will surely be cherished for a lifetime. Memories of a long home run lofted over the stadium scoreboard onto the roof of the Knit-to-Fit factory next door. A home run that might have come off the bat of Rocky Nelson, once described by former major leaguer Bob Oldis as "the only guy who could make conversation, smoke a cigar, watch television, chew tobacco and read a pocketbook - all at the same time!"

But for those who have no first-hand memories of the team and wonder about the importance of a defunct minor-league baseball club, the legacy is no less remarkable. In September of 1959, after Jackie Robinson had retired from baseball and was active in the civil rights movement in the United States, he spoke at a business convention in Montreal. He expressed his everlasting appreciation for the way the city had embraced him in 1946. Without that support, he remarked, "I might not have had the courage to go on."

Roy Campanella, who played for the Royals on the way to a glittering but tragically short career with the Brooklyn Dodgers, once mused that Branch Rickey's plan to integrate baseball might never have worked had he not had a farm team in Montreal. He said he didn't know of any place in the United States where black players would have been so well received. Baseball scholar Jules Tygiel, who has studied baseball integration, feels that given Robinson's courage and determination, he would have succeeded anywhere he played, a sentiment shared by Jackie's wife Rachel. But both Tygiel and Rachel Robinson also believe that Jackie's positive experience in Montreal was a key factor in his success.

"I think it was all-important for his psychological well-being that when he went

Glenn "Rocky" Nelson brought a lot of lumber to the Royals' lineup.

on the road, he felt that he was leaving Rachel in a very warm environment," says Tygiel, adding that the enthusiastic support lavished on Robinson by adoring Montreal fans may have spurred him to even better performances. Rachel Robinson agrees. "We felt secure, respected and embraced in many ways," she recalls. "That allowed Jack to perform at the peak of his abilities."

Robinson wasn't the only player to benefit from the liberal racial attitudes in Montreal at the time. A number of other black players played for the Royals in the years following Robinson. Besides Campanella, there were such future Dodgers as Don Newcombe, Dan Bankhead, Junior Gilliam, Sandy Amoros and Joe Black. They were some of the pioneers who integrated baseball and made it a better game. They were members of the Montreal Royals before big-league clubs such as the New York Yankees, Detroit Tigers, Philadelphia Phillies and Boston Red Sox had even hired their first black player. In this way, the Royals played a crucial role in what has been described as one of the most important social developments of the 20th century.

Attending a ceremony in Montreal in 1996, marking her husband's 50th anniversary since his professional baseball debut with the Royals, Rachel Robinson said, "It was more than fortuitous that Branch Rickey sent us to Montreal. I think it was destiny in some way." It may have been destiny, too, that eight years after the demise of the Royals, Montreal was awarded a baseball franchise in the National League. But the trailblazing done by the Royals certainly didn't hurt Montreal's chances when it made its franchise bid. "You don't have to tell me anything about Montreal," said Dodgers owner and influential expansion committee member Walter O'Malley, when Montreal city councillor Gerry Snyder was lobbying for a franchise in 1968.

A picture is said to be worth at least a thousand words. But the team snapshot of the Royals on that September evening in 1960, didn't begin to chronicle the history of a franchise which was one of the jewels of baseball's minor leagues. Tommy Lasorda, the longest-serving member of the Royals spent nine years of his baseball career in Montreal. Duke Snider and Don Drysdale used it as a brief stopover on the way to stardom. But they, like the hundreds of others who wore Royal blue, are part of a collection of memories that began before the turn of the century, and endure long after the cheering has died.

Rachel Robinson, Chuck Connors and Tommy Lasorda in Montreal to unveil a statue of Jackie Robinson in 1987. Courtesy La Presse.

The 1948 Montreal Royals, lead by Chuck Connors (back row, centre), and Don Newcombe (back row, far right), won the pennant, league championship and Junior World Series.

1890-1907
A Home for Orphaned Ball Tossers

In the late 19th century, Montreal was a growing, bustling city of more than 200,000 people, the largest city in a country only 23 years old. With its large port on the St. Lawrence River and its extensive railway network, the city was a major transportation hub and an important centre for business and finance. Montreal was the head office of the Canadian National Railway, the transportation system built to unite the country from east to west. Culturally, it was unlike any other city in North America because of the large French-speaking and Catholic population. Although baseball was popular in the United States and, to a lesser degree, the neighboring province of Ontario, it was still a minor pastime in Montreal. In the 1860s, a city bylaw was passed prohibiting baseball in the city's parks because it was considered to be hazardous to other users. That led to the establishment of baseball clubs—groups of men who would get together on club grounds to play ball.

It has been estimated that approximately 40 baseball clubs were formed in Montreal in the 20 years following Confederation in 1867, but only a quarter of them survived more than two years. In that era, twice as many lacrosse clubs operated in the summer months, and the sport was recognized as Canada's national game. A new cricket club was formed in 1890 by the Montreal Amateur Athletic Association but the game's popularity was on the wane and its offspring - baseball - was becoming the preferred bat-and-ball sport in the city.

While baseball was a minor pastime in Montreal, played for fun at athletic clubs around town, it was a booming professional enterprise in the United States. Three major professional leagues, the National League, American Association and the short-lived Players' League were in operation in 1890. They represented large urban areas such as New York, Chicago, Boston, Philadelphia, Cleveland and St. Louis. The International League, a minor circuit established in 1884 as the Eastern League, represented smaller cities - Buffalo, Toronto and, briefly, Detroit. In Canada, three Ontario cities - Toronto, Hamilton and London, had been part of the International League in the 1880s. In fact, their inclusion had prompted the circuit to change its name to the International League. But despite the participation of these Ontario cities, Montreal was still reluctant to join the network of major and minor leagues which comprised Organized Baseball.

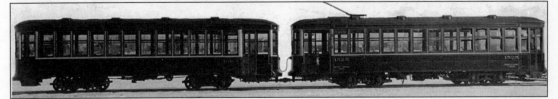

Streetcars and baseball games became increasingly popular sights in Montreal in the early 1900's.

Montreal at the turn of the century. The corner of Ste-Catherine and St-Laurent.

Part of the reason was that all but a few players in the league were Americans - even those who played in Canada - and many Montreal fans, especially those who spoke French, preferred watching local players. French-Canadians enjoyed amateur clubs such as Le National, which had a high content of Quebec-born, French-speaking players. And while the English-speaking community also enjoyed local amateur baseball, there was no great impetus on their part to join the International League. So it was somewhat unexpected when rumors started to circulate in the summer of 1890 that the International League's floundering Buffalo Bisons might transfer to Montreal to finish their season.

The owner of the Bisons, Charles D. White, was losing money because of the Players' League franchise in the city. The upstart league, which grew out of a clash between National League players and owners, only lasted one season but it lured enough fans from the Bisons to chase the team from Buffalo. White came to Montreal in early June to scout for a park where the team could play. He seemed unconcerned by the cool fan reaction to the idea. He saw a big, bustling city that he perceived as a potentially good baseball town, or at the very least, a welcoming port in a storm.

White liked the Shamrock Lacrosse Club grounds at the corner of Ste. Catherine Street and Atwater. A baseball diamond was laid out and Montreal joined Toronto, London, Hamilton, Detroit and Saginaw-Bay City (Michigan) in the International League - at least for a couple of weeks. The team played six games in early June - three in Montreal, one in Hamilton and two in London, losing five of the six games. The three games in Montreal didn't attract much interest, except for the initial one against Toronto. Two thousand fans attended that one hoping to see the Montreal squad "wipe up the earth with the team from Toronto," as one newspaper put it, but the visitors were 11-10

winners. Montreal won the next day before a crowd which was half the size of the first one, and already it seemed the novelty of professional baseball in Montreal had worn off. The league promptly transferred the team to Grand Rapids, Mich.

But before the team could be missed, the Montreal "cranks", as baseball fans were called in those days, received another chance. The Hamilton franchise went broke and was transferred to Montreal. The team played nine games, winning only three, and the two games at the Shamrock Grounds attracted few spectators. Those on hand were unimpressed by the team's play and appearance. The disowned players sported tattered uniforms with the name Montreal stitched sloppily over the faded silhouette of the previous logo.

The club had represented Montreal for nine games when the league suspended play in early July. The Players' League had grabbed enough playing talent to make things difficult for many International League franchises, not just Buffalo and Hamilton. Fortunately for the I.L., the Players' League folded at the end of the 1890 season, and the minor league resumed operations, although it changed its name to the Eastern Association.

It was back in business without Montreal, however, an absence that disappointed only a few diehards. The idea of having a professional team in Montreal appealed to some, but the feeling persisted that it should be home-grown. Most people shared the view expressed by a Montreal Gazette writer who asked indignantly: "Why should Montreal be called upon to father every insolvent aggregation of peripatetic ball-tossers that can find nowhere else to take them in?" The common response was: "It shouldn't! "So baseball went back to being an amateur pastime in Montreal.

The idea of the city having a professional team wasn't permanently shelved. It was simply on hold, until the right moment. In fact, some of the keener baseball people in the city were already mapping strategy. One of them was Joe Page, an American who worked for the Canadian Pacific Railway. He had played baseball in his native state of Indianapolis, and was a good friend of James Edward "Tip" O'Neill, Canada's first major-league baseball star. Tip O'Neill, of Woodstock, Ontario, won two batting titles for the St. Louis Browns of the American Association during an outstanding, 10-year major-league career. He was an all-star four times and became such a beloved figure that many American boys were nicknamed "Tip" in his honor. "Tip" O'Neill, the former speaker of the U.S. House of Representatives, was among those so nicknamed. A monicker that apparently stemmed from the ball-playing O'Neill's ability to foul-tip pitches at will.

Page and O'Neill combined in the mid 1890s to assemble a professional team in Montreal, using itinerant American players and whatever local talent they deemed good enough. By 1896, O'Neill had moved on to other interests, but Page found financial backers and got the team some uniforms—gray, with bottle-green piping and knickerbockers. The team played a few games in the summer of 1896 against teams from the province's Eastern Townships and some American college teams. But it was informal and many of the players quit en masse before a game in Hull, Quebec.

Joe Page, pioneer of professional baseball in Montreal.

Page's dream of a professional team in Montreal and a possible return to the International League (now temporarily calling itself the Eastern League) might have ended there had New England sports promoter William H. Rowe not come aboard, bringing a number of players with him. The season was saved and continued with a new vitality. A month later, 1,200 people were at the Shamrock Grounds to see Montreal confront a team from Plattsburgh, NY. The exhibition tour was a success, thanks to Rowe's timely rescue, and he and Page decided to expand their horizons for 1897. Page spent much of the spring travelling to Ontario and the Eastern US. trying to schedule games.

Several games were lined up but in the middle of June, nine games into the schedule, an opportunity arose in the Eastern League. The Wilkes-Barre, Pa. team was in trouble and Montreal was mentioned as a possible new home. Rowe, who'd been managing the touring Montreal squad, put the season on hold and tackled the new project. He found some investors for the new team, including Major George Cameron of Montreal, and was preparing a bid for the Wilkes-Barre franchise when another Eastern League team was forced to seek new headquarters. The ball park in Rochester burned down and the club, named the Jingoes, needed a home for the rest of the season. Since the Wilkes-Barre option was still uncertain, Rowe shifted gears and pursued this new opportunity.

League president Pat Powers was concerned by the past failures of International League teams in Montreal. He also felt the city was too far from the other franchises. But Rowe was persuasive, assuring Powers he had sufficient money to run the team and suggesting that travel problems could be solved with some creative scheduling. On July 16, 1897, Powers agreed to transfer the Rochester Jingoes to Montreal, and the team joined Syracuse, Toronto, Buffalo, Springfield, Providence, Scranton and Wilkes-Barre in the Eastern League. Rowe used some of the money he had raised to erect a new grandstand and improve the quality of the playing field. The Shamrock Grounds were now the Montreal Baseball Grounds, and would soon be called Atwater Park.

Powers attended the first game in Montreal -- an 11-10 loss to Wilkes-Barre – and approved of both the new facilities and the turnout. Not as pleased was starting centre-fielder and player-manager George Weidman, who didn't like Montreal and quit the team shortly after the first game. His replacement was first-baseman Charlie Dooley, called "Handsome Charlie" because of his brown eyes and bushy handlebar moustache. Dooley was one of the team's better players, along with second-baseman Fred "Snake" Henry and right-fielder Jack Shearon.

The team won a few games in its new city but, inheriting a poor record from the Rochester Jingoes, it finished seventh and was plagued by poor attendance. Fans weren't sure whether they liked this latest "peripatetic bunch of ball-tossers," and couldn't even decide what to call them. The Snowbirds, Canuck Juniors, the Frenchmen and the Eskimos were some of the suggestions (although there were certainly no Canucks, Frenchmen, or Eskimos on the team). It was also suggested the team be called the Royals after Mount Royal, the mountain in the middle of the city. But like a stray cat taken in out of pity rather than affection, the team was never officially named by the public, who generically called it the Montreals, L'Equipe de Montreal, or the Montreal Baseball Club.

Despite the fans' ambivalence, the league decided to keep the team in Montreal for 1898 season. Major Cameron spent some money to improve the club's park, building a new grandstand and adding bleachers in the outfield. He also established a reserved-seating section and sold season tickets: a 68 home-game package went for $20. The changes to the stands raised seating capacity to between four and five thousand. Cameron also built a new clubhouse for the players and overhauled the playing field. In 1987 the infield had been so uneven and pebble-filled it was a nightmare for fielders and hazardous for base runners brave enough to slide on it.

The new grounds were well received but the real surprise of the season was the team's strong play. Dooley and Shearon led the way along with shortstop Shad Barry, pitcher Dan McFarlan and two brothers from Amesbury, Mass., Jimmy and Tommy Bannon. Jimmy, whose nickname was "Foxy Grandpa", was an infielder but could pitch an inning or two if necessary, and his older brother Tommy was an outfielder. Neither brother was particularly big and both were pushing 30, but they were aggressive and emotional players who gave the team a keen competitive edge. The consensus in spring training was that Dooley had assembled a good-looking ball club, but many observers were still shocked to see the team leading the pack in July. But Montreal made believers out of everyone when it clinched the pennant in the first week of September, rising from seventh place in 1897 to a championship the first full season in Montreal.

The pennant surprised and delighted the city's baseball fans. Major Cameron decided to celebrate the triumph on the final day of the season, a home doubleheader against Buffalo (the Bisons had returned after the demise of the Players League). Cameron invited Montreal Mayor J. R. F. Préfontaine to toss out the first pitch, as he had done for the home opener four months earlier. Both teams travelled to the stadium in horse-drawn carriages, accompanied by a military band. Celebrations continued after the teams split a sloppy, lacklustre doubleheader.

A charity game was organized to raise some extra cash for the players, who pocketed $30 each, and the team went on a barnstorming tour of the province of Quebec. Dooley was praised as a fine manager and Cameron was commended for turning Atwater Park into a place where "a gentleman could take a lady, a father his children without fear of unpleasant consequences." It was said that "some of the best people in the city have been regular attendants at the games." It was also mentioned, as often as possible, that in winning the Eastern League pennant, Montreal had accomplished in a season and a-half what Toronto hadn't managed in seven.

Most of the players on the pennant-winning team were back the next season, although Jimmy Bannon left to join Toronto and won the 1899 batting title with a .341 average. Montreal managed to maintain its quota of Bannons, however, by acquiring outfielder George Bannon, Jim and Tom's brother. The team did well but couldn't quite catch Rochester and finished in second place with a respectable .519 winning percentage.

Over the next few seasons, some of the players who had helped Dooley win the 1898 pennant left the club, including Tom and George Bannon, and the team suffered as a result. Dooley scoured the minor leagues for players, but couldn't acquire enough

"Handsome Charlie" Dooley was a popular Montreal player-manager from 1897 to 1902.

talent to keep the team from plummeting toward the bottom of the standings. Montreal finished no higher than sixth in the next three seasons. In 1902, headlines in The Gazette sports section conveyed impatience

(WE LOST ONCE MORE), dismay (THE VERY WORST YET) and abject misery (IT IS REALLY AWFUL).

Although the team was struggling, fan support increased and there seemed to be a loyal, if not large following for professional baseball in Montreal. It was a rude shock when rumblings from Eastern League headquarters hinted that Montreal might be squeezed out of the circuit to make room for Baltimore. The threat arose because of manoeuvring by Ban Johnson, the president of the brand-new American League. After operating for two seasons, Johnson wanted a New York team in the league for 1903, so he dumped the Baltimore Orioles and signed up the New York Highlanders (later the Yankees). The move induced the Orioles to seek a franchise in the Eastern League and, mindful that Baltimore was a proven baseball town, league president Powers was delighted to oblige.

The problem was deciding which existing club to drop. Only two candidates were considered: Rochester and Montreal. The Rochester team had finished seventh in 1902 and was a disaster at the box-office. The Royals had done better in both departments, but many owners still resented having to send their teams on all-night train rides to

The 1902 Montreal entry in the Eastern League was dropped to make room for Baltimore. Courtesy Don McGowan.

get to Montreal. (Rochester would sometimes travel on a steamer across Lake Ontario and then down the St. Lawrence River). Some owners called the Montreal franchise the "thorn in the flesh of the league." There was also the impression fans in Montreal didn't know much about baseball and didn't appreciate the game. One Buffalo sportswriter described his distaste at having to attend a game at Atwater Park amongst a "frog-eating bunch of flannel mouths" who spoke in "French sentences chewed off in the middle, Irish 'come-all-ye's,' and English sputters."

It wasn't a big surprise, therefore, when Powers announced that Montreal had drawn the short straw. "The addition of Baltimore to our league will be an excellent thing for all the cities of our circuit," he said. Not so excellent for Montreal baseball fans, however, many of whom found the news hard to believe until it was reported that Charlie Dooley himself had invested in the Orioles. "Handsome Charlie" was always on the lookout for a good business deal, and at 34 he knew his playing days were near an end. He was offered a piece of the new franchise, and jumped at the opportunity. His departure, after directing the team from his post at first base for five-and-a-half seasons, dashed hopes of a last-minute reprieve for the team.

Montreal applied for a franchise in the New York State League, but was rejected and there was talk of forming a new league, comprising teams from Quebec, Ontario and nearby U.S. states. But when nothing had happened by the beginning of July, with the 1903 baseball season half over, it seemed the year would be a complete write-off for Montreal in terms of pro baseball. Just when fans were about to abandon hope, another floundering franchise landed in their laps.

The Eastern League team in Worcester, Mass., in its fifth season of operation, was in

trouble and its owner, P.H. Hurley, was considering moving the team to Montreal. This got things churning in the city's baseball circles and a Montreal police officer, Timothy Connors, a native of Worcester, visited his home town to speak with Hurley. Laying it on a bit thick, he assured the club owner that "the public at large (in Montreal) cannot be made to stop raving for baseball." Whether it was Connors' rhetoric that turned the trick, or the city's reputation as a suitable foster home for wayward baseball teams, Hurley agreed to move his club to Montreal.

So after only a few months' absence Montreal was back in the Eastern League, replete with another motley collection of orphaned ballplayers. Fans had just been getting used to the old crew, agreeing on the Royals, or Les Royaux, as a nickname, but what about this new group? What should they be called? The safest thing seemed to be a return to something generic like the Montreals - at least until they got to know the players better. Indeed, the only player the least bit familiar to most fans was the manager-second baseman, Eugene Napoleon DeMontreville. He had enjoyed a distinguished career in the major leagues for several clubs, compiling a .303 average in 11 seasons. As it was in 1897, when the city inherited the Rochester team at mid-season, Worcester was near the cellar when it was transferred and the change of scenery didn't help much. The team ended the season in seventh place with a record of 37-94.

Professional baseball was back in Montreal but several years of instability and disorganization loomed. In 1904, the team was bought by Buffalo businessman John Kreitner, who fired DeMontreville and put Charles Atherton, the team's third baseman, in charge. But by the second week of August, with the team in fifth place, Atherton was traded and Edward G. Barrow was hired to run the team. Barrow had bought into the Toronto franchise in 1900 and, as manager,

Montreal was back in the Eastern League by 1904, with a brand new squad. Courtesy Don McGowan.

led the team to the Eastern League pennant in 1902. He was snapped up by the American League's Detroit Tigers the following year but left during the 1904 season. Barrow was a respected manager and might have improved the troubled Montreal team had he returned for the 1905 season. But he quit, eventually re-joining the Toronto club, and that forced Kreitner to again beat the bushes for a replacement.

Kreitner's next move was to hire old Montreal favorite Jimmy Bannon, a member of the 1898 pennant-winning team. Bannon, now 33, was pried loose from the Eastern League's Newark squad for $500 and given the job of managing and playing second base. His return seemed to establish a link with the past and the nickname "Royals" was back in vogue. But Bannon could lift the team no higher than sixth place in the next two seasons. In fact, his stubborn personality often hurt the club. He pulled his team off

the field once during a game against the Jersey City Skeeters, after arguing a ruling which had actually gone in his favor. With the score tied 1-1 in the fifth inning, the home-plate umpire made a tough call against Jersey City and a few of the players argued vehemently. Several Skeeters were ejected which should have pleased Bannon, but he complained about which Skeeters were ejected and refused to resume play. The game was awarded to Jersey City by forfeit.

A staunch supporter of unionized labor, Bannon almost forfeited another game, this time in Rochester, when he discovered the bus driver hired to take the team to the ball park was a non-union worker. The stand earned him a gold badge from the Central Trades and Labor Union, but didn't win any accolades from his employers. Nor did it help matters when George Bannon, who had returned to Montreal to play for his brother, was suspended for punching out an

Future Hall of Fame baseball man, Clark Griffith was a part owner of the Montreal Royals.

"Wee Willie" Keeler, a future Hall-of-Famer, also had a stake in the Montreal team.

After buying the club Farrell sent a few players to shore up the roster. He also tried to replace Bannon as manager. Griffith, who was a good friend of former Montreal manager Ed Barrow, tried unsuccessfully to coax him to leave Toronto and return to Montreal for the 1906 season. When that ploy failed Farrell re-hired Bannon, but by mid August he was so exasperated with the manager's shenanigans, he suspended him without pay for insubordination and started seeking a replacement.

Farrell again approached Barrow about leaving Toronto but struck out. He considered offering the job to the Highlanders steady infielder Joe Yeager, who had played for the Royals in 1904 and won the Eastern League batting title with a .332 average. Finally, he decided to hire Malachi Kittridge, just winding up a 16-year career as a major-league catcher. He had played for six big-league teams, including a stint as player-manager for the Washington Senators in 1904. As the 1906 season waned, Kittridge was seeing only limited action with Cleveland and decided to take the job in Montreal.

Kittridge had never been much of a hitter, but was regarded as a top-notch catcher. In one of his first outings behind the plate for Montreal, at the age of 36, he threw out four baserunners. His credentials as a player weren't in doubt, but as a manager, he was parachuted into the middle of a losing season and wasn't able to improve things much. The team ended up seventh, a familiar spot, winning 57 games and losing 83. The only positive development was that support for baseball in Montreal remained steady, despite the chaos. The fans didn't turn out in huge numbers but they were loyal. The last day of the season, a crowd of 1,000 were on hand at Atwater Park, on a day so cold and rainy even the umpires

umpire. The Battling Bannon Brothers were a colorful pair but the team's new owners, who took baseball very seriously, were fed up with them.

Following the 1905 season, Kreitner sold the Royals to a New York group headed by Frank Farrell, the owner of the New York Highlanders of the American League. Also involved in the deal was the Highlander's player-manager Clark Griffith, a talented future Hall-of-Famer who made his name as a pitcher, manager and - when his playing days were over - the long-time owner of the Washington Senators. Highlanders outfielder didn't show up. A player from each team had to officiate in the umpires' absence.

Such enthusiasm continued into 1907, when 4,000 people showed up for the home opener against Buffalo despite virtually unplayable conditions. Rain and melting ground frost created puddles and ponds all over the field. Players donned hip-waders and rubber boots. Some even stood on planks of wood. Buffalo protested having to play in the swampy conditions but the game was played nonetheless, and the Bisons won 10-3. The teams tried to play the next day at the Shamrock Grounds, the new home of the Shamrocks lacrosse team, but conditions weren't much better. Once again, 4,000 fans braved the abysmal conditions.

A correspondent from The Sporting Life, taking in a Royals' game in 1907, remarked that although a crowd of three or four thousand was considered a good draw for a baseball game in Montreal, a lacrosse match could attract three times as many. But he was impressed with the enthusiasm for the game. "The French-Canadians are great ball-fiends," he wrote. Indeed, support for the team was steady and use of the nickname Royals or Les Royaux was becoming widespread, even though the team continued to struggle. Before the end of July, with the squad in last place, Farrell fired Kittridge and replaced him with the team's third baseman, Jimmy Morgan. That didn't solve much. The Royals finished the season in the cellar with an atrocious 46-85 record and Morgan wasn't re-hired. The team was now looking for its ninth manager in 12 seasons. From both an organizational and a baseball standpoint the Royals were a mess heading into the 1908 season. The nightmare worsened when a fire destroyed the grandstand at Atwater Park.

The future of minor-league professional baseball in Montreal was again murky. But unlike other times, when the coming or going of the team brought only a yawn, the Royals were now part of the Montreal sports scene and there was a growing sentiment that something should be done. Many thought the team should be re-claimed by Montrealers instead of being run out of the office of the New York Highlanders. As it turned out, the feeling was mutual. In the winter of 1908, Frank Farrell sent an emissary to Montreal to gauge local interest in buying the Royals. The emissary was George Stallings, one of the Eastern League's most distinguished citizens and a man would play an enormous role in the future of baseball in Montreal.

Joe Page (right), not just a baseball promoter, welcomes heavy-weight champ Gene Tunney to Montreal.

1908-1917

Growing Pains and the Heartache of Rejection

George Stallings was called "Gentleman George" because of his dapper appearance.

George Tweedy Stallings was a prosperous southern gentleman of 40 when he arrived in Montreal in January, 1908. The son of a Confederate general and the owner of a successful plantation, he was in the process of making a name for himself in another field of endeavor. Following a brief, unimpressive career as a major-league player and manager before the turn of the century, Stallings bought into the Buffalo Bisons of the Eastern League and, as manager, led

them to pennants in 1904 and 1906. Both times the team participated in a Little World Series against the champs of the rival American Association and won the title. These were the first two Little World Series ever played. (The series was omitted in 1905 and dropped after 1907, only returning for good in 1920. Its name was changed to the Junior World Series in 1931.)

It was first assumed that Stallings was interested in buying the Royals himself and rumors circulated that Charlie Dooley, a former minor league teammate of "Gentleman George", would return as manager. But Stallings made it clear he was in Montreal on behalf of Frank Farrell, who hoped to sell the Royals because of other business demands. In the three years he had owned the team, Farrell never once set foot in Montreal. He believed Stallings, who knew the city fairly well, would be a suitable agent. Stallings had made a number of contacts on his trips to the city as Buffalo manager and he looked them up during his visit in 1908.

In late January, Stallings successfully brokered a deal between Farrell and three Montreal businessmen who would become the new owners of the Royals. They were E.R. Carrington, manager of the Thiel Detective Service, Hubert Cushing, vice-president of The Montreal Brewing Company and Sam Lichtenhein, a local sports promoter. The Montreal group paid $10,000

Atwater Park (seen here after the Royals had moved to Delorimier Stadium) was where the team played for 21 seasons.

for the franchise and the 16 players under contract and spent $1,500 on a 38-year-old Brooklyn Dodgers third baseman named James "Doc" Casey. A dentist from Lawrence, Mass., Casey reached the majors at the advanced age of 28 and stayed there for 10 seasons. He was considered to be a solid citizen in every way and the Royals hoped he would be a solid player-manager.

None of the new investors had much experience in baseball but they realized they needed a good park for the team to be successful. That meant re-building the charred stands at Atwater Park, or finding a new place to play. During his visit to Montreal, Stallings had scouted a few sites and was especially impressed with Mascotte Park at the corner of Delorimier (now de Lorimier) and Ontario Street, in the city's east end. The park was the home field of the Mascottes amateur baseball team. One advantage to relocating was that the Royals

could play home games on Sunday, something the seminary that owned Atwater Park forbade. It would save the team having to play its Sunday games at the Shamrock Grounds as it did now. On the other hand, the seminary was willing to lower the rent because of the damage to the grandstand, so Carrington, Cushing and Lichtenhein decided to stay. They rebuilt the stands, restoring the seating capacity to approximately 5,000.

The home opener in 1908 against the Providence Grays, was a tremendous success for the new owners, although they probably wished they had added a few seats to the park while the were rebuilding it. About 5,200 fans showed up, filling the brand-new grandstand and overflowing the bleachers onto the outfield grass, occasionally getting in the players' way. The Royals booted two plays, allowing the Grays to tie the score 5-5 in the ninth. It was still tied after 11 innings, when the umpire called the game because of darkness and it was re-scheduled for a later date.

The 1908 Royals were improved over the previous year, winning 18 more games and climbing out of last place, but they were still out of pennant contention and had to settle for fifth spot in the standings. They were the best hitting team in the league, led by batting champ Jimmy "Sheriff" Jones with a .309 average, but their defense was the worst. It was almost the reverse in 1909, with infielder Joe Yeager, back with the Royals after leaving the Highlanders, anchoring a tighter defense, but centre-fielder Jones had a sub-par year at the plate.

By the end of the season the Royals were in the middle of the pack, prompting Lichtenhein, the team's president and majority shareholder, to fire Casey. Despite the Royals' mediocrity and the fact they went through managers like wads of chewing tobacco, Montreal baseball fans stood by their team. On July 1, 1909 - Canada's national holiday - a record 7,000 fans crammed into Atwater Park, with hundreds straddling the foul lines, to watch the Royals play.

In 1910, Lichtenhein improved the club by accomplishing what Frank Farrell had been unable to do: he brought back Ed Barrow to manage the team. Barrow had been out of baseball for a few years, but Lichtenhein was sure he could build a winning team in Montreal. After signing Barrow, a man he hoped would be with the organization for years, Lichtenhein spruced up Atwater Park. The team had been short of seating a few times in 1909 and didn't want a repeat scenario, so about 1,000 seats were added. Lichtenhein also joined the third-base bleachers to the main grandstand, covered the entire structure with a roof and made the playing diamond smoother and more uniform. The park could now seat between six and seven thousand, depending on how

Ed Barrow, the man the Royals couldn't hang on to.

many could be squeezed into the bleachers. The final touch in the off-season improvements was a new uniform featuring grey pants and jerseys with blue trim, blue stockings and caps and a blue "M" on the left side of the jersey and sleeve.

Lichtenhein was so thrilled to have Barrow, a man of long-term baseball vision, he gave him a free hand to operate the club. "We have given Barrow absolute control over the team," he said. "We will not interfere with him in any way." Although the club only marginally improved under Barrow in 1910, Lichtenhein threw a party for him following the season, presenting him with a gold-watch fob and reiterating he could manage the Royals as long as he wanted. There were toasts all around, with Lichtenhein drinking to the health of U.S. President William Taft, and Barrow reciprocating by proposing a toast to King George V.

But Lichtenhein's dreams of Barrow building a winner in Montreal were dashed when Pat Powers stepped down as Eastern League President and Barrow was hired to replace him. In retrospect, Lichtenhein was right to value Barrow's baseball acumen. After eight seasons as league president (during which he re-named the circuit the International League), Barrow went on to become a successful general manager in the major leagues, most notably in New York, where he was an architect for the Yankees' dynasty of the 1920s and '30's.

Barrow's departure signalled a resumption of the Royals' roller-coaster ride. The team's business manager, Eddie McCafferty, was named manager for the 1911 season and his first move was to release centrefielder Jimmy Jones. The "Sheriff" was a wild character who aspired to one day succeed his brother as sheriff of London, Ky., his home town. He was said to be a quick draw with a pistol and had a hair-trigger temper to match. A couple of seasons earlier, after being criticized by McCafferty for not hustling, Jones attacked and beat up the business manager. As soon as McCafferty assumed the Royals' reins, he decided Montreal wasn't big enough for both of them and he rode "Sheriff" out of town.

Jones's spot was more-that-adequately filled by Ward Miller, who led the team in hitting with a .322 average and was the league's top base-stealer with 63. Joe Yeager and Chick Gandil (a future member of the notorious Chicago White Sox who threw the 1919 World Series) had good years at the plate for Montreal, both hitting .300. But overall the team showed little improvement under McCafferty, reclaiming its usual fifth spot. The team's minority shareholders, Hubert Cushing and E.J. Carrington, were unhappy. They wanted Lichtenhein to fire McCafferty but the team president refused. The issue caused a serious rift and Lichtenhein offered to sell out to his associates for $50,000. He had other

Chic Gandil, a member of the infamous 1919 Chicago "Black Sox", was a Montreal Royal in 1911 and 1912.

interests besides the Royals. He owned the Montreal Wanderers hockey team and Montreal's Jubilee Ice Skating rink and wanted to sell the Royals anyway. But Cushing and Carrington didn't take

Lichtenhein up on the offer and the matter was still unsettled with the 1912 season just a few months away.

McCafferty realized that even if Lichtenhein pulled rank and retained him as manager, he would still have Cushing and Carrington on his back. He didn't want to work under those conditions, so he decided to go into business with one of the team's pitchers, Fred Burchell, who had just bought the Syracuse franchise in the New York State League. Burchell had obtained his release from Montreal to become the Syracuse manager and he offered McCafferty the club presidency. McCafferty accepted but told no one. Sometime in January, 1912, his name was spotted on the Syracuse team's letterhead and all hell broke loose. Why, it was asked, had the Montreal manager kept the matter secret?

Newspaper stories appearing in New York and Buffalo claimed the whole thing was an attempt by Barrow to move the Montreal franchise to Syracuse, and that Barrow's old buddy Lichtenhein was in on the scam. The stories asserted Lichtenhein was tired of paying the high transportation costs associated with having a team in Montreal and had bought the Syracuse team himself, using Burchell and McCafferty as front men. The stories sent shock waves through Montreal baseball circles. Was Montreal about to lose its team again? Was Lichtenhein involved in the caper?

All parties denied the reports and the conspiracy theory fell apart when no evidence surfaced to support it. Fears that the team would be lost were allayed, but Lichtenhein was left on the defensive and without a manager a few weeks from spring training. He searched for an experienced hand to steady the team and found Billy Lush, a former major leaguer most recently the coach of the Yale University baseball team. It was a good choice on paper but

accomplished nothing, and in late July, with the team wallowing near the bottom of the standings, Lush was replaced by William "Kitty" Bransfield, a 12-year major-league first baseman.

The mid-season managerial change was no more successful than it had been in the past and the Royals finished sixth. It was decided, however, not to fire Bransfield after only a half-season and he was hired for the following year. Montreal improved marginally in 1913, finishing fifth with a record of 74-77, a .490 winning percentage. It was the closest the team had come to playing .500 baseball since their .519 record of 1904. The performance earned Bransfield a contract for 1914, a rehiring made easier by the steady fan support. Seven thousand fans had come out for the 1913 home opener, inducing one sports reporter to comment that "baseball is commencing to look like the national game."

But by the early summer of 1914 the Royals were floundering again and Bransfield's job was in jeopardy. The manager seemed to have lost the respect of some of his players. In June, during a tight game against Toronto, he yanked a pitcher who had just loaded the bases. The pitcher was so angry he didn't wait to give the ball to Bransfield. He stormed off the mound and threw the ball into the crowd. A month later, Bransfield was fired by Lichtenhein and one of the team's catchers, Dan Howley, became the 14th Montreal manager in 18 seasons.

If Howley believed in omens he had to be worried when, shortly after inheriting the job, the main grandstand at Atwater Park burned down for the second time in seven years. Lichtenhein erected some temporary, carnival-style stands and said he would check his finances at the end of the year to determine what could be done about rebuilding for 1915. The team fell to last place after the change in managers and stayed there until the bitter end, winning only 48 games and losing 106, its worst season ever.

Lichtenhein had a few things to consider about the fate of Atwater Park in the spring of 1915. Canada was several months into the fighting in Europe and Montrealers were preoccupied with the war effort. War stories dominated the newspapers and there was less coverage of sports. But Lichtenhein decided to rebuild anyway, erecting a new grandstand at Atwater Park and moving the diamond closer to the stands, creating more intimacy for the fans. The team staged its home-opener in mid-May, but Lichtenhein probably wondered if he had done the right thing when a scant 1,500 souls were scattered throughout the refurbished ball yard. The 1915 season brought another fifth-place finish, despite the efforts of centre-fielder Lucky Whiteman, who hit .312 and led the league in homers (in an anemic year for power hitters, he only needed 14 to accomplish it).

Howley was a capable manager, although he wasn't afforded much in the way of talent on the field. There were tough times off the field, too. In the spring of 1916, while in Manhattan, Howley fell in the path of a moving streetcar as he sprinted across Broadway and narrowly missed being run over. Fortunately, neither he nor the Royals stumbled too badly during the season. In fact, the team finished in third place, the best showing since 1899, when it was second. Second baseman, James Smythe won the batting title by hitting .344 and pitcher Leon Cadore went 25-14 to lead the league. At last the team seemed on an upward swing, a reason for optimism as Howley led his troops into the 1917 season. That optimism, however, was tempered by some troop movements elsewhere.

In April of 1917, President Woodrow Wilson committed the United States to the War in Europe and baseball players joined the service. That exacerbated a player

shortage which had started with the launching of the Federal League in 1914. The rival major league lasted only two seasons but they were years in which baseball had to compete with movies and increased automobile travel to attract fan attention. The player raids conducted by the Federal League added to an already difficult situation. Of the 42 minor leagues in organized baseball in 1914, only 20 started the 1917 season. Now, with players enlisting in military service, only half of those minor leagues survived the the 1917 season.

Canada had already been at war for three years by this time and it was obvious that baseball interest was waning. Coverage of Royals' games in newspapers was limited to brief accounts from a news wire, often lacking the usual statistical information such as box scores. Attendance was down throughout the minor leagues and Montreal was no exception. Schemes were devised to revive interest in the minors: one was to restore the Little World Series in 1917. That was accomplished, but it was subsequently dropped again until 1920. The other plan was for teams in the two leagues to meet in intra-league games during the season but that fell apart at the last minute.

For Royals' supporters, the glow from the 1916 season quickly faded in 1917, when the team lost its home-opener 12-2 against Providence. It was generally agreed that Mayor Médéric Martin, who threw out the ceremonial first pitch, was the best Montreal pitcher of the day. By the end of June the team was in last place. During one game in late July the Royals committed eight errors. By the first week of September the team had clawed its way into seventh place, but just when it seemed about to make a move on a long homestand, heavy rains forced the transfer of some games to opposing parks. The Royals were one of many franchises which had to cope with a record number of rainouts in 1917.

The Royals managed to stay out of last place by a handful of games, finishing seventh with a 56-94 record. But as soon as the season concluded there was talk the league might suspend play until the end of the war. In December of 1917, the owners narrowly voted to continue in 1918. But the teams eager to keep going - Baltimore, Toronto, Rochester and Newark - wanted some changes. According to International League historian Bill O'Neal, some owners felt that for the league to survive it had to get rid of the teams on its geographical fringes: notably Montreal, Richmond and Providence. The owners maintained that travel restrictions imposed by the war effort would make commuting to these cities too difficult. It was also noted that the owners of all three of these far-flung franchises had voted against the league resuming play.

While Lichtenhein was willing to operate again in 1918, he wasn't enthusiastic. "We don't believe in operating the league under existing conditions for the benefit of a couple of clubs who will make money," he said. It was clear Lichtenhein wasn't going to put up much of a fight if a majority of other owners wanted Montreal out of the International League.

In the end, it was decided to oust Montreal, Providence and Richmond and replace them with Binghampton, Syracuse and Jersey City - cities a little closer to the other franchises. Lichtenhein had done his part, running the club for 10 seasons, rebuilding the stadium twice and changing managers five times. But now he was bowing out. And after a tumultuous two decades involving hundreds of players; 13 managers; a half-dozen owners; one pennant; a second-place finish; and 20 less impressive outcomes, Montreal, which had dropped out of the league and resurfaced three times, was disappearing again, and most people didn't seem to care.

The season ended on a freezing day in September, with only a handful of fans at Atwater Park to watch the team's main rival, the Toronto Maple Leafs. The teams combined for eight home runs, 28 hits, six errors and an assortment of walks and wild pitches. The Royals trailed by six runs in the ninth, but scraped and clawed and scored six times to tie it 16-16. Toronto eventually won with three 12th-inning runs. It was the last game the Royals would play in Montreal for more than a decade. Afterwards, the reporter covering the game for The Gazette said the fans came to the ball park in a state of disgust and "they were glad the final game of the season was being played. It was too much for anyone with a weak heart to stand for a whole season."

International League owners in 1915. Montreal's Sam Lichtenhein is in the bottom row, far right. Two years later, Montreal, Richmond and Providence were banished from the league.

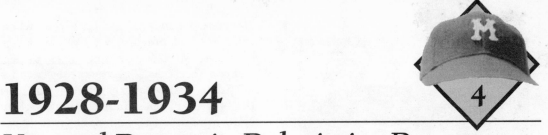

1928-1934

Ups and Downs in Delorimier Downs

Brilliant sunshine and a clear blue sky blessed Montreal on the first Saturday in May, 1928. It was cool but an occasional warm breeze suggested summer was on the way, following two weeks of wet snow and rain. The abysmal weather had delayed the home-opener of the Royals, now returning to the International League and professional baseball for the first time since the 1917 season.

As the sun gradually warmed the chilled city, it dried the soggy turf of a new stadium nestled among the houses and factories of an east-end neighborhood. For the last few days, groundskeepers had worked frantically to prepare the field. There was no grass in the infield yet and the turf was soft and spongy, but the ball park, located at the corner of Delorimier and Ontario Street, was ready for the Royals, who had started the season on the road and returned home in third place with a 6-4 record.

Many of Montreal's baseball fans couldn't wait to see the new Delorimier Stadium. On the Friday before the game, hundreds wandered into the park to look around and get a feel for the place. They walked up and

Construction of Delorimier Stadium began in January, 1928, and was completed just in time for Montreal's re-entry into the International League.

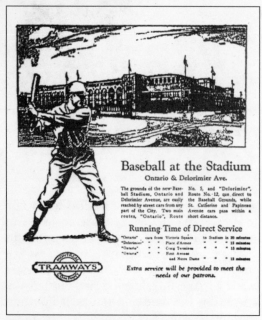

Baseball at the Stadium
Ontario & Delorimier Ave.

The grounds of the new Baseball Stadium, Ontario and
Delorimier Avenue, are easily
reached by street cars from any
part of the City. Two main
routes, "Ontario", Route

No. 5, and "Delorimier",
Route No. 12, run direct to
the Baseball Grounds, while
the St. Catherine and Papineau
Avenue cars pass within a
short distance.

Running Time of Direct Service

"Ontario"	cars from Victoria Square	to Stadium in 20 minutes	
"Delorimier"	"	"	Place d'Armes	"	"	15 minutes
"Ontario"	"	"	Craig Terminus	"	"	15 minutes
"Ontario"	"	"	Fort Avenue		
	and Notre Dame	"	"	15 minutes

*Extra service will be provided to meet the
needs of our patrons.*

TRAMWAYS

*Extra streetcars were in operation to bring thousands of
"baseball-starved" fans to the 1928 home opener.*

down the aisles and peered into the dugouts
as the areas around the bases were being
dried with portable furnaces. They examined
the freshly-painted seats and gave them a try.
Some sat in the shady area of the stands and
chatted about the weather, others sat alone
and read the newspaper as load after load of
sand was dumped on the field and packed
down with rollers pulled by teams of horses.
Royals executive Ernest Savard joked that
one day a horse and cart sank out of sight
near third base. The pre-game stadium
inspection showed that the city's baseball
fans eagerly awaited the Royals' return. After
all, they'd been waiting for this moment for
almost 11 years.

By 2 p.m., more than an hour before game
time, hundreds had lined up for tickets
outside the stadium. Many had arrived on
one of the special streetcars organized for the
event. More than 20,000 fans jammed into
the new stadium, setting a record for a
sporting event in Montreal. Many were awed
by what they saw. Delorimier Stadium was
nothing like the multi-purpose field at the

corner of Atwater and Ste. Catherine, where
the team had previously played. It was a
state-of-the-art ball park, constructed of steel
and concrete. A local newspaper described it
as "palatial", and it was generally regarded as
the biggest and best minor league park in
North America. The commissioner of Major
League Baseball, Judge Kenesaw Mountain
Landis, said it was even better than some
major-league parks.

Just before 3 p.m., a marching band
paraded into the stadium escorting the
mayor of Montreal, Camillien Houde, and
members of the Royals' front office. Houde
was joined by International League president
John Conway Toole and other top executives
from the minor leagues. When Houde and
the marching band entered the stadium,
players and officials from both teams lined
up in rows and the entire procession
marched to the flag pole in deep centre field.
The band played "God Save the King" and
"O Canada." The Union Jack was raised by
Royals second baseman and team captain
Chick Fewster. The players and officials then
followed the band back toward the infield
while a drum major entertained the crowd
by juggling a baton. The public-address
announcer introduced the starting pitchers
and catchers through a large, hand-held
megaphone. The Royals' pitcher, Bob
Shawkey, drew a big cheer from the fans. He
was a former Yankees star and an instant
hero because of his days with the World
Series-winning team. Another hero was
starting centre-fielder Bucky Gaudette, a
Franco-American.

Joining in the ceremony was the team's
60-year-old manager George Tweedy
Stallings. As one of the few baseball
managers who wore street clothes in the
dugout, "Gentleman George" sported a
fashionable suit, bow-tie and an expensive
hat. A respected manager in both the minor
and major leagues, Stallings had earned the
nickname "Miracle Man" for rallying the

1914 Boston Braves from last place at mid-season to a National League pennant and World Series victory. Stallings also performed wonders in Montreal, working feverishly to restore the city to the International League. Stallings was a teammate of another Montreal manager, Charlie Dooley. He had also played and managed in the International League and competed against the Royals at Atwater Park. In 1908, when Frank Farrell decided to sell the Royals, Stallings acted as the middleman in the deal with the Lichtenhein group. He considered Montreal to be a good baseball town and kept an eye on the city's baseball scene after the Royals folded in 1917.

Between 1917-28, when Montreal was without a professional team, baseball - as a pastime and spectator sport - continued to grow in popularity throughout Canada. In Montreal, amateur and semi-pro baseball leagues flourished at places such as Atwater Park, the Shamrock lacrosse grounds and other parks throughout the city. Montreal teams joined high-calibre circuits such as the Class B Eastern Canadian League and the Quebec-Ontario-Vermont League. Major-league baseball was extensively covered in local newspapers. In 1926, Joe Page, a Royals pioneer, convinced Babe Ruth to play in an exhibition game with a local team at downtown Guybourg Park. The Babe had been to Montreal before, facing the Royals as a pitcher for the Baltimore Orioles in 1914. Now he was a New York Yankees slugger, fresh off a season of 47 home runs and 146 RBIs, which led the American League. Four thousand Montrealers saw the Babe hit two homers on his barnstorming trip. Legend has it that one homer travelled 600 feet, although the distance seemed to grow each time the story was told.

As baseball soared in popularity in Canada, interest in lacrosse, the national sport, ebbed. A Canadian manufacturer of sports equipment reported that demand for lacrosse sticks had dropped just before the start of the First World War and continued to slide for the next decade. There seemed to be a connection between lacrosse's decline and baseball's upsurge. For Stallings, the time was ripe for Montreal to rejoin the International League. When the Jersey City franchise was available in 1927, he returned to Montreal seeking financial backers, as he had done in 1908. This time, he wanted in on the deal himself.

Stallings contacted Louis Athanase David, a Montreal-born lawyer who was also a provincial Liberal politician, representing the riding of Terrebonne in the Quebec Legislative Assembly. David was widely known throughout the province of Quebec and had lots of contacts. He relished the idea of Montreal rejoining the professional baseball ranks and contacted Ernest J. Savard, a successful Montreal investment dealer, stock broker and avid sports fan. Savard found investors for the project and formed two companies. Le Club de Baseball de Montreal handled the operations of the ball club, under the direction of Savard, while La Compagnie de L'Exposition de Montreal was formed to build and administrate a new stadium. That would be run by David, assisted by Carlos Ferrar and Walter E. Hapgood, associates of Stallings. (Ferrar left the team four months into the season and Hapgood succeeded him as the team's business manager).

The Savard-David group bought the franchise for about $225,000, a price some baseball people felt was a bit steep, and the Royals re-entered the I.L., joining Baltimore, Buffalo, Rochester, Toronto, Reading, Newark and Jersey City (whose owners purchased the Syracuse franchise when Jersey City was bought by Montreal).

Back in business, the first matter on the Royals' agenda was to build a baseball stadium which could accommodate the large crowds the new team owners hoped to attract. Atwater Park had been a decent baseball spot, but was deemed too small by the ownership group. The club acquired some property at the corner of Delorimier and Ontario, a busy intersection in the city's east end, and construction started in January, 1928. It was the home park of the old Mascottes amateur baseball team, a facility Stallings had first noticed while in Montreal 20 years earlier.

Some of the concrete for the new stadium was poured on days with sub-zero temperatures and the finishing touches to the ball park were still being applied the night before the home-opener. Sources estimated the total cost at $850,000. Others said it was more like $1.5 million. But the result was a facility hailed as the best minor-league ball park in North America. It had a few official names over the years - Royals' Stadium and later Hector Racine Stadium (after a team president), but it was usually referred to either as Delorimier Stadium, Le Stade Delorimier, or Delorimier Downs.

Like many ball parks of the era, it was rectangular in shape, configuring itself to the city block in which it was built. The right-field fence was a scant 293 feet from home plate. That was the only easy-home-run field, despite the fence and scoreboard which were a combined 40-feet high. Left field was 341 feet away, farther than some major-league power alleys are today. Home runs to left field were made even tougher by a 24-foot fence. Centre-field had only a 12-foot wall, but it was a forbidding 441 feet from home plate. It was a park that favored left-handed pull hitters and left-handed pitchers. Over the years, the Royals tried to stock their roster with these two commodities.

So, on this glorious spring day in early May of 1928, the Royals were back, playing before an appreciative audience. Stallings was in his first game as the Royals' manager, and it was a triumph all around. Trailing 3-0 against Reading, the Royals caught fire in the sixth inning, staging a rally that brought the fans to their feet, yelling and waving their hats in an attempt

The right field fence at Delorimier, only 293 feet from home plate, was tailor-made for left-handed sluggers who often hit home runs onto the Knit-to-fit clothing factory beyond. Courtesy Don McGowan.

to distract opposing pitcher, Jack Wisner. A newspaper report the next day said the fans staged "goat-getting stunts to help Wisner down the greasy chute." Spurred by the fans, the Royals came back to win 7-4. One of the new heroes was Gaudette, who knocked in a run with a sacrifice fly and made six catches in centre field. By all accounts, the fans were suitably impressed - one report said they "took the Royals to their hearts." The next day, another 12,000 were on hand, prompting one reporter to call the enthusiastic weekend reception for the club "the greatest tribute to professional sport ever known in Montreal." The Royals had bounced in and out of the International League over the years, but now there was a feeling the team was back for good.

In early June, with the Royals in second place and still riding the wave of enthusiasm following the home opener a month before, Stallings had a serious heart attack while on a road trip in Toronto. Coach Ed Holly, a former Royals shortstop, took over as manager while Stallings went home to Georgia to recuperate. At first, it seemed that Stallings would be back in a matter of weeks. But his return was delayed several times and eventually it was clear the "Miracle Man" would never be well enough to resume his duties. A year later, he died at the age of 61. An old baseball story had it that when Stallings was asked on his death bed what had put him there he replied, "Oh, those bases on balls."

With Stallings out of the picture and the Royals having to adjust to a new manager, the club did well to manage an 84-84 record and fifth place in its first year back from a long hiatus. The team was actually in second place as late as the first week of August but faltered, no match for the powerful Rochester Red Wings, a St Louis Cardinals' farm team.

Some of the Royals' personnel had come

Ed Holly, a former Royals shortstop at Atwater Park, took charge when George Stallings fell ill.

from the Jersey City team, others were grabbed by Stallings from various I.L. and minor- league squads. In general, the acquired players performed better for the Royals than they had for their previous teams. There were seven .300 hitters on the Royals in 1928 (it was the "lively ball era" when averages were somewhat inflated for a few seasons) and, in all but one case, the batting averages were an improvement over the previous season. Gaudette, for example, hit .318 for the Royals, 27 points better than his output for Jersey City and Baltimore in 1927. Outfielder Tom Gulley, the team's best hitter, fashioned a .347 average, 57 percentage points higher than his 1927 season in the Southern Association. The team's best pitchers, Roy Sherid and Roy Buckalew, also improved their respective performances. This didn't win the Royals a pennant, but it showed Stallings and Hapgood had assembled the team well.

Many of the key players - outfielders Gaudette, Gulley and Henry "Hinkey" Haines, infielders Bill Urbanski and Fred "Snake" Henry, along with pitchers Buckalew and Herb Thormahlen - were returnees in 1929. But Holly and Hapgood didn't stand pat. They obtained a veteran second baseman, five-foot-four, 129-pound Walter "Doc" Gautreau, pitcher Elon "Chief" Hogsett (who would lead the league with 22 wins that season) and Jimmy Ripple, a 19-year-old sensation from Jeannette, Pennsylvania.

Ripple was a switch-hitting outfielder (he later hit left-handed only) who attracted attention for his home runs and acrobatic catches as a centre-fielder in the Mid-Atlantic League. Hapgood decided to scout him. He sat in the stands in a business suit and sombrero, smoking a cigar. His mind sometimes strayed, until the sixth inning when a Jeannette player clouted a long home run to tie the score. Hapgood looked around, removed his cigar and asked: "Who's that?" Told it was Ripple, he played close attention for the rest of the game. In

the ninth inning, Ripple hit a hard liner to drive in the winning run and Hapgood was impressed. He signed the kid immediately after the game.

Ripple wasn't an instant success with the Royals but one night, late in the season, he got into a game against the Buffalo Bisons, after Hinkey Haines was ejected for throwing his bat. Ripple hit a double that scored a key run and prolonged a rally that led to a 6-4 victory. It was the first of many game-winning hits Ripple would deliver as he became, over the next several seasons, one of the best players in the Royals' history.

Montreal-area Iroquois honor Royals pitcher Elon Hogsett (centre), by making him a full "Chief".

After improving to fourth in 1929, the Royals continued their ascent in 1930, with largely the same core of players and pitching additions such as Gowell "Lefty" Claset and John Pomorski. Haines distinguished himself by leading the league with 45 stolen bases, helping the Royals to third place and an impressive .571 winning percentage.

While there was solid progress on the field, the effects of the stock-market crash were being felt at the box-office. Attendance was down at all ball parks and many minor-league teams started to experiment with night baseball to attract more fans during the week. The idea of playing baseball under artificial lights had originated before the turn of the century but it didn't really catch on until 1930, when a few owners of minor league teams, including the legendary Kansas City Monarchs of the Negro Leagues, installed lights in their ball parks.

The idea spread and, in 1930, the Buffalo Bisons decided to bring night baseball to the International League. The first game under the lights was on July 3, 1930, between the Bisons and the Royals. Bisons president Frank J. Offermann organized an extravagant pre-game ceremony, inviting baseball executives from all over the Eastern United States and Canada. The Bisons expected such a large crowd they decided to maximize profits by cancelling their usual Thursday "Woman's Day" promotion. About 12,000 fans turned up for the 8:30 p.m. game, a close contest which the Royals won, thanks in part to the inadequacy of the artificial lights.

With one out in the ninth inning and the score tied 4-4, Montreal shortstop Bill Urbanski drilled a ball up the middle into a poorly-lit centre field. By the time the Bisons outfielder could locate the ball and relay it to the infield, Urbanski was standing on third base. He soon scored the go-ahead run on a base hit. Snake Henry then lifted a routine fly ball that would have easily been caught in the daylight but was dropped under the lights, allowing what proved to be the winning run to score.

The arrival of night baseball in the International League brought mixed reviews, although the players were unanimous in their disapproval. Like the Bisons, the Royals encountered problems. Doc Gautreau, Montreal's sure-handed second baseman, had dropped an easy pop-up that led to a Buffalo run early in the game. The lighting was so poor at Offermann Stadium that fly balls cast a long shadow, resembling baseball bats hurled into the sky. The visibility wasn't much better on ground balls as players had difficulty seeing the ball at their feet. Urbanski was covered in bruises after the game.

Jimmy Ripple made enough waves in his home-town of Jeannette, Pa. to get the Royals' attention.

Another problem seemed to be that the lights were too low. Players had to pull their caps way down to keep the glare out of their eyes, "like second-story men," as someone cracked. Some players insisted that night baseball was dangerous, fearing that someone would get killed by a line drive. Many minor-league club owners agreed with the players' assessment but they knew they needed something to help them survive the Depression. That meant night baseball, for all of its flaws, was in the minor leagues to stay. In the International League alone, four teams joined Buffalo in installing lights at their stadiums. The gimmick didn't catch on as quickly in the majors, however. It was another five years before Cincinnati Reds general manager Larry MacPhail took the initiative and had lights installed at Crosley Field.

As the 1931 season dawned, there were no plans to install lights at Delorimier Stadium, but fans believed that prospects were bright for a great year. Most of manager Ed Holly's charges were back, along with a few additions, the most notable being centre-fielder Jocko Conlan, a proven I.L. hitter. Holly shared the fans' optimism, saying this was the best edition of the Royals since he became manager in 1928. But, as is often the case in baseball, things didn't go according to script.

From the start, the 1931 Royals seemed to lack a competitive edge. They were inconsistent, sometimes lapsing into "extraordinary trances," as one observer remarked. The club was in first place at the end of May but slipped to fourth by the first week of August and remained there with an unspectacular record of 85-80. One of the few players worth watching was Lefty Claset, who pitched complete games in both ends of a doubleheader against Reading, winning 1-0 and 3-1 and allowing only 10 hits on the day.

Boos echoed more and more from the dwindling crowds at Delorimier Downs. On

Tom Gulley, Montreal's best hitter, 1928 through 1931.

the Ontario Street streetcars, riders regularly discussed the woes of the ball club. They laid much of the blame on a front office that seemed more interested in the balance sheet than the standings. Like many minor-league teams of the day, the Royals tried to sell some of their players to the major leagues to make some money. This was never a popular move with fans, especially when the team made bad deals. The Gazette's D.A.L. MacDonald noted that Savard and Hapgood had blown a chance to sell 22-game winner, Chief Hogsett, in 1929. Eventually, they released him and got nothing in return.

The Royals' uninspired play was reflected at the gate. The team was lucky to attract a few thousand fans for a weekday game and seven or eight thousand on the weekend. Many felt like MacDonald: if the team wanted to attract more fans, it should spend some money on building a winning ball club. One way of achieving that would be to improve the organization's ties with the major leagues. Although some clubs, such as the Rochester Red Wings, were owned outright by a major-league organization, others had less formal working agreements which seemed to benefit both teams. A typical arrangement involved the major-league team sending players to the minor-league organization for some seasoning. The players could be recalled at any time, but while they were in the minors they remained on the major-league team's payroll. The arrangement meant the minor teams relinquished some control of their operation but they enjoyed the services of some talented future major leaguers without having to pay them.

There were suggestions in Montreal that the Royals seek such a working agreement, or at least try to make a few major-league connections to broaden their horizons. But it seemed that neither Savard nor Hapgood had many contacts in the majors. And Holly, although respected around the league as an astute manager, seemed unable to help in that regard. The front office went on the offensive responding to the criticism, declaring it was committed to winning the pennant in 1932. A possible deal with the New York Yankees for a third baseman, a catcher and an outfielder was raised, but nothing materialized. Savard made one

move, however, that unquestionably improved the Royals' organization. He hired Frank J. Shaughnessy to replace Hapgood as business manager.

A native of Amboy, Ill., "Shag" Shaughnessy was a well-respected sports figure in Canada. He had moved to Montreal in 1912 to coach the McGill University football team. He was a former Notre Dame football player and helped introduce the forward pass to Canadian football during his years at McGill. He also brought the university two football championships. In the off-season, Shaughnessy managed semi-professional baseball teams in Ottawa and Hamilton and had also managed in various minor leagues, including Syracuse of the International League. He had played in a few major-league baseball games for Washington and Philadelphia in the American League at the turn of the century and had also been a coach for the Detroit Tigers. He was in the stands scouting the Royals for the Tigers when Montreal inaugurated Delorimier Stadium in May, 1928.

Shaughnessy had some contacts in the big leagues, especially in Detroit, and it was a former Tiger, Ivey "Chick" Shiver, who was

The 193? Royals arrive at Montreal's Windsor Station for the home opener. Left to right:: Joe Page, John Grabowski, Clarence Fisher, Frank Barnes, Walter Brown, John Pomorski, Warren Hogden, Oscar Roettger, Doc Gautreau, Herbert Thomas, Jimmy Ripple, H. Walker, Jocko Conlan, Bill O'Brien

the team's best newcomer in 1932. Taking the spot left vacant by the departure of power-hitter Tom Gulley, the last remaining member of the 1928 team, Shiver hit .311, second only to Jimmy Ripple, and had the team's best power stats with 27 home runs and 111 RBIs. On the mound, Lefty Claset won 23 games and third-baseman Bucky Walters impressed with his defensive play. (Walters later went on to win 198 games in the major leagues as a pitcher). But despite some solid individual performances, the pennant race promised by Savard never developed. The Royals finished in fourth place again, well behind the Newark Bears, a recent acquisition of the New York Yankees who had wrested International League supremacy from the Rochester Red Wings.

Before the season ended, the Royals front office started making some moves. Shag became the general manager and he relieved an exhausted Holly of his managerial duties. Holly had collapsed in Jersey City and was sent to relax at a resort in the Laurentian Mountains, north of Montreal. But he was no longer up to the task of managing the team and Shaughnessy replaced him with the team's second baseman Doc Gautreau. An excellent fielder, Gautreau had played errorless ball for the team's first 52 games and committed only 12 all season.

While these moves seemed like the actions of a healthy team planning for the future, the Royals were actually on the verge of financial collapse. The Savard-David group had paid a lot for the franchise and, ravaged by the Depression and poor attendance, the club was no longer able to pay its bills. The Royals owed $51, 000 in back taxes to the city of Montreal and the mortgage company that owned the stadium was about to foreclose. In the months following the 1932 season, it appeared the Royals were about to fold again, only five seasons after their triumphant resurrection. But late in the year Ernest Savard, the club's

J.C.E. "Charlie" Trudeau, relaxing at Old Orchard Beach, dug the Royals out of a deep financial hole

major shareholder since the departure of L. Athanase David, started to speak optimistically about the future of the team. He alluded to a deal that would bring in enough new money to keep the team afloat. In early 1933, Savard announced a major re-organization of the team's financial structure.

The key investor in the new setup was Montreal businessman Jean-Charles Emile Trudeau, "Charlie" to his poker buddies. Trudeau, father of future Canadian Prime Minister Pierre Elliott Trudeau, had become a millionaire during the Depression by selling a successful chain of service stations to Imperial Oil. Although Trudeau enjoyed sports, it wasn't easy convincing him to invest in the Royals. He was said to have written the words "In Protest" on the back of a $25,000 cheque investing in the team. Trudeau was likely more confident about the investment than he let on, since he brought in an acquaintance, Lt.-Col. Roméo J. Gauvreau, as a major investor (although it may have been a case of misery loves company).

Gauvreau, a civil engineer by trade had also derived his riches from the oil business. The new owners were willing to put up a lot of money, but in return they wanted to ensure their investment was well managed - a reasonable request considering the current financial state of the organization. They insisted their mutual friend, Hector Racine, be appointed president of the Royals. Savard agreed, stepping down as president to become the secretary-treasurer. He soon left the Royals to become the president and part-owner of the Montreal Canadiens hockey team.

Racine was involved in a number of Montreal business interests, mostly in the garment trade, and was a council member of the city's Board of Trade. He was also president of the Canadian Wholesale Dry Goods Association. It wasn't a typical resume for a baseball executive, and Racine admitted he had only seen a handful of games in his 46 years. But Trudeau and Gauvreau were convinced their friend's business acumen was what the Royals needed. Racine immediately immersed himself in the technical and financial aspects of baseball. As with the hiring of Shaughnessy, the arrival of Racine immediately made the Royals a sounder organization. He would be an important part of the club until his death more than 20 years later.

With the money matters resolved, Shaughnessy could focus on making the Royals a more competitive team. Early in 1933, he traded Walter Brown, one of the team's best pitchers of the previous two seasons, to the Boston Red Sox for catcher Bennie Tate and power- hitter "Long Tom" Winsett. Tate hit well over .300 for the club, while Winsett clubbed 19 home runs, some of them pulled onto the roof of the Grover Knit-To-Fit clothing factory beyond the right-field fence.

Chick Shiver produced another terrific season, hitting for average and power. The other two offensive stalwarts for the team were Jimmy Ripple and Oscar Roettger. The clutch-hitting Roettger led the Royals with 117 RBIs and topped the league with 52 doubles. Shaughnessy was so impressed with the 33-year-old infielder's leadership abilities he relieved Gautreau of his managerial duties and made Roettger the team's new player-manager.

Shaughnessy also tackled the task of attracting more fans to the stadium. He believed it was time to bring the Royals into the era of night baseball. It would be a way to improve gate receipts during the week and give working people a chance to see the Royals without having to play hooky from work. Shaughnessy felt that even one night game a week, or a couple a month, would improve the bottom line.

Four light stands were installed on the roof of Delorimier Stadium and two 90-foot lamp standards were erected in the outfield, one in right-centre the other in left-centre. On the day before the system was to start, Shag stayed up all night with technicians, checking all corners of the ball park for shadows. He wanted to avoid the disaster the Royals were part of part three years earlier in Buffalo. As the night wore on he got a little playful, inviting reporters to take the field while he hit some high flies to test the lights. One reporter disgraced himself and his colleagues by diving for a ball and missing it by three feet. The ball hit the ground and rebounded off his chest as he stretched. Shag decided the lights weren't to blame for that one and he continued testing the new system until sunrise. Shag was confident the lights would work well, but to be on the safe side, he scheduled the game for 9:15 p.m., so that it would be completely dark and the lights would have maximum effect.

The Royals inaugurated their new lighting system on July 18, 1933, in a game against the Albany Senators. When the lights were switched on, there was an excited buzz from the fans who had showed up early for the event. Players hit high fly balls in practice to test the visibility, much as Shag had done the night before. Things looked fine, except for a shadowy region in deep centre field. Thirteen thousand fans came to witness the spectacle, an indication that Shaughnessy was on to something. They were treated to a brilliant view of the illuminated field and the awesome sight of the towering-steel light standards studded with lights, reminding one spectator of giant diamond stick-pins. Most of the players on the field had played under artificial light before but many still weren't used to it. There were six errors in the game, five by the Senators, including a mistake by an Albany outfielder, who lost a ball in the lights in the bottom of the ninth, allowing the Royals Oscar Roettger to score the winning run.

Night baseball in Montreal was a success,

and with each passing season more and more of the Royals' weekday games were played under the lights - both at home and on the road. But the installation of the lights was the only real positive note of the 1933 season. The team finished in sixth place, below the .500 mark for the first time since returning to the league in 1928. Placing sixth now had further repercussions. Because of the efforts of Shaughnessy, the I.L. now had a playoff system that allowed the top four teams to compete for the league championship, so a decent season would have put the Royals in the playoffs.

During the 1932 International League meetings, Shaughnessy had convinced the owners to adopt a playoff structure similar to the one used in the National Hockey League. It wasn't an easy sell; most of the owners were vehemently opposed to tinkering with baseball tradition. But Shag persisted and won the argument. He felt that fans got bored near the end of a season if their team was out of the pennant race. With the depression at its worst, most clubs agreed that a playoff system would be good for business, even if it went against tradition. Shag suggested that the top four teams in the league advance and compete for a Governors' Cup.

The Cup was donated and named for the state governors and provincial premiers represented in the International League in 1933, the first year the playoff structure went into effect. The new post-season structure was adopted by other minor leagues, including the two other Double-A circuits, the American Association and the Pacific Coast League. Many people credited the "Shaughnessy Plan" with saving the minor leagues from the decimation of the Depression. Shag had become one of the most respected men in minor-league baseball.

With the 1934 season looming, Shaughnessy's priorities were on the home

Oscar Roettger had sure hands, but his leg gave out and Frank Shaughnessy had to step in to replace him as manager.

front, trying to improve the Royals' pitching staff. His first deal was for Detroit farmhand Ray Fritz, no ace but a dependable starter. He had a durable arm that allowed him to pitch in 41 games in 1934, going the distance 17 times. Two other deals brought pitchers Harry Smythe and Chad Kimsey. Both had been in the major leagues and were pushing 30, but the similarities ended there. Smythe was a stocky, bow-legged southpaw, somewhat shorter than his listed five foot 10. He relied on a nasty curve to fool batters. Kimsey was a tall, beefy right-hander who went right at batters trying to strike them out.

Shaughnessy also made some moves to strengthen the middle of the infield. He signed svelte shortstop Ben Sankey, a slick fielder and a good hitter with big-league experience, and bought Lafayette "Fresco" Thompson from the New York Giants. The Royals had needed a steady shortstop since selling the talented Bill Urbanski to the Boston Braves in 1931, and with Gautreau gone, they also needed a second baseman. Sankey and Thompson meshed well, and with Hal King at third base and Oscar Roettger at first, the Royals now had the best infield in the league.

The season-opener was more stylish in 1934 than it had been in recent years. Trying to add some color to the proceedings, Shag had the players from both teams introduced to the fans though loudspeakers. He also jazzed up the ceremonial first pitch, inviting Mayor Camillien Houde out to the mound to fire a pitch to the team's main investor, Charlie Trudeau, instead of just lobbing a ball from his seat. Houde, a southpaw, loved throwing out the first pitch, a job he had done several times before, and he and Trudeau hammed it up. Trudeau crouched behind the plate and held up two fingers for the mayor and everyone else to see. Houde, a somewhat roly-poly man, wound up and threw a curveball, that actually curved. It was a bit low, but it seemed to paint a corner and the fans whooped when Trudeau caught it. The opening-day crowd was in a good mood, but it wasn't an impressive turnout - only 6,000 people were on hand to see the Royals beat Syracuse 2-1.

The crowds were modest for the rest of the season as the Royals were never really in contention for a playoff spot. By the end of August, when they were 15 games behind the powerful Newark Bears and four games out of the playoffs, most fans had written them off. On Wednesday, August 29, only 500 fans braved the cool weather to see the Royals play the Toronto Maple Leafs— usually a good draw because of the keen Montreal-Toronto rivalry. The Royals lost the game 5-4, but adding insult to injury for Shag was that the season's smallest crowd turned out for a night game. Was the novelty of night baseball already wearing off, only a year after it was introduced?

That gave Shaughnessy another thing to think about as he surveyed a mediocre 1934 season. The team's 73-77 record was its worst since rejoining the International League and it finished sixth for the second straight season. Player-manager Roettger hurt his leg near the end of the summer and was laid up for a while. The injury not only kept him off

the field, it prevented him from running the club and Shaughnessy took over as manager. By the end of the season, Hector Racine had decided that Roettger, obviously worn out, would not be offered a contract for the 1935 season, either as a player or manager. Racine convinced Shaughnessy to continue in the manager's job for the 1935 season.

Shag seemingly had his work cut out for him in 1935, since none of his recent acquisitions were overly impressive in 1934, with the exception of Fresco Thompson, who hit .311 with 12 homers and 96 RBIs. But Smythe, Kimsey and Sankey still represented a solid pitching nucleus and trader Shag worked to complete a couple more deals which, in 1935, would finally bring the Montreal fans what they wanted most: a winning team.

Shaughnessy's new lights were installed in the outfield in 1933 so the Royals could play night games.

1935-1936
The Team That Shag Built

By the winter of 1935, the Royals were again in a precarious financial state, as slender attendance for two straight seasons led to a shortfall. The club's new business manager, Guy Moreau, was handed the unpleasant task of begging for a bank loan to finance spring training. He also had to cajole a railway company to delay billing the Royals for transporting the players to and from Florida. Moreau had to put the company off until the first road trip to Newark, where he collected a sizeable cheque for the visitors' share of a well-attended series.

Once the team arrived in Orlando for training camp, baseball took precedence over finance and, in that regard, the team was quite healthy. In the off-season, Shaughnessy had again worked his Detroit contacts and obtained outfielder Bob Seeds, a journeyman major-leaguer who'd been traded so often his nickname was "Suitcase." While "Suitcase" never stayed in one place for long, he had a reliable bat and a very good glove. Another newcomer in the outfield was Quebec-born Gus Dugas, acquired from the Albany Senators following several outstanding seasons in the minors. Dugas was born in St-Jean-de-Matha, north of Montreal, but had moved to the United States as a young boy.

Another acquisition from the Senators, also with Quebec roots, was Del Bissonette, born in a logging camp in Maine to French-Canadian parents. Like Dugas, Bissonette could speak French, and in 1922 he had

played in the Quebec Provincial League for the Cap-de-la-Madeleine Madcaps. Bissonette had reached the majors with Brooklyn as a 28-year-old rookie and enjoyed four productive seasons as the team's first baseman. His best year was 1930, when he hit .336, drove in 113 runs and slammed 16 home runs. Bissonette was now 35, but Shag felt he still had some power and, hopefully, some leadership to provide the Royals. Another former big-leaguer joining the

Frank Shaughnessy: The "Fighting Irishman".

Royals in 1935 was pitcher Pete Appleton. He could easily have been called "Suitcase" Pete, since he'd played for four major-league teams and was pushing 31 when he arrived in Montreal as Shag's right-handed ace.

Obtaining Appleton was a key move in a series of deals by Shaughnessy since becoming the general manager. Everything seemed to finally be coming together. Bissonette was at first base; Fresco Thompson at second, Hal King at third; Ben Sankey at shortstop ; Dugas, Seeds and Jimmy Ripple in the outfield; Bennie Tate behind the plate; and Harry Smythe, Appleton and Chad Kimsey anchored the pitching staff. The Royals could now boast a starting lineup with seven experienced major-leaguers.

With spring training about to conclude and Shag and his players eagerly awaiting the start of the new season, they were knocked off stride by the sudden death of Charlie Trudeau, the team's vice-president and principal shareholder. Trudeau was with the team in Orlando when he caught pneumonia and died. Shaughnessy spent a lot of time at the hospital with his boss and was with him in his final hours. Trudeau was enthusiastic about attending spring training and had looked forward to periodically traveling with the team during the season. He was a popular figure among the players and the entire team was at the train station to send his remains north to Montreal. Royals president Hector Racine said Trudeau would be missed from a personal and professional standpoint, but the team would survive with Romeo Gauvreau assuming much of the former vice-president's responsibilities.

Following a pause in the team's spring-training schedule to mourn Trudeau's death, the Royals resumed preparations for their season-opening series against the Baltimore Orioles. It was a four- game series that turned sour, partly because of a bet between the managers. Shaughnessy, a notoriously competitive man, wagered Baltimore manager Guy Sturdy that the Royals would outhustle his Orioles in the opening game. Shag allowed Oriole owner Charles Knapp to judge the contest since Knapp was also the president of the International League and presumably capable of impartiality. On the surface, only a new hat was at stake, but both managers took it a lot more seriously than that.

The first game, won 13-12 by Baltimore in the bottom of the ninth, was out-and-out warfare. It was obvious that the "friendly bet" was off midway through the game when Shaughnessy got into a fight with Baltimore pitcher Beryl Richmond. It started with some needling, followed by shouting and then a shoving match. Both benches emptied and players converged in a knot of arms and legs near the pitcher's mound. Once umpire Cal Hubbard restored order and dodged a few pop bottles from the stands, the game resumed. In the eighth inning, however, Hubbard made a close call that favored Montreal. This time the hail of bottles forced Hubbard to run for cover. Sturdy had to come out of the Baltimore dugout and plead with the crowd to restrain themselves.

The game was completed without further incident, as were the next two games, which the Royals won. But there was bad blood as the teams took the field for the fourth and final game. Sturdy warned of trouble but it didn't occur until the game was almost over. The Royals were leading in the ninth when Harry Smythe laid down a bunt which sent Orioles second baseman Irvine Jeffries scrambling to cover first. When the two players met at the bag, Smythe stepped on Jeffries' foot. When Smythe made a show of apologizing for the spiking, Jeffries swore and cocked his fist. But Smythe was quicker off the mark and flattened Jeffries with a dandy left hook. The benches were empty before Jeffries hit the ground.

A mob of Orioles went straight for Smythe, who was seriously outnumbered until Ben Sankey came charging in from second base, where he was a baserunner, and Chad Kimsey, the team's only real heavyweight, came barreling in from the bullpen. There was a confused scrum around Smythe, who eventually crawled out between a pair of legs and headed to the on-deck circle for a bat. He was just about to rejoin the fray, brandishing lumber, when Bob Seeds stepped in and disarmed him. Meanwhile, Sturdy belted Fresco Thompson, only to be felled himself by an onrushing Hal King, who slammed the Baltimore manager to the ground. Thompson, dazed by Sturdy's assault, was searching for his cap when he ran smack into beefy Baltimore slugger George "Pooch" Puccinelli. "I don't want any part of you Pooch," said Thompson. But Pooch picked him up anyway and tossed him on his head. By this time, a Baltimore player had pinned King to the ground and Sturdy, his face covered in blood, kicked the Royals third baseman in the chin.

Montreal aces Pete Appleton (left) and Harry Smythe.

At its peak, the brawl involved 40 players. Even the two trainers - Montreal's Bill O'Brien and Baltimore's Doc Widener - sparred for a while, until O'Brien doubled Widener over with a knee in the stomach. The scene worsened when spectators and sports reporters made their way onto the field for a piece of the action.

After about 20 minutes of what was later called the I.L.'s "worst riotous outbreak in years," the combatants started to tire and the police moved in to separate the players and clear the field of spectators. The last civilian escorted from the diamond was the sports editor of a Baltimore newspaper. No one was arrested and, astonishingly, none of the combatants were ejected from the game. Somehow, the players controlled themselves long enough to finish the game, won 7-4 by Montreal.

After losing the next three games at a stop in Newark, the Royals headed north for their home opener. As luck would have it, their opponent was their old feuding partner, the Baltimore Orioles. Both teams vowed they were ready to resume hostilities but league officials were determined to make sure that didn't happen.

President Knapp would be on hand, as would the league's umpire-in-chief.

As the train pulled into Montreal's Windsor Station on a winter-like April night prior to the home-opener, the players gathered on the platform for team pictures and interviews. But Frank Shaughnessy couldn't be found. He had left the train a few stops early, near his home in Montreal West. If he was trying to give reporters the slip, it didn't work. They made their way west and landed on his doorstep at around midnight looking for quotes. Shag appeared sleepy-eyed before the reporters, in brown-striped pajamas, a black silk dressing gown and brand-new slippers. He told the visitors the addition of Appleton and Seeds would make the Royals pennant contenders. He also told them to keep their eyes on pitcher Lauri Myllykangas, who would be getting the start the next day. Finally, realizing the game was only a matter of hours away, the men pulled their fedoras down firmly on their heads and wandered out into the snowy night. They joked about how the opening game would be "Red Flannel Baseball."

There were fewer jokes the next afternoon as the reporters sat shivering in the press box at Delorimier Stadium. Those in attendance, some 7,000, were asked to stand for a moment of silence in memory of Charlie Trudeau, the team's fallen benefactor. Once the umpire called "Play Ball", the players did just that, without resorting to the shenanigans of a week earlier. The Royals outplayed the Orioles once again, beating them 9-3.

After the game, Orioles manager Sturdy hurled one of his spiked boots into the corner of the clubhouse - the same boot applied to Hal King's chin during the recent melee. Sturdy complained about having to play baseball in winter weather and being held to four hits by Myllykangas, a pitcher he'd never heard of, with a Finnish name he found absurd. What displeased him the most was again being stomped by the Royals, this time without throwing a punch.

Most of the damage that afternoon was done by centre-fielder Jimmy Ripple, who hit a home run over the right field scoreboard and added two singles for a three-RBI day. In his sixth full season with the Royals, Ripple was off to a torrid start, hitting .459 with three homers and 15 RBIs in the team's first 15 games. Since joining the team in late 1929 at the age of 19 and winning a regular spot the following season, Ripple had become one of the best players in the International League. He was an smooth outfielder, able to catch a ball off his shoetops or make a grab out of thin air and hold on while crashing into a fence. One of the few times he failed defensively was the time in Rochester, when he was chasing down a ball and caught his pants on a loose wire on the outfield fence. He was trapped, the ball a few inches from his wiggling fingers as the tying and winning runs scored.

By the end of June, Montreal nudged into first place, then won 11 of the next 16 games for a three-and-a-half-game lead over the Buffalo Bisons. The Royals lost the lead briefly in mid-August but quickly regained it and all but locked up the pennant on the first Sunday in September with Gus Dugas crashing three homers in a convincing 16-6, 5-0 doubleheader sweep of Buffalo.

The Royals clinched the regular-season crown against the Toronto Maple Leafs on September 6, the same date on which the franchise had won its first pennant in 1898. Most of the players had won minor-league pennants before - they were an experienced bunch – but they celebrated like rookies. Shaughnessy hadn't been involved with a pennant-winner since he managed Ottawa in the semi-pro Canadian League 20 years earlier, so he let himself enjoy the moment before concentrating on his first appearance in the playoffs.

The 1935 I.L. pennant-winners. left to right, back row: Hector Racine, Bill O'Brien, Pete Appleton, Curly Ogden, Ray Fritz, Leon Chagnon, Chad Kimsey, Hal King, Lauri Myllykangas, Harry Smythe, Aurthur Normandin, Guy Moreau middle row: Buddy Lewis, Billy Rhiel, Bob Seeds, Eddie Montagu, Fresco Thompson, Frank Shaughnessy, Jimmy Ripple, Del Bissonette, Glen Chapman bottom row: Bennie Tate, George Granger, Larry O'Brien, Ben Sankey, Gus Dugas.

Ike Boone, the Toronto manager, came into the dressing room after the game to congratulate the Royals. He clasped Shag's hand and told him he deserved the pennant. Many people agreed. The Royals had compiled a 92-62 record, and a few days later Shaughnessy was presented with a silver tray from R.B. Bennett, the prime minister of Canada. The inscription read: "To Francis Joseph Shaughnessy From The Prime Minister of Canada. In recognition of his keen ability in sport, his sincere enthusiasm for fair play and, especially, the honest efforts he has made throughout his career to inspire Canadian youth toward clean living and clear thinking. R.B. Bennett."

Although Shaughnessy was the only member of the team to receive recognition from the Prime Minister, other Royals earned laurels. Jimmy Ripple, Fresco Thompson, Harry Smythe and Pete Appleton were all named to the International League all-star team. Ripple had his finest season, with a .333 batting average, 12 homers and 115 RBIs. Thompson hit .314 and knocked in 75 runs. He also played well at second base and, as team captain, was an on-field leader.

Appleton led the league with 23 victories and Smythe was 22-11.

The supporting cast made huge contributions. Chad Kimsey won 16 games, Gus Dugas batted .308 with 22 home runs and 96 RBIs and Bob Seeds hit .315. Seeds was such a valuable member of the team, Shaughnessy once remarked the $10,000 he spent to acquire him had bought the pennant for Montreal. Del Bissonette, Hal King and Ben Sankey also had good seasons. There were a few flaws, but nothing the Montreal front office couldn't solve. The catching combination of Bennie Tate and Pete Stack had been disappointing, so Shag traded for Buddy Lewis from the Cardinals system, solidifying that position. As the season wound down, Shag filled the need for an experienced reliever by obtaining Leon Chagnon - not a Quebec native, despite the surname - from the Giants.

A tall right-hander, Chagnon was effective out of the bullpen and as a spot starter. But the trade was unpopular with the fans because Ripple, the team's best and most popular player, was sent to the New York

Giants for the 1936 season. In return, the Royals got Chagnon and $35,000, an important sum because the team, despite improved attendance in 1935, was still in a tenuous financial state. Chad Kimsey was sold to the Detroit Tigers, although like Ripple, he was to remain with Montreal for the rest of the 1935 season. The cash put the Royals in a more comfortable financial position for 1936, although there would be a couple of large holes to fill on the roster.

The immediate challenge facing the club was an appearance in what some people still called the "Shaughnessy playoffs." In 1933, the first year of the new post-season format, the first-place team faced the second-place squad. That changed the following year to a first-third, second-fourth matchup. That meant the Royals would play Buffalo, with home-field advantage as the regular-season champion. It was an important edge, since the Royals hit .301 at Delorimier Stadium in 1935 and had a winning percentage of .675 at home. The team's overall batting average was a league-best .294.

The two teams split the first four games of the semi-final series, with late-season-addition Chagnon winning twice, the second victory coming in Game 4 on two days' rest. Emulating his teammate, Kimsey won Game 5 on two days' rest, tossing a 3-0 shutout. As he had been throughout the series, Del Bissonette was a big man with the bat and glove, contributing a homer and a base hit and smothering a dangerous Buffalo rally in the ninth inning with a diving grab at first base. After snaring the ball, Bissonette flipped it to Kimsey, covering the bag, for the third out.

It was a close play for umpire Vic Campbell and Buffalo manager Ray Schalk bolted from the dugout to argue, actually staging a shoving match at one point with the umpire. The Bisons' bench emptied and fans jumped down onto the field, chased by 15 Buffalo police officers. The cops escorted

Del Bissonette swung a hot bat in the 1935 playoffs.

Campbell to the umpire's dressing room and dispersed an angry mob bent on getting their hands on the official.

It was to be the last game in Buffalo. The Royals took the series in Game 6, a tight pitching duel between Appleton and Buffalo's Ken Ash until Montreal had a seven-run seventh inning and went on to an 8-0 victory. Bissonette was superb again, going 2-for-4, and Bob Seeds, also a steady performer in the series, blasted a three-run home run. Bissonette, Seeds and Thompson had been the best Royals offensively in the series. Bissonette was 11-for-21, a gaudy .524 average, while Seeds and Thompson both hit over .300.

The opening-round win meant the Royals had snapped a jinx by becoming the first I.L. pennant-winner to advance to the Governor's Cup final. The Newark Bears were eliminated in the first round in each of the previous two years. But breaking the hex didn't seem to do the Royals much good in the first game of the Governor's Cup final against the Syracuse Chiefs. Montreal trailed 7-5 in the ninth inning when Ripple, a playoff slumper at that point, smacked a two-out, RBI double. But 7-6 was as close as the Royals got.

Harry Smythe, the team-leader in innings pitched during the regular season, was used sparingly in the post-season, but he started the second game of the series and pitched well until a seven-run eighth inning as Montreal lost 10-5. But Kimsey came to the rescue with a six-hitter in the third game, beating the Chiefs 5-2. In the fourth game, Appleton scattered seven hits in a Royals' victory, highlighted by Hal King's four RBIs. King led Montreal to a 3-2 series lead with a two-run homer in Game 5.

Attendance at Delorimier Stadium had increased slightly in 1935, especially in the playoffs, and 19, 000 fans came out on a Sunday afternoon to see the next game, hoping the Royals could bag the Governor's Cup. It was the largest crowd at Delorimier since the the 22,000-plus for the first-ever game there, opening day of 1928. Helped by five double plays, the Royals were tied 2-2 in the ninth inning of Game 6. They looked to be the Governor's Cup winner when Gus Dugas yanked a ball into the screen over the scoreboard in right field. Usually when a ball hit the screen, it dropped onto the top of the scoreboard for a home run, so when the ball

cleared the board it seemed that Dugas had a dramatic, game-winning blow.

But this time, for some reason, the ball rebounded back onto the field and Dugas' home-run trot was interrupted by the umpires, who awarded him only a ground-rule double. Dugas eventually advanced to third, but his teammates were unable to bring him home. Syracuse scored the go-ahead run in the 10th inning and Montreal responded by loading the bases in the bottom of the inning, with Dugas again at the plate. This time the Royals' slugger struck out, capping a heart-breaking loss which seemed unfair because Dugas had been denied a homer. The ground rule was changed the following season so that any ball hitting the screen was an automatic home run.

The sixth-game setback seemed to leave

Quebec-born Gus Dugas. Author's collection.

the Royals in a lousy mood for the seventh and deciding game against Syracuse southpaw George Hockette. They scraped together four hits in the first four innings and managed a run, but didn't get another hit. Royals starter Appleton didn't have his best stuff but he battled and the team was only trailing 2-1 when it came to bat in the bottom of the ninth. With one out and "Suitcase" Seeds at second base, Ripple, already destined for New York in 1936 as part of the Royals' recent trade, had the chance to go out in grand style. He had already made two great catches in centre field to keep the team in the game. Now the fans were pleading for him to be a hero one more time. All it would take was something he'd done many time before: a fly ball over the right-field fence. How about one more for old time's sake?

Ripple made contact, and though the ball wasn't heading out of the park it appeared it might drop just behind second base, allowing Seeds to score the tying run. Seeds thought that way, too. He was off like a shot heading for home, while Syracuse second baseman George "Specs" Toporcer also took off, scampering behind the bag and hauling in the short pop fly before it sailed over his head. Seeds was a dead duck as the Chiefs stepped on second base for a double play that won Syracuse the Governor's Cup. It was a sad moment for Royals' supporters, especially since it was Ripple's last at-bat in a Montreal uniform. What no one knew at the time was that Ripple would be re-acquired a few years later.

For the moment, it was a painful ending to the Royals' best season. The team had accomplished a great deal, winning the pennant and almost claiming the Governor's Cup. More than 300,000 fans had come to see the Royals play at home in 1935, the team's best attendance mark thus far. And with the sale of Ripple and Kimsey and a third transaction that sent Appleton to the

Washington Senators, the team was stronger financially, although decidedly weaker on the field. Still, the core of the 1935 team would be back and there was optimism that Shag could mine his contacts again to fill in the gaps and maintain the Royals' contending status in 1936.

Much of the pennant-winning squad was intact in 1936, starting with the crackerjack infield of Bissonette, Thompson, Sankey and King. Dugas and Seeds were holdovers in the outfield, while pitchers Smythe, Chagnon and Myllykangas also returned. Seeds, a good all-around outfielder, was shifted to centre field, replacing Ripple, and Billy Rhiel, a utility player and part-time first-base coach, was pressed into action as the team's third outfielder. Rhiel was yet another former Tiger who found his way to Montreal during the Shaughnessy years.

The club needed to bolster its pitching staff, so Shag obtained two right-handers - former major-leaguer Henry Johnson and Crip Polli. The duo looked like winners during the first homestand of 1936, when they combined to shut out Syracuse in a Sunday doubleheader. In the first game, before close to 10,000 fans who cheered while the I.L pennant was raised up the centre-field flagpole, Polli scattered six hits for a 2-0 win. In the nightcap, Johnson had a no-hitter through nine innings but the Royals had also failed to score. Johnson pitched into the 11th inning and finally earned a one-hit, 2-0 triumph. The sweep put the Royals in first place ahead of the Newark Bears. One week later,19,889 fans came to Delorimier Downs for another Sunday afternoon doubleheader.

Things turned sour after that. The Royals struggled for the next month, eventually surrendering first place to the Bears. By mid-June, the club had fallen to fifth place. It was a team in disarray and the seeds for the downfall had apparently been planted at the the start of

Fresco Thompson, never afraid to get his uniform dirty.

the season, when Shag was overheard muttering bitterly about being second-guessed by players with managerial aspirations. It was quite evident he was talking about Thompson and Bissonette, two veterans who weren't shy about giving the manager some free advice about how to run the club.

The first confrontation came with Thompson, the team captain. Shag felt Thompson was undermining him in the clubhouse. Already, the infielder wasn't too popular with president Hector Racine, after asking for more money when he was named captain. Thompson got his raise, but at the expense of his relationship with management. By the first week of July, the Royals were looking for someone to replace him in the infield. They signed Irvine Jeffries, a .302 hitter with Baltimore in 1935 and the man Smythe had spiked that season to ignite one of the league's worst brawls. Thompson was released shortly after Jeffries arrived. Bissonette wasn't far behind. At 37, he was no longer hitting the ball well or getting along with Shaughnessy. Suddenly, the team was without two more of its pennant-winning players, and the Royals no longer resembled that talented squad that had performed so well several months earlier.

While Shaughnessy unloaded two players who had complicated his life, things didn't get any easier for him. The large crowds at Delorimier Stadium tapered off as the Royals fell out of playoff contention. By the first week of August, Montreal was 17 1\2 games behind first-place Rochester and 6 1\2 games from a playoff spot. Many fans blamed Shaughnessy, and some started to boo him during games. There were reports of petitions circulating factory floors demanding that Shag be fired. It was tough thing for the 53-year-old "Fighting Irishman" to accept. He was a proud man, tall and lean, with snow-white hair and a ruddy Irish face. He had a habit of arriving at the ball park early so he could be alone to reflect and say a quiet rosary. He had never asked for the manager's job. Racine had talked him into it, and now Shag decided it was time to go.

In the first week of August, Shag surprised everyone by announcing his resignation, saying the team's poor performance was affecting his health. "The club had me worried until I couldn't sleep. Now I'll have time to rest and play some golf," he said. Racine said it would be extremely difficult to replace the man who'd been pulling double-duty as manager and general manager since late in the 1934 season. The team's president lauded Shag for his baseball and business acumen. "Montreal owes him much for winning the pennant last year and keeping the city in the league before that," Racine remarked. Released from the daily pressure of running a ball club, Shag spent his first day of freedom on the golf course, while Harry Smythe took over as interim manager.

As it turned out, Shaughnessy didn't get in as much golf as he planned. The president of the International League, Charles Knapp, died in 1936 and his successor, Warren Giles, left the post after only a few months to join the Cincinnati Reds. Shaughnessy was offered the job and he took it, starting a

reign that would last until his retirement in 1960 at the age of 77.

Royals President Hector Racine tried to change the team's luck by hiring Rabbit Maranville.

Meanwhile, in Montreal, the Royals continued to play mediocre baseball in front of sparse crowds and finished the 1936 season in sixth place, with a 71-81 record. Although fan interest waned near the end of the season, strong attendance early in the season enabled the team to break even financially. Money was still scarce, however, and the team had to sell catcher Tate and pitcher Chagnon to the Baltimore Orioles. In a much bigger move, Racine signed a working agreement with William Benswanger of the Pittsburgh Pirates. Racine was tired of scrambling to keep the club afloat and Benswanger agreed to supply the Royals with some cash and a half-dozen young players for the 1937 season. It was the team's first link-up with a major-league organization and Racine was optimistic the partnership would save the franchise.

Racine also hired Walter "Rabbit" Maranville as the team's new manager for the 1937 season. Smythe, who'd replaced Shag as interim manager, wanted to return but Racine had other plans.

1937-1938
A Rabbit out of a Hat

6

The Pittsburgh Pirates weren't the only team Hector Racine had spoken with about a working agreement, although they were the only organization offering both money and players. Unfortunately, the arrangement never worked the way it was devised. The Pirates weren't very generous in sending young talent to Montreal. They also flatly refused to supply any pitchers, a commodity the Royals needed the most. Thus, despite finally having an affiliation with a major-league team, the Royals' best deals in 1937 season were the ones Racine made with organizations other than Pittsburgh.

The best of these deals was a four-player swap with the Yankees that sent "Suitcase" Bob Seeds to New York - his sixth major-league organization, for catcher Normie Kies, outfielder Paul Dunlap and pitcher Marvin Duke. Seeds was one of the team's steadiest players, offensively and defensively, but the three-for-one swap was too good to turn down. Other deals brought former Albany Senators second baseman Sammy Bell and Dave Harris, 36, an outfielder with lots of major-league experience. With Seeds gone, only four players remained from the 1935 champions - Harry Smythe, Lauri Myllykangas, Gus Dugas and Ben Sankey.

The new manager, Walter "Rabbit" Maranville, had his hands full piloting a club that had been virtually dismantled and rebuilt over the past few months. But "Rabbit", a veteran of 23 major-league seasons, knew all the tricks. Born on

After 23 seasons in the big leagues, Rabbit Maranville, had seen, and done it all.

October 11, 1891, in Spavinaw, Oklahoma, Maranville broke into the majors as a shortstop with the George Stallings-managed Boston Braves in 1912. A diminutive five foot five, 155 pounds, he was nicknamed Rabbit because of the distinctive way he hopped around while fielding a ground ball. Other players taunted him, suggesting his nickname stemmed from his floppy ears. He was also teased about his height. Baseball Magazine once described him as "The Midget Marvel".

Maranville won the shortstop job with the Braves by impressing Stallings so much that the manager cut his own nephew to make room for him. Stallings had been a brainy, if not gifted player and he sensed the same intelligence in Maranville. In 1914, the Braves' miracle pennant-winning season, second baseman Johnny Evers won the National League MVP award, but many felt Maranville was more deserving. Although he hit only .246, Maranville drove in 78 runs, almost twice as many as Evers, and saved countless games with his fielding. Modern statistical methods show that Maranville, by a wide margin, prevented more runs from being scored against his team than any other National League shortstop in 1914. Maranville never won an MVP award; he came close a couple of times and was in the top 20 in balloting on seven occasions.

Noted for his superb fielding, aggressive leadership and his colorful "basket catches", Maranville was infamous for his wildness off the field. There are loads of stories about Maranville's drunken pranks, such as the time he jumped into a hotel fountain, fully clothed, and emerged with a goldfish in his teeth. Or the time he dangled a teammate out a 12-story window. He apparently enjoyed walking along the ledges of hotels. Dan Howley, a former Montreal catcher and manager, enjoyed recounting a story about Maranville going off on a three-day binge, getting into trouble with the law and having to jump off a bridge to elude police. Howley insisted the cops actually took a few shots at the fleeing Rabbit.

Maranville often clowned around on the field as well, pulling the bill of his cap down over his ear to coax a laugh and making a great production of handing a pair of glasses to an umpire in the middle of a game. But his off-field escapades were the ones that got him in trouble with managers. Between 1920 and 1925 he was sent around the horn from

Boston to Pittsburgh to Chicago. The Cubs made him player-manager in 1925 but regretted it immediately. Maranville celebrated the new job by getting drunk on the team train and dousing his sleeping players with ice-water. "Rabbit" was chased out of Chicago after only eight weeks. The next season he wound up in Brooklyn, where he quickly wore out his welcome and was sent to the Cardinals in 1927. By then, Maranville's drinking was affecting his performance on the field and the Cards demoted him to the Rochester Red Wings. That's when Maranville decided it was time to quit drinking.

Maranville returned to the Cardinals in 1928. Asked for his thoughts on prohibition, he replied: "There is a lot less drinking now than there was before 1927 because I quit drinking on May 24, 1927." In the 1928 World Series, back in top form, he hit .308 in a losing effort against the Yankees. He was traded again the next season - back to the Boston Braves - and became a key performer for four seasons at shortstop, second and third base. In 1932, at the age of 41, Maranville led the National League in fielding and putouts. But while he stayed away from alcohol, he couldn't fully shake his reputation. Once, a Boston fan dropped a bottle in the stands and the crash was heard near the Braves' dugout. A leather-lunged fan hollered: "Hey Rabbit, you dropped your pint," and Maranville grabbed a bat and hopped into the stands after him.

Though Maranville was in his forties, he seemed capable of lasting a few more seasons in the majors. But his career suffered a fatal blow in a spring-training game against the Yankees in 1934, when he broke his leg in a home-plate collision and was out for the season. He played a few games in 1935 but wasn't himself and he decided to retire. He left the major leagues as the all-time leader in putouts with 5,133, and as the only player to lead the National league in that category six times. Both marks are still standing. In

Some 1937 Royals: from left: Gus Dugas, Crip Polli, Irvine Jeffries, Joe Benning, Sammy Bell, Rabbit Maranville.

1954, a few weeks after his death from a heart attack, he was elected to the Hall of Fame. With a .258 career batting average and only 28 home runs in more than 10,000 at-bats, he's one of the few men enshrined at Cooperstown mostly for his fielding and leadership abilities.

After retiring from the majors, Maranville took a job as a player-coach for the Class-A Elmira Pioneers and, at the age of 44, hit .323 as a back-up second baseman. That's where the Royals spotted him and offered him the managerial job. As soon as he arrived at spring training he encountered a familiar face, albeit one that may have resurrected unpleasant memories. The Royals' new catcher, Normie Kies, was the Yankees' player Maranville had collided with in the 1934 exhibition game, when he broke his leg. But the new skipper had more important things to worry about, like making the Royals a contending team again.

In fact, the Royals were a better team in 1937, collecting 11 more wins and climbing from sixth to second place in the standings. It was difficult to say whether Maranville or team president Hector Racine deserved the lion's share of credit for the club's improvement. Racine's deals, for example, reaped dividends. Paul Dunlap and Irvine Jeffries were the team's best hitters and sure-handed second baseman Sammy Bell hit .296. Dave Harris played a significant role, batting .294, leading Montreal in home runs with 18 and tying first baseman Bernie Cobb for the lead in RBIs with 74. The only Montreal pitcher to have a good season was 21-game winner Marvin Duke, part of the Bob Seeds trade. All but Cobb, who hit .300, were obtained from clubs other than the Pirates, the team with which the Royals were supposed to have a special relationship.

The Royals made the playoffs in 1937 but they never came close to winning the pennant. The Newark Bears had first place wrapped up by the end of June, when they had a 49-14 record and a 15-game lead over the Royals, a gap that widened as the season progressed. The Bears finished with 109 wins and only 42 losses, capturing the pennant by 25 1\2 games.

The Newark club had become

Four Royals batsmen from 1938. Left to right: Normie Kies, Bob Porter, Sammy Bell and Tom Oliver.

increasingly dominant since the Yankees bought the franchise and made it their top farm team in 1932. New York owner, Col. Jacob Ruppert, was trying to build a network of farm teams, the way Branch Rickey had done with the St. Louis Cardinals. The result had an immediate effect on the balance of power in the International League, as the Bears won the pennant in 1932, 1933 and 1934. Now they were back at the top of the league following a couple of off-years, boasting one of the strongest lineups in minor-league history. The Bears had future Yankees stars such as Charlie Keller and Joe Gordon, and other future major leaguers such as Babe Dahlgren, George McQuinn and Joe Beggs. "Suitcase" Bob Seeds, whom the Royals had traded to obtain Marvin Duke, Normie Kies and Paul Dunlap, was Newark's centre fielder. The talented squad was managed by an experienced major-leaguer, Oscar "Ossie" Vitt.

In the past, the Bears hadn't done well in the playoffs, but they cruised through to the Governor's Cup in 1937, beating Syracuse and Baltimore in straight games. They faltered in the Junior World Series, dropping the first three games against the American Association Columbus Red Birds, a Cardinals' farm team. But the Bears mounted a Herculean comeback, winning the next four games in Columbus to win their first JWS title.

Herculean was not a word to describe the Royals in the playoffs. They won the first game against Baltimore, thanks to a good outing by faithful Harry Smythe, but blew 5-1 leads in the next two games. The pivotal fourth game turned into one of the wildest in International League playoff history.

It was 9-4 for Montreal after five innings when, for the third straight game, the Royals blew a lead, yielding six runs in the sixth inning. Both teams traded a run here and there and by the bottom of the ninth the Royals were back on top, 13-11. But Montreal pitcher Ed Chapman surrendered a two-run, game-tying homer to first baseman Les Powers, his second of the game. Chapman struck out the next Baltimore batter for the second out, and with pitcher Harry Matuzak coming up, the Royals seemed likely to survive into extra innings.

But Matuzak got a base hit and Chapman walked the next two batters, loading the bases. Chapman was the third Montreal pitcher in the game and Maranville decided to let him work his way out of trouble. It wasn't a good decision. Chapman served up three straight balls to catcher Milt Gray, then two strikes, then a fourth ball to walk in the winning run. Baltimore had won 14-13 and had a commanding series' lead. The game featured seven home runs, 36 hits and a near riot in the eighth inning when umpire Chuck Solodare made a close call in Montreal's favor. It prompted a familiar scene in Baltimore: a hail of pop bottles and a hoard of fans trying to get onto the field. This time the police maintained control and the game was completed with only a minor delay.

It was a stunning, humiliating loss for the Royals, who offered little resistance in the fifth game and the Orioles captured the series with a 4-2 victory. In his game account the next day, The Gazette's D.A.L. MacDonald wrote that clubhouse man Bill O'Brien's folding of the team's uniforms following the game was a gesture that best symbolized the club's performance in the playoffs.

Although disappointed by the arrangement, the Royals' renewed their working agreement with the Pirates for the 1938 season. But, as he had done previously, Racine continued to make deals with other organizations and moved to solve the team's pitching problems by obtaining Ben Cantwell from the Brooklyn Dodgers. Cantwell had won 20 games for the Boston Braves a few seasons earlier and, after spending the last year in the minors, was hoping for a return to the majors. He refused to report to Montreal and Racine complained to Dodgers general manager Larry MacPhail, who resolved the matter. Cantwell arrived for spring training, bragging that he would win 25 games. Racine also struck a deal with MacPhail for the services of Art Parks, although the outfielder would remain the property of the Dodgers. Racine then acquired outfielder Arnold Moser from the Cardinals and two players from the Class-A Southern Association - pitcher Bob Porter

and first baseman Alex Hooks. The only good prospect to come from the Pirates was infielder Bill Schuster.

With all the roster shuffling, it was difficult to predict at the start of the 1938 season whether the Royals would be an improved club. The answer came swiftly, when they lost 11 of their first 14 games and were 9 1\2 games out of a playoff spot before mid-season. By the second week of July, with the team in last place and on a 2-12 skid, the club's directors held a closed-door meeting to discuss ways to improve the team. Some directors felt that Maranville was too easy-going and had let the players get out of shape. They wanted Racine to fire him. Instead, the president tried to shake up the team by trading Gus Dugas and Ben Cantwell to Baltimore for power-hitting outfielder Ab Wright.

Dugas was a popular player in Montreal, an adopted favorite son whose relatives from Joliette, north of Montreal, would often come to the stadium to watch him play. He had also been a productive player over the years but was now slumping, and the Royals were desperate for anything that would snap them out of their lethargy. As for Cantwell,

The Royals in early 1938. Left to right: Alex Hooks, Ed Chapman, Ben Sankey, Harry Smythe, Normie Kies, Paul Dunlap, Bill Schuster, Morris Sands, Sammy Bell, Mercer Harris, Rabbit Maranville, Oadis Swigart, George Kadis, Del Wetherell, Bob Porter and Gus Dugas.

he had failed to fulfill expectations, so the Royals were glad to see him go. The team escaped the cellar, but by mid-August it was still 11 games from a playoff spot, leaving Racine with no choice but to fire Maranville.

In his brief tenure as manager, Maranville was liked and respected by most of the players but some of the team's investors found him to be a curious character. He wasn't the type of fellow whose clear-thinking and clean-living would ever be praised by a prime minister, as was the case with Shaughnessy. Occasionally, while the team's catcher strapped on his gear between innings, Maranville would go behind the plate and warm up the pitcher. After receiving the last warm-up toss, he would crank his arm backwards, over his head, and fling the ball back-handed down to second base. The trick usually drew a round of applause from the crowd, which Maranville would acknowledge with a deep bow before trotting back to the dugout.

Maranville also enjoyed kidding around with the players, often performing a ceremonial bow in mock respect when a batter returned to the dugout after hitting a home run. It was the type of behavior that was tolerable if the team was winning but wearisome if it was not. It was the latter for the Royals, who changed managers at mid-season for the fourth time in 10 years (not counting George Stallings' departure due to illness). First baseman Alex Hooks inherited the job for the rest of the season, becoming the team's 10th manager since 1928.

The managerial change had little impact. The Royals finished in sixth place with a 69-84 record, their worst since 1917, when they won only 56 games and then went out

Sammy Bell, acquired from the Albany Senators, was a great defensive second baseman for the Royals and held his own with the bat. Author's collection.

of business. Racine was fed up with the unprofitable working arrangement with the Pirates and decided to sever ties and seek an affiliation with the Dodgers. Not only did Brooklyn seem to have more young talent to offer but Racine got along well with GM Larry MacPhail.

MacPhail was one of baseball's most dynamic personalities. While running the Cincinnati Reds in 1935, he had introduced night baseball to the major leagues. He was a fiery red-head who was a heavy drinker with a quick temper. MacPhail was unpredictable but Racine liked doing business with him. MacPhail was an avid sportsman and Racine often invited him to the Laurentian Mountains to do some fishing. The Dodgers had no Double-A affiliate, and MacPhail was interested in acquiring one. That led to MacPhail and Racine negotiating a working agreement by the end of 1938.

An early indication the Dodgers were taking the affiliation more seriously than the Pirates was their decision to name Burleigh Grimes as the Montreal manager. Grimes, a former major league all-star pitcher, had been the Dodgers' manager for the last two years, succeeding Casey Stengel. Like Maranville, Grimes had enjoyed a long and successful big-league career and - also like Maranville - he had become one of the game's true eccentrics. A former spitball pitcher, Grimes was a notorious hothead, constantly feuding with umpires. In his two seasons managing the Dodgers, the team finished in the second division both times. MacPhail fired him and, in what turned out to be an inspired move, handed the post to the team's shortstop, Leo Durocher. But MacPhail wanted to keep Grimes in the organization, so he sent him to Montreal.

Entering their 12th season since returning to the International League, the Royals had their ninth manager, along with a deal for players and financing that Racine believed would truly benefit the club. Now, Racine had to also hope that replacing the patient Maranville by the hard-nosed Grimes would add some life to a listless bunch of ball players.

Game scene in 1939. On the mound is Montreal's dependable Harry Smyth. Archives nationales du Québec.

1939-1940
Donning Dodger Blue

When Burleigh Grimes was introduced to the Montreal media at a reception in mid-December, 1938, some reporters were astonished to see him wearing an expensive, impeccably tailored suit with a white gardenia in the buttonhole. They were both amused and chagrined to see him clean-shaven and well-coiffured as he held a long cigar between his manicured fingers. One playful reporter wrote that Grimes' pleasant manner and dignified air heightened "the aspect of general well-being, poise and good nature," which seemed in direct contrast to the ball-playing Grimes, who was one of the scruffiest and scrappiest players the game had ever seen.

In his playing days, Grimes was a right-handed pitcher of average build who used his brains and any available tool to retire a batter. In 19 years as a major-league pitcher, Grimes won 270 games with seven different teams, and he did it the old-fashioned way - with a spitball. Defacing the ball was declared illegal in 1920, five years into Grimes' career, but because of a grandfather clause, the 20 or so known spitballers were not forced to abandon the pitch. Urban Shocker, a star with the St. Louis Browns, and future Hall-of-Famer Stan Coveleski were among those granted an exemption. Since Grimes was the last of the group to retire, he is credited with throwing the last legal spitball in major-league history. His spitter was regarded as one of the best ever thrown, sometimes breaking several inches.

Burleigh Grimes, "Ol Stubblebeard", cleaned up his act when he become a manager.

The spitball was only one of the things for which Grimes gained recognition. He was nicknamed "Ol' Stubblebeard" for his habit of refusing to shave on a day he pitched. Grimes believed the whiskers made him look more intimidating. He was also notorious for his vicious arguments with umpires and the delight he took in ridiculing them in front of the fans. He was once ejected from a game for tying a red bandanna over his nose to let an umpire know what he thought of a call. Grimes was a fierce, aggressive competitor but he once admitted that his spitball was as much psychology as it was saliva. He said he used the pitch sparingly but faked a gob of spit on every pitch to keep the hitters guessing. He was a shrewd, determined man who fought his way to the major leagues in an era before big-league teams had extensive scouting systems. The major leagues didn't find Grimes, he found them.

As a child in Clear Lake, Wis., he was a baseball prodigy, the only boy on a team of men managed by his father. When he was 16, Grimes headed off on his own and played for a number of semi-pro teams in Wisconsin, Minnesota and Iowa. One of the teams had him working as a ticket-taker when he wasn't pitching. Another club paid him $125 a season to pitch in the afternoon and run a pool hall at night. In his spare time, Grimes would go home and help his father on the farm. It wasn't until he went south to play for a team in Birmingham, Ala., and allowed only 18 hits in six games, that he attracted some interest. He signed with the Pittsburgh Pirates in 1916 and would win 20 games five times over the next 19 seasons. His best years were with Brooklyn in the 1920s, where he averaged 18 wins over a seven-season stretch. He was an intimidating force. It was often said that his idea of an intentional walk was four pitches at the batter's head.

Although Grimes was undeniably a winner, he also had his share of failure and frustration in the big leagues. He was 3-4 in seven World Series starts and was roughed up in his only two post-season relief appearances. He made it to the World Series four times, with the Brooklyn Robins,

Chicago Cubs and twice with the St. Louis Cardinals, but won only once - with the Cards in 1931.

Pitching for Brooklyn in the 1920 World Series, Grimes was tagged for the first grand-slam homer in Series' history, a blow by Cleveland right-fielder Elmer Smith. Grimes had even harder luck in his attempts to pitch a no-hitter. Five times in his career he was one out away from this baseball rarity only to lose the no-hit bid. He once pitched 20 innings against Philadelphia and allowed only one hit in the final 10 innings, only to have the game called because of darkness with the teams tied at nine runs apiece. Still, his successes far outnumbered his setbacks and Grimes was elected to the Hall of Fame in 1964, 30 years after he retired.

When Grimes was named manager of the Royals, he was authorized to make any trades he deemed necessary. He'd only had the job for a few days when he showed Montreal baseball fans he wasn't about to be ruled by sentiment. Grimes sold veterans Harry Smythe and Alex Hooks to the Chattanooga Lookouts of the Southern Association. The grey-haired Smythe had been with the club for five seasons and was an effective pitcher, winning 74 games, including 16 the previous season. Hooks, 32, had been a dependable first baseman with some power. He also impressed the fans by the way he handled the team after replacing "Rabbit" Maranville.

Smythe and Hooks were popular players, and the Royals' front office received a lot of mail protesting the move. The media speculated the two players were traded because both had stints as manager, and Grimes felt threatened by them. Explaining his actions at the reception where he was introduced as manager, Grimes said that Smythe and Hooks were simply too old to fit into the Royals' plans. He said the 1939 squad would be built around youth and speed and

Steady first baseman Alex Hooks was sent packing by Burleigh Grimes. Archives nationales du Québec.

Association in batting in 1938 with a .337 average. To help the fans forget about Smythe, the Dodgers sent a couple of southpaws, including Kemp Wicker, who had played on the powerful 1937 Newark Bears.

The Royals also added players from other organizations, such as infielder Don Ross, who saw some action with the Detroit Tigers in 1938 and had played in the International League for Toronto the year before. Outfielder Maurice Van Robays was invited to camp. He had led the Southern League in home runs and RBIs in 1938 and had been Royals' property for a couple of years.

On the eve of their first regular-season game against the Baltimore Orioles, the Royals had some familiar faces in the lineup, but also plenty of new ones. Outfielders Arnold Moser and Art Parks had hung on to their starting jobs but Paul Dunlap, who had hit .295 the previous year, lost his to Lindsey Deal. The infield was still anchored by Ben Sankey and Sammy Bell but with former Dodger Haas at first and Ross at third. On the mound, Marvin Duke and Bob Porter were back, giving the starting rotation some International League experience. The team also had new uniforms of Dodger-blue, signifying its new association with Brooklyn.

Many people around the league expected the link with the Dodgers would work out well for the Royals. Some predicted the team would contend for the pennant, along with Newark and Rochester. But Grimes seemed less confident. He felt the team was good defensively and adequate offensively but the pitching worried him. Grimes really didn't know what to expect when the Royals faced the Orioles in the season-opener in late April.

Baltimore manager Rogers Hornsby, a future Hall-of-Famer who'd been Grimes' teammate, opponent and manager over the years, joined Grimes in addressing the crowd before the game, as part of the opening-day

neither player had those assets. Although he didn't promise a pennant, Grimes predicted the Royals would steal more bases than any team in the I.L. "We'll be the runningest team in the league," he vowed.

Four months later, as spring training at Lakes Wales, Fla., neared its end, Grimes seemed to have everything functioning according to plan. The team ran well in Grapefruit League play and executed a number of double steals. The youth movement continued, with more fuzzy-cheeked prospects from the Dodgers' camp arriving to replace aging players. Among the newcomers was Bert Haas, a right-handed-hitting first baseman who led the Southern ceremonies. Grimes told the fans Hornsby was the best hitter he had ever faced. Hornsby didn't return the compliment, naming Grover Cleveland Alexander as the best pitcher he had faced. If the remark annoyed Grimes, he extracted some revenge when the Royals whipped Hornsby's club 10-4. Wicker was the winning pitcher and a combination of the new and old guard - Parks, Haas, Deal and Bell - supplied the offense. The game set the tone for an impressive start as the Royals spent the first 10 days of the season in first place. They started to slide, however, as the pitching problems Grimes had feared started to surface. The Royals were in third place with an 8-6 record by the time they arrived in Montreal for the home opener in early May.

Only 5,500 fans showed up on a bitterly cold day afternoon to see the team in its new outfit. Although the fans recognized only three of the starters from the previous year, they witnessed a fine performance by the home team as it walloped the struggling Orioles 8-1. Wicker won his fourth straight game and the fans got a brief display of Grimes' explosive temper in a mild but spirited argument with an umpire. The win lifted the team into second place, but it had dropped to seventh by the end of the month, spurring the front office into some personnel moves.

In early June, Ben Sankey was released after more than four years of steady service at shortstop. Hector Racine said the veteran had lost a step and the team could no longer afford to keep him. A native of Alabama, Sankey had enjoyed living in Montreal. Unlike most of the players who came to the city, he had learned to speak French. With the departure of Smythe earlier in the season, Sankey had been the only player left from the 1935 pennant-winning team.

Three weeks later, the Royals completed a four-player swap with the Dodgers, sending Art Parks, their best hitter and the league's RBI leader, for pitchers Gene Schott and Cletus "Boots" Poffenberger. They also obtained Toronto-born outfielder Goody Rosen, who had played well for the Dodgers in 1938 but was now a part-time player. Poffenberger was the best known of the three. He was considered by some to be the "ranking screwball of the major leagues," a label that had nothing to do with his repertoire of pitches. Poffenberger got into trouble for breaking curfew and occasionally going AWOL while playing for Brooklyn and Detroit. He was also known to sometimes butcher the English language, once declaring as he limped off the field that he had just "pulled a tenement". His latest bit of after-hour carousing - about a month before the trade to Montreal - had again landed him in the Dodgers' doghouse, as manager Leo Durocher sent him home on a suspension.

Cornered in the clubhouse following the trade announcement, Grimes seemed pleased by the deal. He regaled reporters with a few baseball stories, pausing only to use the spittoon (which he could hit dead-centre from several feet away). But once he ran out of stories Grimes admitted he was concerned about the team's shaky pitching. He claimed to have lost 12 pounds fretting about it since the start of the season. Grimes was so desperate for pitching help that he was heartened when the flaky Poffenberger was quoted as being eager to join the Royals. The newspaper report didn't mention that "Boots" had recently been spotted trying to pitch himself into shape with a semi-pro team in Williamsport, Maryland, and was getting clobbered. As it turned out, Poffenberger never joined the Royals or made it back to the majors.

That meant the Royals had traded their best hitter for a marginal pitcher and a utility outfielder. There was talk that Dodgers GM Larry MacPhail, needing some extra power for his club, had strong-armed Hector Racine into the deal, and some suspected the so-called "working agreement" with the Dodgers might be a one-way street. But the Royals president insisted that both he and Grimes had approved of the deal because they felt it would benefit the Royals. In the final analysis, the trade did little to help the Royals in their bid for a playoff spot. By early August the team was still mired in seventh place, two games ahead of Toronto and 13 games out of a playoff berth. Many fans believed MacPhail hadn't done enough to help the Royals, even though some of the prospects he sent were doing well. Rumors were circulating the team would be sold or the association would be severed. Racine shot down such speculation and expressed confidence the Dodgers would send better players for the 1940 season.

By the end of August the team was still out of playoff contention and the frustration surfaced one night during a tight game in Buffalo. The Royals and the Bisons were tied in the ninth inning with Bill Crouch, a tall right-hander, pitching for Montreal. Crouch argued a call with home-plate umpire Chet Swanson and was ejected. He reacted so violently that he had to be restrained by teammates and practically carried off the field. Then Grimes got into the act and harangued Swanson for 10 minutes, his anger increasing as the argument escalated. Finally, Swanson ejected Grimes, ordering him to leave the field or forfeit the game. Grimes was firmly escorted off the field by Royals coach Red Rollings.

A few days later, whatever chance the Royals still had of making the playoffs vanished, as the team lost Maurice Van Robays, its best hitter and brightest prospect. He was acquired by the Dodgers and then traded to the Pittsburgh Pirates. Shortly after, Montreal tumbled into last place for a spell, with a coinciding decline in attendance. One game in early September attracted only 107 fans. The team clawed its way back into seventh spot on the last day of the season by

splitting a doubleheader against Toronto. Bob Porter collected his 18th win as the team fashioned a 64-88 record. The first year of the working agreement with the Dodgers had been a disappointment, and many blamed MacPhail for failing to provide enough quality players. Grimes, who admitted to making a few mistakes, was criticized by some players for his badgering style. One veteran complained that the hard-nosed manager was always on somebody's back and that made everyone nervous.

Racine decided he needed someone who could get along with the players. A few months after the season it was announced that Grimes had resigned, even though he had a year left on his contract. Sportswriter Baz O' Meara said Grimes had alienated the fans by breaking up the Sankey-Bell double-play combination. There was also the trade of Harry Smythe, inexplicable considering the team's obvious problems on the mound. Grimes was roasted for his failure to make good on his one promise: speed on the basepaths. It was noted that the Royals were by no means "the runningest team in the league." Most of the running had been done by the shellshocked pitching staff as it made a beeline for the showers.

Hector Racine was looking for two things as he prepared for the 1940 season: a new manager and a new deal with the Brooklyn Dodgers. Racine felt the Royals needed a more formal association with a major-league club to keep pace with teams such as Newark, Rochester and Jersey City. Racine wanted the Dodgers to buy a controlling interest in the Royals and MacPhail, who saw how the Yankees and Cardinals had benefited from their Double-A teams, was interested. Before he agreed, however, he demanded extensive renovations to Delorimier Stadium. The stadium had been a state-of-the-art ball park when it was built in 1928 but it was neglected over the years. New grass was needed in the outfield and the infield required a smoother surface. The park also needed a new watering system and additional groundskeepers, so that it could be properly maintained. MacPhail also wanted to enhance the facility's revenue potential by expanding the concession stands and improving the washroom facilities.

While negotiations continued on that front, Racine came up with a short list of managers that included Rogers Hornsby, who had left Baltimore, and former Royal Del Bissonette. He surprised everyone by choosing Clyde Sukeforth, an unknown Dodgers' farmhand. Sukeforth had been a second-string catcher for 10 seasons in the National League, first with Cincinnati and then with Brooklyn. In 1935, the Dodgers converted the slight, wiry New Englander into a manager and dispatched him to run various farm clubs. His last job prior to joining the Royals was as manager of the Elmira Pioneers of the A-calibre Eastern League. The Pioneers finished near the top of the league both seasons under Sukeforth.

Sukeforth was 38 when the Royals hired him with a boyish face and earnest, almost doleful eyes. He had studied at Georgetown and looked and acted more like a young executive than a baseball manager. In fact, he often joked - usually when his team was losing - that he should have listened to his mother and become a banker. Sukeforth was a soft-spoken, even-tempered widower from Maine who only considered the job when he was assured that Bissonette, his friend and fellow

Maine resident, had been eliminated from the running. He was less of an entertainer than Grimes but he had a dry sense of humor that rewarded the attentive listener. When asked if he planned to catch a few games for the Royals, as he had done at Elmira, Sukeforth said he wouldn't be behind the plate but he knew he'd catch plenty if the Royals didn't win. He admitted he didn't have any revolutionary ideas to help the Royals improve. "You can't do tricks with the baseball," he said, a statement that would have been challenged by the spitballing Grimes.

Clyde Sukeforth, a soft-spoken Mainer.

Sukeforth's approach to the looming spring-training camp was simple. None of the often-romanticized rites of spring for him. He boiled training camp down to "taking a fungo bat and a bag of balls and a half-dozen fat pitchers and making them run for two hours while my hands are blistered and raw from batting." Racine, meanwhile, believed that Sukeforth's finest asset was his ability to get along with players and inspire them to play hard, something he felt Grimes hadn't been able to do.

Once Sukeforth was hired, Racine pursued his negotiations with the Dodgers. Things had started to come together by the middle of February, 1940, and it was agreed that the $30,000 cost of stadium renovations would be shared equally by the stadium owners, the concession owners and the Dodgers. Also, the Dodgers would buy a controlling interest in the Royals and make them their No.1 farm team. While Racine would still run the

*Things started looking up for the Royals after they were taken over by the Brooklyn Dodgers.
Left to right: George Staller, Tuck Stainback, Arnold Moser, and Pete Reiser.*

club on a daily basis, the Dodgers would now own - and control - most of the players. Racine said it was the greatest deal ever for baseball in Montreal because, next to the Cardinals and Yankees, the Dodgers owned the best minor-league ball players. It was an equally good arrangement for the Dodgers. Later, after MacPhail left Brooklyn, he boasted about his coup, saying he had earned his paycheque with that one deal.

The Royals opened training camp in Lake

Wales in the spring of 1940 as the jewel in the Dodgers' crown. Now that the team was part of the Dodgers' family, MacPhail seemed to pay more attention to it. After a few exhibition games in early April, which the Royals lost, he barked at Racine, "Hector, your ball club looks like hell!" Despite this lapse in front of the boss, the Royals were indeed much improved. They had acquired veteran minor-league shortstop Louis "Bosey" Berger, major-league outfielder Tuck Stainback and two promising outfielders whom Sukeforth had managed at Elmira - Pete Reiser and George Staller. Reiser had been an infielder with Elmira, but shifted to the outfield after hurting his arm. He was a good hitter who always aimed for the fences with his looping swing. Among the Royals' returnees were infielders Sammy Bell and Don Ross, catcher Joe Becker and Bob Porter, the team's best pitcher in 1939.

The opening series of the season in Jersey City was cancelled because of five straight days of rain. The Montreal front office wasn't pleased by the washout at Roosevelt Stadium because it cost the Royals a healthy cut of what was always a huge gate for opening day. But while the team lost a few thousand dollars because of the rainouts, it was able to start the season a little richer in talent. The Dodgers sent Bert Haas back to the Royals in time to open the season against Newark. Haas had started the 1939 season with the Royals but ended up in A-ball for most of the year. The Montreal organization hoped he could stick around this time and provide some power.

The Royals clobbered the Newark Bears 12-1 when they finally launched the season, a week later than scheduled. They stroked 19 hits and Kemp Wicker pitched a complete game, allowing only two hits and two walks. It was a good day for the newcomers; Staller and Reiser each got three hits and Stainback and Berger collected two. Haas, who arrived from Brooklyn just in time to don his

uniform, hit a home run and Bell went 4-for-5. The Royals continued to sizzle during their opening road trip, with the exception of Reiser, who was demoted to Elmira and eventually bypassed the Royals on his way up to the Dodgers. Spotty pitching, however, had the team in third place when it finally arrived in Montreal for the home opener.

Wicker, who had won three opening games since joining the Royals, again got the call for the home debut against first-place Jersey City. He pitched a three-hit, 1-0 shutout on a cold, foggy day. Nine thousand fans turned out to see the brilliant pitching performance. They also witnessed an impressive debut by Stainback. In the fourth inning, the Giants had a runner at third with one out when the Stainback snared a fly ball in centre and fired a bullet to the plate to nail the runner. In the bottom of the inning, Stainback blasted a Frank Pearce pitch off the left-field wall for a triple and scored the only run on a double by Haas.

The following Sunday, the free-swinging Royals attracted more than 21,000 for a doubleheader against Newark. One thousand fans were put in a special roped-off section of centre field and ground rules were devised in case a ball went into the crowd. The team disappointed the overflow crowd by losing both games.

Slipping in the standings by late May, the Royals acquired two players they hoped would help them land a playoff spot. One was Gus Suhr, a former all-star first baseman with the Pittsburgh Pirates. The other was Jimmy Ripple, one of the most popular players in Royals' history. Ripple had done rather well with the New York Giants since leaving the Royals following the 1935 season, but he was unable to win a starting job and landed in Brooklyn in 1939. Now 30, Ripple was at least 20 pounds heavier than his early days with Montreal, but he provided a spark as soon as he put on the uniform. By the middle of July, the Royals had fashioned an eight-game winning streak and climbed back into fourth place. Ripple hit over .300 throughout the summer and helped the club stay within reach of the playoffs. But the race got tougher for the Royals when the Dodgers recalled Ripple for the month of September and sold Stainback to the Detroit Tigers.

The Royals' flickering playoff hopes were all but extinguished in early September when George Staller, the team's home run and RBI leader, snagged one of his spikes running to second base against Rochester and snapped his ankle. The team made a late-season run at fourth spot but came up one game short. The Royals finished at 80-80, an improvement over the previous year but still not enough to qualify for the playoffs. Some fans complained that the washed-out opening series against Jersey City had cost the Royals a playoff berth because it forced them to play too many doubleheaders. But the disappointing outcome had more to do with personnel than the weather.

The team's major weakness in 1940, as it had been in 1939, was pitching. Only one of the starters (Wicker, 18-10) had a good season and the bullpen was unreliable. An epidemic of sore arms accounted for some of the pitching woes. Red Lucas, for one, couldn't raise his arm above his shoulder for much of the season. Max Macon's arm was so sore he couldn't sleep at night, and Porter, an 18-game winner 1939, could barely get the ball up to the plate. One afternoon the three pitchers were in the clubhouse being treated for their aching arms when one of them ragged his teammate about being "a softball pitcher." The spat escalated to the point where Sukeforth came to investigate. He saw the three pitchers heading onto the field to determine who could throw the ball the farthest. Sukeforth told them to sit down and give both their arms and mouths a rest. "Hell," he cracked, "you don't even have to leave the room to settle that bet."

After Larry MacPhail left Brooklyn (seen here with Yankee manager Bucky Harris) he often bragged about having landed the Royals as the top Dodger farm club.

1941

The Junior World Series Comes to Montreal

Sukeforth (centre) points out some of the nuances of playing ball in Montreal. His pupils are Pete Reiser (right) and George Staller.

The Royals were in need of an overhaul and heading into the 1941 season it was clear that few jobs were safe. In late April, MacPhail called Racine and promised he would be sending some quality talent. He mentioned the name of Ed Head, a 23-year-old right-handed pitching prospect. Head had played little for the Dodgers the previous season, but he showed promise and there was no doubt he had character. He was a natural southpaw, but had learned to pitch

with his right arm after severely injuring the left one, almost requiring an amputation. The Royals also signed Chet Kehn, a cocky 19-year-old curveballer who had pitched for the Elmira Pioneers in 1940. Racine was high on Kehn, especially after he'd watched him pitch for the Dodgers in an exhibition game against the Detroit Tigers. Kehn twice struck out Tigers slugger Hank Greenberg with men on base. Racine also had high expectations for veteran Cardinals farmhand

Al Sherer and Max Macon, the only returning pitcher from the previous season's sore-arm brigade.

Shortstop was the next concern for the Royals' braintrust. "Bosey" Berger was a disappointment and he often complained about playing in Montreal. He didn't like Canada's high taxes compared to the United States, nor did he appreciate the infield playing surface at Delorimier Stadium. Little had gone right for him in 1940. At one point he went to a doctor to have his eyes examined and was given a prescription for glasses. The first time he wore them for batting practice he couldn't hit a thing and he claimed the glasses worsened his vision. Sukeforth thought Berger was just being difficult, so he ordered him to follow the doctor's orders and wear the glasses. Berger insisted he couldn't see the ball and called the doctor for an explanation. After some checking the doctor reluctantly admitted he had mistakenly given Berger someone else's prescription.

Aware of Berger's unhappiness in Montreal, the Royals had acquired Billy Rogell near the end of the 1940 season, a few days after he was released by the Chicago Cubs. Rogell had been a solid major-leaguer for 14 years but his brief stint with the Royals was less than spectacular. In an early September game he fell while chasing a pop fly in shallow left field, landing on his rump as the ball fell beside him. It was one of five errors Rogell made in the game and the small but ornery crowd at Delorimier Downs razzed him as he jogged off the field late in the game. Rogell fired his glove at a group of jeering fans behind the Montreal dugout. Flashing better defense than Rogell, the fans caught the glove and ripped it to shreds.

Roy Hughes, the team captain, excelled at third base.

Clyde Sukeforth was surrounded by talented players.

The Royals didn't re-sign Rogell. They traded outfielders Arnold Moser and Gus Suhr to the Milwaukee Brewers of the American Association for Claude Corbitt, a slick-fielding shortstop who had played baseball at Duke University with Sammy Bell. He could run hit and field and seemed tailor-made for Montreal. The deal brought a smile to Sukeforth's face. "If you don't write before this season is over that he is the best player in the league, I'll buy you a new hat," he promised a reporter. The move also allowed Sukeforth to shift infielder Don Ross to the outfield, where he'd likely be needed with the departures of Tuck Stainback and Jimmy Ripple (traded to Cincinnati) and the injury to George Staller. The outfield was further bolstered by acquiring 33-year-old Woody Jensen, a .285 hitter in nine seasons of mostly second-string duty with the Pittsburgh Pirates, and by trading Berger to

Newark for Jack Graham, a six-foot-two, 200-pound slugger. A vacancy at first base was filled by Paul Campbell, a good young prospect the Dodgers had obtained from the Red Sox organization.

The biggest surprise of the 1941 spring-training camp was the comeback of third baseman Roy Hughes. A member of the Royals early in 1940, Hughes had encountered a string of bad luck. First, he collided with Rochester shortstop Frank Crespi while running the bases and severely separated his right shoulder. Then, while recuperating at home, he was badly burned by hot tar while repairing his basement floor. The tar scorched his neck and injured shoulder. When he reported to camp, showing off the ugly red welts on his skin, he insisted his shoulder was better than ever. He claimed the doctors had told him the

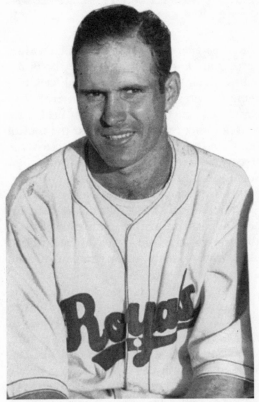

Paul Campbell, a master at double plays from first base.

Ed Head was the Royals best pitcher in 1941.

burning tar somehow accelerated the healing process. Whether it was fact or fiction, Hughes was throwing well enough to win the job at the hot corner.

The Royals played their first game of the season against the Newark Bears, the defending Junior World Series champion and a favorite to repeat. Despite a four-run rally in the ninth inning, the Royals lost 7-6, although there were some encouraging signs in defeat. Catcher Herman Franks, the most recent roster addition, started behind the plate and hit a home run, two doubles and collected four RBIs. A last-minute cut by the Dodgers, Franks was offered a trade to another National League club, but he decided to stay with the Brooklyn organization, even if it meant a stint in the minors. He made up his mind to join Montreal on the morning of the game in Newark and MacPhail sent him from Ebbets Field to Ruppert Stadium in a cab. Franks arrived an hour before the first pitch and signed a contract while he put on his uniform.

The Royals won seven of their next 11 games and returned for the home opener at spruced-up Delorimier Stadium. In another tough battle against Newark, the Royals staked Ed Head to an early three-run lead. Head faltered in the third, walking the first three men he faced. Sukeforth noticed the young pitcher was rushing his delivery and releasing the ball too early, so he visited the mound and suggested he hold onto the ball a little longer. Head settled down but Sukeforth got into an argument with the home-plate umpire a few pitches later and was ejected. It was an uncharacteristic loss of composure by the Montreal manager, who'd been criticized a year earlier for being too passive.

Sukeforth spent the rest of the game in the clubhouse, chain-smoking, but he was constantly updated about developments in the game. In the ninth inning, someone relayed the news that Ziggy Sears, a 200-

Shortstop Claude Corbitt could run, hit and field.

pound catcher known for his tape-measure home runs,was pinch-hitting for the Bears. Sukeforth shuddered as he flashed back to a game the previous season, when Sears had blasted a home run over the right-field fence at Delorimier Stadium and onto the roof of the Grover Knit-To-Fit factory across the street. "There's nothing to do but pray," Sukeforth told himself as Sears prepared to bat. "There isn't a thing we can pitch to that guy that he can't hit." Sukeforth buried his head in his hands and was thinking wistfully about a job in a bank when he heard Head had thrown something Sears couldn't hit and the game was over.

Things continued to go well for the Royals as the season progressed. They stayed close to the first-place Bears, even overtaking them for a few days at the end of May. Sparked by Corbitt's 19-game hitting streak, the Royals had compiled a lofty .302 team batting average, the best in the league by 35

The carousing Mungo, no fun at all for opposing hitters.

percentage points. The front office was also on a roll, acquiring infielder-outfielder Alex Kampouris and hard-throwing right-hander Van Lingle Mungo from the Dodgers. Kampouris had played for Newark the year before and slugged 36 home runs - one shy of the league high - and knocked in 97 runs.

Mungo had pitched well for the Dodgers from 1932 to 1936. He was heralded by some as the next Dizzy Dean, but he had a nasty habit of arguing with managers and teammates and trouble seemed to follow him wherever he went. In Cuba, during spring training, Mungo had been caught in bed with one of the dancers at a night club he visited. The matter came to the attention of the woman's husband, a former bullfighter, who attacked Mungo on the dance floor. The nightclub sued the Dodgers for $20,000 in damages. The pitcher was sent to the Royals as penance for his sins.

The 29-year-old pitcher was unpredictable and hot-headed but reporters loved him because he was a colorful story-spinner, especially about some of his former managers. Mungo liked to recall how revered Dodgers manager Wilbert Robinson mistakenly called him Fungo instead of Mungo for an entire season. He remembered how Robinson would clean his dentures in the middle of a game, usually during a tense moment. Mungo would imitate Brooklyn catchers peering frantically into the dugout for a signal, only to see the manager scraping his false teeth with a pen-knife. Mungo was irreverent but he brought experience to the Royals' bullpen, along with a blazing fastball that he delivered with a dizzyingly high leg kick.

Shortly after the team picked up Mungo and Kampouris it lost its top catcher, Herman Franks, to the Dodgers. Franks was hitting .292 at the time and delivering key hits from the bottom of the order. The Royals made a quick deal with Indianapolis of the American Association and recovered dependable Joe Becker to assume the catching chores. Despite losing key players, the 1941 Royals seemed unshaken. They had more depth than the 1940 squad and a June 19 meeting against arch-rival Newark demonstrated just how much the Royals had improved.

It was scoreless into the seventh inning, as the Bears' ace left-hander Tommy Byrne had a two-hitter. Montreal's s Ed Head was pitching even better. He had retired the first 18 batters he faced and took a perfect game into the seventh, with the top of the Bears' order due to bat. Lead-off batter Tommy Holmes fouled a 3-and-2 pitch high behind the plate. Becker scrambled after it, throwing his mask aside, and manoeuvred underneath the pop-up. But as he set himself to make the catch, he stumbled over his mask and dropped the ball. Holmes walked on the next pitch, moved to second on a sacrifice bunt and took third on a base hit. He remained there as Head retired Frank Kelleher, the league's leading home-run hitter, on a grounder.

The Royals were still in trouble because old nemesis Ziggy Sears, second in the league in homers, was up next. Head had retired Sears in a key situation in the home opener but Sukeforth played it safe this time and gave Sears an intentional walk, loading the bases with two out. The next batter, first baseman Fred Collins, lifted a routine fly ball to Jack Graham in left field. Graham drifted under it but, inexplicably, he slipped and fell. Head got the final out of the inning, which he'd started with a perfect game and now trailed 3-0, despite allowing only one hit. The Bears added two more in the eighth and the Royals, after a run in the bottom of the inning, went to the last of the ninth trailing 5-1.

A tiring Byrne walked Graham to lead off the inning. He then hit Woody Jensen and walked Alex Kampouris to load the bases with none out. Up came George Staller, still limping from the ankle he'd broken last season. Many of the fans, smelling a comeback, hollered for a home run, but others moved toward the exits, and they hurried their pace when Staller struck out. Becker followed with a two-run single and wildness by George Washburn, who relieved Byrne and issued a walk and a bases-loaded wild pitch, made the score 5-4. Washburn then walked Paul Campbell to re-load the bases, but Claude Corbitt hit a ground ball, forcing a runner at home for the second out, and now it was up to Roy Hughes.

The hard-luck man of 1940, Hughes showed no ill effects from his tar-scalded shoulder. As the fans who'd been wending their way to the exits stood frozen in the aisles, Hughes belted a single that brought home the tying and winning runs. It was the type of dramatic late-inning rally that Montreal fans hadn't seen in a long while. It also gave the Bears a hint of what they might

expect from the Royals should the two teams meet in the playoffs. And as the season progressed, it was obvious the Royals were destined to make the playoffs for the first time since 1937.

Late in the season, with this playoff prospect in mind, the Royals made a few moves to solidify their lineup. They traded Sammy Bell, Joe Becker and George Staller to Rochester for catcher Homer "Dixie" Howell, one of the best young prospects in the International league. Bell had played second base for the Royals for five seasons and was having a good year, but MacPhail had stated in spring training he was on the trading block. The team also signed outfielder Jake Powell, a steady performer in the American League since 1930 and a .455 hitter for the Yankees in their 1936 World Series' triumph over the Giants. Powell was acquired for his experience team in clutch situations - and he'd find himself in several before the season was over.

The Royals couldn't catch Newark, who won the pennant by 10 games, but they were good enough to nose out Buffalo for second place, finishing the season at 90-64. It was the team's best record since 1935. Ross and Hughes hit over .300. Jensen, Corbitt, Campbell and Graham all hit above .280 and the Royals posted a team batting average of .269, second only to the mighty Bears. Graham had the best year overall at the plate, knocking in more than 100 runs and hitting a team-record 31 homers. Defensively, the team was the best in the league, led by Campbell, who set a league record by starting 26 double plays from first base. Campbell, who led the league in stolen bases with 24, combined with Corbitt to make the Royals the "runningest team in the league," which had been promised by Grimes two years earlier. The starting pitching was also much improved, as Head led the staff with 18 wins, followed by Kehn and and Sherer with 16 and 14 respectively.

The bullpen, anchored by wily veterans Mungo and Macon, was finally a crew that Sukeforth could count on.

The playoff set-up had been changed slightly since 1937, the last time the Royals had qualified. The first-place team no longer faced the third-place finisher in the opening round, but was matched against No. 4. That meant the Royals went up against Buffalo, and because they had edged the Bisons out for second place, the Royals had home-field advantage. Second place also earned the players $2,000, but by the time the money was divided up, each player pocketed a paltry $83, four dollars less than "Shorty", the clubhouse boy, received when the players passed the hat for him.

Kemp Wicker pitched a strong game for Montreal the next night and Roy Hughes hit a two-run homer as the Royals won 4-2. But Hutchinson made it 10 straight wins over Montreal, tossing a three-hitter to take the fifth game and a 3-2 series lead. Returning home Sunday afternoon for Game 6, the Royals had 14,000 fans cheering them as Van Lingle Mungo preserved a win with a gritty ninth-inning save, forcing a seventh and deciding game. More than 15,000 came to Delorimier Stadium the following night and looked on glumly during the Bisons' three-run first inning. They soon cheered up, however, as the Royals scored eight runs in the bottom of the inning, capitalizing on Buffalo errors - the Bisons made six in the game - for an 11-8 victory. The Royals had

The first Royals team to make the Junior World Series. Front row, left to right: G. Lefebvre (clubhouse boy), Steve Rachunok, Ed Head, Homer Howell, Fred Walters, Jack Graham, Wes Flowers, Don Ross, Max Macon, Tex Carleton, Van Mungo, Fran Pearce, Gene Karst (traveling secretary). Back row: Chet Kehn, Roy Hughes, Claude Corbitt, Alex Kampouris, Woody Jensen, Paul Campbell, Jake Powell, Kemp Wicker, Clyde Sukeforth (manager), Al Sherer, Bill O'Brien (trainer).

In the series opener, Montreal faced league MVP Fred Hutchinson, a towering right-hander who had won 26 games in 1941, including seven straight against the Royals. He continued that dominance in the opening game, retiring the first 13 batters and going on to a three-hit, 4-0 victory. Montreal's Ed Head evened the series with a two-hitter in Game 2, but Hutchinson, in a relief role, notched another win in the third game.

advanced to the Governor's Cup round for the second time in their history, but they'd now have yet another confrontation with the Newark Bears.

Montreal started shakily, blowing the first game 6-5 before rebounding the next night, parlaying 13 walks and 12 hits into a 12-4 victory. The Royals then won 6-4 before a home crowd, helped by Jack Graham's homer and a clutch double by Alex Kampouris. The team took a firm 3-1 series' grip, using tight defense and a solid pitching performance by Chet Kehn, hospitalized because of a bad back a few days before the fourth game.

A record Delorimier Downs crowd of 24,732 were on hand for Game 5, anticipating the Royals' first Governor's Cup triumph. Spectators were four deep in a special roped-off section of centre field and another row of fans stretched along the fence from centre field to the left-field foul pole, much like a gallery at a golf tournament. The game was a spine-tingling tug-of-war that had the home team up by one run after the second inning, down by two after the sixth and scrambling to tie the score in the ninth. The Royals came close but fell one run short as Newark cut their series' lead to 3-2.

More then 11, 000 fans filed into Roosevelt Stadium on a warm, foggy night to watch the Bears battle for their lives. Newark was ahead 4-2 in the ninth but Montreal sent the game into extra innings with a two-run homer by Don Ross. It was a sizzling day in Newark and as the temperature cooled around midnight, a thick fog enveloped Roosevelt Stadium. The mist was so thick that a couple of ferry boats collided on the Hackensack River near the ballpark. In the 11th inning, with pitcher Max Macon doing emergency duty in left field for the Royals and reliever Steve Rachunok on the mound, the Bears loaded the bases with two out. Ziggy Sears came to bat as the fog thickened and Rachunok served him three consecutive balls before throwing a strike. Sears then fouled off a few pitches before getting under a ball and sending a pop fly toward left field that disappeared in the fog. Macon hesitated, uncertain where the ball was. He broke toward the infield, then stopped as the ball sailed over his head and landed 20 feet behind him. The field was so shrouded it took the fans a few moments to figure out

what had happened. They soon caught on and they erupted with joy as the Bears scored the winning run.

The Royals were frustrated and angry heading into the deciding game. Their exasperation grew as things continued to fall in place for Newark, who grabbed an early 3-0 lead in Game 7. Montreal picked up two runs in the fourth, but another questionable call by an umpire brought Sukeforth out of the dugout in the eighth and he was ejected. The Royals entered the ninth inning trailing Newark's ace pitcher Tommy Byrne by a run. It was like a replay of the Royals' home opener against the Bears, with the two clubs in a one-run game and Sukeforth calling the shots from the clubhouse.

But it was at this point the Royals' luck started to change. Roy Hughes led off the inning with a seemingly routine pop fly in foul territory that wasn't caught because of confusion between catcher Tom Padden and first baseman Fred Collins. It appeared the Royals weren't going to cash in on the break when Hughes bounced an easy grounder to third baseman Hank Majeski. But the ball took a wild hop in front of Majeski and bounced over his head into left field for a double. Clean-up hitter Jack Graham, followed with a score-tying, RBI single.

Byrne gave way to reliever John Lindell, a 23-game winner with a league-leading 2.05 earned-run-average. A sacrifice bunt moved Graham to second for Jake Powell, the late-season addition who was acquired specifically for such a pressure situation. Powell lived up to his clutch-hitting reputation, lining a ball past the outstretched glove of Newark shortstop George Scharein into left field to score Graham with the go-ahead run. Three outs were all that separated the Royals from their first Junior World Series appearance.

Sukeforth, in solitary suffering inside the

Montreal clubhouse, sent word to get Van Lingle Mungo into the game and the big right-hander induced the lead-off batter to ground out. Then, in a deja-vu of the home opener, a player came into the clubhouse to tell Sukeforth that Ziggy Sears would be pinch hitting for the Bears. Again, the manager found himself with his head in his hands, sweating through a crucial at-bat he could only picture in his mind. With a full count on Sears, Mungo tried to jam the big catcher inside. But Sears was ready for it and yanked the ball toward the right-field foul-pole. For a few heartbreaking seconds, it appeared that the ball would stay fair, but it veered foul at the pole. Mungo wiped the sweat from his brow as he contemplated his next pitch. Guessing that Sears wouldn't expect a breaking ball, Mungo threw a slow curve that froze the slugger as he watched the ball float over the plate for strike three. Breathing a sigh of relief, Mungo got Joe Mack on a popup to third baseman Roy Hughes and the Royals had won the Governor's Cup. They celebrated gleefully on the field and then came bounding into the clubhouse, shrieking and howling, to greet Sukeforth, who told them they deserved all the credit for the win.

The Royals would now face the Columbus Red Birds, who had defeated Louisville for the American Association crown, in the Junior World Series. The Red Birds had been taken over by Branch Rickey and the St. Louis Cardinals in 1931 and, like Newark, they were perennial contenders. They had three Junior World Series' appearances in the last seven seasons and had won the title twice. Several Cardinals stars came up through Columbus, including Enos "Country" Slaughter, pitchers Paul "Daffy" Dean (Dizzy's brother) and Max Lanier. The 1941 Red Birds were managed by former Phillies and Reds skipper (and future Dodger manager) Burt Shotton. They featured the pitching of ace right-handers Murray Dickson, 21-11, and John Grodzicki, 19-5. At the plate, Columbus had a team batting average of .291, the best in the American Association. The club was led offensively by shortstop Lou Klein, the American Association batting champion (.370), and former Royal Bert Haas, who hit .315 and led the league with 133 RBIs.

The first three games of the series were to be played in Montreal and the rest would shift to Columbus. Ten thousand people, including Branch Rickey, came out to see the Junior World Series get under way at Delorimier Stadium, where the home team got off to a good start. Second baseman Alex Kampouris hit a grand slam in the first inning and Jack Graham hit another in the third that reached the Knit-To-Fit factory roof. The Royals cruised to a 12-6 victory, their only misfortune occurring in the eighth inning when Kampouris was hit in the head by a pitch. The injury wasn't serious but Kampouris was ordered to sit out the rest of the series. The next night the Royals played horribly, committing five errors and handing Red Birds pitcher John Grodzicki an early lead that he never relinquished. Montreal rebounded to win the third game 9-6 with a seven-run, sixth-inning outburst.

Red Bird Stadium, where the rest of the series now shifted, was almost completely surrounded by graveyards and, since the brick wall around the outfield was exceptionally far from home plate, the park was a graveyard for potential home runs. The left-field fence was an especially long poke. A batter had to launch a ball about 460 feet to clear the fence, something nobody had accomplished in the stadium's nine-year history. (Joe DiMaggio was the first to do it in a 1946 exhibition game.) That was bad news for the Royals, who'd been hitting a lot of home runs in the playoffs. They could have used the long ball in Game 4, which Columbus won by one run. The next night, Montreal roughed up John Grodzicki for three first-inning runs but the Red Birds battered Royals starter Max Macon on the way to a 13-run output for a 3-2 lead in the series

Two days of rain interrupted the series, and it didn't resume until Sunday, the same October afternoon as a memorable World Series game between the Brooklyn Dodgers and New York Yankees. Ironically, both games would games would come down to a costly error, resulting in a heartbreaking defeat. In Brooklyn, the Dodgers were leading in the ninth inning, one out from tying the series 2-2, when catcher Mickey Owen dropped a third strike on Tommy Henrich. The mistake opened the door for Yankees to stage a rally that helped them win the game and, ultimately, the World Series. At Columbus, the Royals were ahead 8-5 in the ninth, thanks to a five-run upsurge in the sixth. With two on and one out in the bottom of the ninth, Royals starter Chet Kehn induced Hugh Poland to pop up to left-fielder Jake Powell. Powell drifted under the ball, ready to pocket the second out but, somehow, the ball popped out of his glove and a run scored. Rochester had closed within two runs when the dangerous Harry "The Hat" Walker came to the plate. He battled Kehn fiercely, fouling off seven pitches, before pulling a 2-2 pitch over the right-field fence to win the game and the Junior World Series for the Red Birds.

Sukeforth was heartbroken but gracious in defeat. He consoled Powell after the game and insisted there was nothing wrong with Kehn's pitch to Walker. Shotton, the Columbus manager, said his team had simply "out-lucked" the Royals. It was a disappointing end to a remarkable season in which Sukeforth brought the Royals from fifth place in 1940 to a Junior World Series appearance. Now, there was optimism that next year would be just as good, even though some players wouldn't be returning. No one knew it at the time, but a lot of teams would be deprived of some of their players in 1942, when they were called into military service.

A practice at Delorimier Stadium. The H and E of the Black Horse Beer billboard (background, left) was wired with electric lights to indicate a hit or an error.

1942-1945

9

Cheering on the Native Sons

A couple of months after the end of the 1941 baseball season, Japan attacked Pearl Harbor, drawing the United States into the Second World War. Hoping that baseball would boost public morale, U.S. President Franklin D. Roosevelt asked baseball commissioner Kenesaw Mountain Landis to keep the game going despite the war. Baseball continued throughout the conflict, although the quality of play in the major and minor leagues was somewhat diluted as many players left their teams for military service. In many cases, the departing players were replaced by aging veterans, such as

former Royal Tuck Stainback, who landed a job in the Yankees outfield after Joe DiMaggio left for the service. Many raw youngsters also got jobs in the minors and majors, players who might otherwise not have made it. But while it was business as usual at the major league and Double-A levels, things weren't as secure in the lower echelons. Most of the 40 or so minor leagues that started the 1941 season closed down and didn't get going again until 1946.

For the Royals, the next few seasons were disappointing compared to the exciting 1941

Les trois amis. Local heroes Roland Gladu (left), Stan Bréard (centre) and Jean-Pierre Roy.

Governor's Cup victory and Junior World Series appearance. The Royals had a decent season in 1942, finishing in second place. (Newark won its seventh pennant in 11 years.) But because of player turnover, they were no longer the same battling bunch from a year earlier. Dixie Howell and Jack Graham were among the few returnees. Howell provided leadership behind the plate and Graham continued to hit monster home runs. Newcomer Les Burge, a six-foot-two, 200-pound outfielder who won the American Association MVP award in 1941, wore the International League home-run crown in 1942, hitting 28. He teamed with Graham and major-league journeyman Gene Moore to give the Royals a formidable home-run punch (they hit 77 between them, more than the entire 1941 team). Also joining the Royals in 1942 was a 20-year-old outfielder named Carl Furillo, who had a potent bat and a rifle-like arm. Furillo won the left-field job and hit .284 with 51 RBIs.

Montreal baseball fans also got a brief look at the legendary Lynwood "Schoolboy" Rowe, whom the Dodgers had obtained from Detroit halfway through the season. A tall Southerner, Rowe was an all-star with the Tigers in the mid-1930s but had struggled the last few seasons. Rowe was just passing through Montreal (he caught on with the Phillies the following season) but he was remembered by local reporters for eating Tums by the handful to soothe his churning stomach, and also for a comment he made on a train ride to Syracuse during the playoffs. A teammate mentioned seeing Albert Einstein aboard the train, explaining the scientist was spending the summer in the Adirondacks. "You mean Eisenstadt?" asked Rowe. "He was with us in Detroit for a while."

Rowe recorded the Royals' lone playoff win in 1942. The team lost to Syracuse in the opening round, manhandled by Red Barrett and Ewell Blackwell, a six foot six 19-year-

As soon as Branch Rickey, the man they called "The Deacon", took over the Brooklyn organization, he vowed to reform the hard-drinking Montreal Royals.

old with a confusing array of sinkers, forkballs and changeups - a repertoire that would serve him well during several all-star seasons with the Cincinnati Reds.

The Royals' lacklustre performance in the playoffs led to some off-season changes, which were part of a greater transformation in the Brooklyn Dodgers organization. Larry MacPhail, the Dodgers president since 1937, left the team to join the army and was succeeded by Branch Rickey, one of baseball's true innovators. In his 23 years as general manager of the St. Louis Cardinals, Rickey had changed baseball forever by establishing an extensive network of minor-league teams that supplied St. Louis with a steady stream of talent, recruited from every corner of the U.S. Rickey's farm system allowed the Cardinals to compete with the richer teams, such as New York and Chicago. At the time he joined the Dodgers, St. Louis had just won the National

League pennant and its American Association farm team, the Columbus Red Birds, had won two straight Junior World Series. The system of farm teams had been adopted by the Yankees, and one of MacPhail's duties in Brooklyn had been to set up a Rickey-like system for the Dodgers.

Rickey was a good judge of baseball talent, a sharp businessman and a firm believer in discipline. A devout Methodist, he abhorred drinking, gambling and loose-living of any kind. When he ran across an unmarried player with a girl friend on his arm, he often urged the player to marry the woman, sometimes even suggesting a date for the wedding. He once offered shortstop Stan Rojek $1,000 to get married by a certain date and questioned him when he missed the deadline. "My fiancee told me to hold out for $2,000," he explained. When Rickey joined the Dodgers he instructed manager Leo Durocher to put an end to poker games on trains and in the clubhouse. He also grilled Durocher about rumors he was hanging out with unsavory characters. (Five years later Durocher was suspended because of alleged connections with professional gamblers). But Rickey's concerns didn't end with the Dodgers. He believed there were also problems to clear up with the organization's top farm team.

Rickey had heard that a number of players on the 1942 Royals liked to break curfew and carouse until dawn. Team president Hector Racine admitted there was a problem, disclosing that hotel managers had often complained to him about the behavior of certain players when the club was on the road. No incidents were reported in the newspapers (possibly because some of the reporters may themselves have been involved in the carousing) but some reporters occasionally made passing references to anonymous players who "liked to finish a flagon" or "enjoyed a beaker of beer." Rickey blamed the indiscipline on

Clyde Sukeforth's easy-going style. At a news conference late in 1942, Rickey said, "My information is that the club got away from Sukeforth. I was told there was far too much drinking going on and that Sukeforth was unable to enforce discipline." Rickey then announced he was relieving Sukeforth of his duties as the Royals manager.

Recalling the developments 50 years later, Sukeforth said the Dodgers' farm system was in its early stages when he managed the Royals, and it wasn't very productive. Instead of showing patience and seeking players with character, MacPhail signed a lot of people on the cheap, without conducting much of a personality study. "We got a lot of undesirables at half-price - players the other teams didn't want," Sukeforth recalled. "Some of their habits weren't the best." There were changes as soon as Rickey arrived. Sukeforth was made a coach and

Witty Fresco Thompson, returned to manage the Royals in 1943, but was soon at his wit's end.

later a scout for the Dodgers, and he helped build the great Brooklyn teams of the 1940s and early 1950s. While other teams cut back during the war, Rickey had scouts scouring the continent for talent, and he signed as many players as he could. "If we win the war, it's worth it," he reasoned. "And if we lose the war, what difference does it make?"

Requiring a replacement for Sukeforth in Montreal, Rickey wanted to hire Freddie Fitzsimmons, who was nearing the end of a long and distinguished career in the National League. But Fitzsimmons wasn't interested in the job, so Rickey's son, Branch Rickey Jr., suggested hiring former Royals infielder Fresco Thompson. Rickey Sr. wasn't as enthusiastic, but he agreed. Thompson had a number of minor-league managing jobs since retiring as a player in 1938. Most recently, he worked with Rickey Jr. overseeing the Dodgers' farm teams. Thompson had a sharp wit and was regarded with enough esteem during his playing days with the Royals that he was offered the team captaincy. But he turned the offer into a point of contention by demanding to be paid for his extra responsibilities. The Royals reluctantly agreed but it poisoned his relationship with the front office, and many were surprised to see him back in Montreal.

As a manager, Thompson enjoyed using his wit to tease opposing players. Gene Mauch, a Royals infielder briefly in 1943, says Thompson had "a needle as sharp as any around." Thompson would sometimes bait Newark infielder Joe Buzas, who wore No. 4, like Lou Gehrig. "If Gehrig knew you were wearing No. 4, he'd be spinning in his grave," Thompson would bellow from the dugout. He also liked to tease his bosses, telling how one of them was so impressed with a triple play the Royals had executed, he urged Thompson to use the play more often. In his playing days, his teammates were often his victims of his needling. On train rides with the Royals in 1935

Thompson would invite passengers to hang up their coats on the teeth of the buck-toothed Bob "Suitcase" Seeds.

Although he was usually joking and wisecracking, Thompson was unhappy as manager of the Royals. At one point in the season he wondered aloud to sportswriter Dink Carroll about why he took the job. "I must be crazy," he moaned. "Here I am half out of my mind and giving my wife reason for divorce on incompatible grounds." Things had started to get tough for Thompson midway through the season, when he lost Jack Graham and Dixie Howell to military service. Then the Dodgers recalled outfielder Luis Olmo, one of the team's most productive players. Stripped of talent, the Royals finished the season with a 76-76 record and were swept in four games by Toronto in the first round of the playoffs. The Maple Leafs were managed by Burleigh Grimes, a much-improved skipper since his unsuccessful season with the Royals.

Thompson was fired following the season and replaced by a 49-year-old former infielder with the St. Louis Cardinals named Bruno Betzel. He was named Christian, Frederick Albert John Henry David Betzel at birth by a mother who didn't want to disappoint any of the boy's six uncles, but called "Bruno" after the family dog. His managerial career started in the 1920s as a player-manager in the American Association, where he won the Little World Series in 1928. He was then a skipper in the Eastern League and, most recently, he managed the Durham Bulls, another Dodgers' farm team. The grizzled Betzel, who lived on cigarettes, Alka-Seltzer and aspirin, was a decided pessimist. Once, while Betzel was with the Indianapolis Indians of the American Association, the team's owner, Jim Perry, invited him to go for a ride in his private plane. But Betzel missed the flight because a hotel switchboard operator forgot to give him a wake-up call. The plane crashed and

Nothin' in my hat! Thompson's successor Bruno Betzel used all the tricks he knew to get the Royals back on top.

Perry was killed. Instead of feeling he'd been smiled on by fate, a morose Betzel was convinced he was a marked man. He told people he was "livin' on borrowed time."

Kermit Kitman, a Brooklyn native who played for Betzel in Durham and later in Montreal, says Betzel was a tough customer, who could be "a mean son-of-a-bitch." His most vivid memory of him is that he was always spitting, making a 'pit, pit, pit' noise as he did so. Despite his hard-boiled exterior, there was a softer side to Betzel that was in evidence during one game, when he pulled the hidden-ball trick on Fred Merkle. Merkle had gained notoriety back in 1908 for a base-running blunder that cost the New York Giants the pennant. Merkle was on first base when Al Birdwell singled in the game-winning run from third base. Seeing the crowd swarming onto the field, Merkle didn't bother touching second base, and Chicago Cubs infielder Johnny Evers retrieved the ball and touched second. Merkle was declared out

and the run was nullified. Because the field couldn't be cleared of fans, the game could not continue. It was decided the game would be replayed if it had a bearing on the final standings. Sure enough, the Cubs and Giants ended in a first-place tie and the Cubs won the replayed game to capture the pennant on "Merkle's Boner."

Seven years later, Betzel decided to catch Merkle on one of the oldest tricks in the book. He pretended to give the ball to the pitcher but stuffed it into his back pocket instead. He waited for Merkle to take a lead off second base, and then hopped in between him and the base. The ball was jammed inside Betzel's back pocket, so he stuck out his rear end and tagged Merkle with his backside. Despite the unorthodox tag, Merkle was called out and fans at the Polo Grounds derisively chanted "Bonehead, Bonehead, Bonehead." Betzel recalled how Merkle walked off the field with tears streaming down his face. "At that moment," said a sensitive Betzel, "I could have cut my arm off."

As the manager of the Royals, almost 30 years later, Betzel may have felt the same way several times during the 1944 season. With more players heading off to the war, the talent shortage persisted. Many of the players at the Dodgers'-Royals' training camp at Bear Mountain, NY (the war-time training site because of travel restrictions) were teenagers. One of the youngsters was a 17-year-old outfielder named Duke Snider. He was given a good look by the Royals but Snider was still a few years from making it in Double-A ball.

The Royals were briefly in first place in July but gradually slipped from contention and finished in sixth place, seven games below .500. While 1944 was unsuccessful in the standings, it was marked by the arrival of several players who would play important roles in the future. Among them was Elmer "Red" Durrett, a power hitter who could also

Wartime travel restrictions prevented teams from heading south for spring training. Here the Royals and Dodgers work out at West Point Military Academy in Bear Mountain, New York.

hit for average. He joined the club after spending the last two years in combat. He would prove to be a consistent run producer for Montreal over the next few seasons, despite the occasional attack of malaria, which he contracted while overseas.

Also arriving in 1944 was right-hander John Gabbard and slugging first baseman Ed Stevens. The year's most popular move, however, was the signing of shortstop Stanislas Bréard, a native of Montreal's working-class neighborhood of Pointe-St-Charles. Bréard, 23, grew up playing sandlot ball in Montreal and was active in a number of amateur and semi-pro leagues. He was a small but gutsy player with an excellent glove and a quick delivery to first base that

compensated for an average arm. Although Bréard grew up in the Royals' back yard, it was Baltimore Orioles manager Tommy Thompson who first invited Bréard to work out with his team during one of its trips to Montreal, early in 1944. Thompson was impressed by Bréard's fielding but he decided not to offer a contract, probably because of Bréard's feeble hitting. But the Royals gave the local kid a shot and he was in their starting lineup shortly after that, to the surprise and delight of the fans.

Bréard played so well in the field and was so popular with his fellow francophones in the stands that he soon had a lock on the shortstop's job, despite his slender batting average. He was the first Montreal-born player to earn a regular spot with the Royals. But if Bréard felt lonely as the only French-speaking player on the team, he didn't have to wait long for company.

Midway through the 1944 season, the Royals acquired pitcher Jean-Pierre Roy from the Rochester Red Wings. Like Bréard, Roy was born in Montreal and grew up playing ball at a park which was located in the shadow of where Olympic Stadium, the home of the Montreal Expos, stands today. Roy was starring for Trois-Rivieres in the Quebec Provincial League in 1940 when Royals executives Hector Racine and Roméo Gauvreau arrived to see him pitch. The 20-year-old Roy wowed the visitors by pitching 11 scoreless innings and winning the game 1-0. Racine and Gauvreau praised his performance but told him after the game that, at 160 pounds and barely five foot 10, he was too small to be a big-league pitcher.

The St. Louis Cardinals saw some potential in Roy, however. They signed him

"Mr. Double", Roland Gladu hit the ball to all fields and led the league in two-base hits

to a minor-league contract in 1941 and Roy spent most of the next three seasons with the Rochester. But now, realizing the value of having a home-town hero, the Royals bought his contract. Roy had been an average pitcher with Rochester but he seemed to blossom as soon as he donned a Royals' uniform. He won 12 games in little more than a half-season.

The addition of another French-Canadian to the lineup was so popular with Montreal fans, the Royals decided to go after Roland Gladu, also a Montreal native. The Royals were first attracted to Gladu at the end of the 1930 season, when he showed up at an open practice. Gladu was only 19 at the time, but he'd been playing sandlot ball for money, apparently since the age of 15. The Royals signed Gladu but didn't elevate him to the

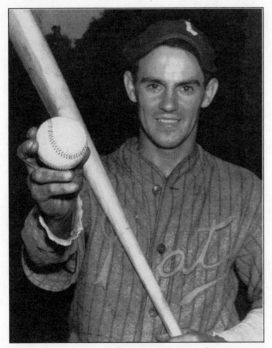

Stan Bréard was a sandlot star in the Royals' own backyard until they finally signed him up in 1944.

International League until late in 1932. He delivered a game-winning, pinch-hit homer on the final day of the season and was a strong candidate to make the club out of spring training the following year. But he wasn't impressive with the bat and the Royals eventually released him. Since then, he had gone on to star for Quebec City in the Provincial League and later the Canadian-American League. His manager in Quebec City was Del Bissonette, the former Royal who was about to join the Boston Braves organization as a minor-league manager. Bissonette recommended Gladu to the Braves, who were seeking some war-time help at third base. The five-foot-eight, 185-pound Gladu was a poor fielder but his potent left-handed bat had produced several .300-plus averages at Quebec City. The Braves signed Gladu, who was nearing his 33rd birthday (although he said he was 30) and invited him to their 1944 training camp.

Gladu had a good spring and it appeared he would make the club until he volunteered to throw batting practice one day and injured his shoulder. But he was in the lineup on opening day and tripled in his first big-league at-bat. With his shoulder still aching, he slumped after that and was sent to the Braves' Eastern League club in Hartford. His shoulder improved and he was among the top hitters in that league, posting an average in the .370s. By next spring training, the war was nearing an end and players returned from the service looking for their old jobs. Gladu never got another shot at the majors. When the Royals heard he was available they bought his contract from the Braves for $10,000.

So it was three native sons that graced the Royals' lineup as they headed into the 1945 season. Manager Bruno Betzel had every right to expect big things from the trio. Roy had undergone off-season surgery for a nagging hernia and was now in the best shape of his career. Gladu was happy to have the

opportunity to perform in front of the home folks. And there was no doubt Bréard would continue to be one of the better-fielding shortstops in the league. There was even reason for optimism that he'd raise his feeble .190 batting average of 1944, since he spent most of spring training working with Clyde Sukeforth and George Sisler learning how to hit from both sides of the plate. When it came to hitting, Sisler knew what he was talking about - he hit .400 twice for the American League's St. Louis Browns in the 1920s.

In addition to the three Montrealers, Betzel could count on Ed Stevens, the club's RBI leader in 1944. He was expected to do a better job at first base, now that the Royals had shelled out $15 for orthopedic baseball shoes to deal with Big Ed's flat feet. Thin on catchers, the Royals added the venerable Al Todd, who was listed as being 44 years old but, like Gladu, he shaved a few years off his age for the record. Todd had caught in the majors for 11 seasons but he was best known for a run-in he'd had with Dizzy Dean in a Texas League game in 1931.

Still steaming because Todd got a hit off him in his previous at-bat, Dean threw inside when Todd next came to the plate, forcing him to hit the deck. Todd threatened to throttle Dean if it happened again. No sooner had he uttered the words when Dean fired the next pitch at his head. Todd went straight for Dean, who was prepared for a verbal confrontation. He was about to unleash a wisecrack when the burly catcher belted him in the mouth. "I seen more stars than there is in Florida on a clear night," Dean recalled in his memoirs. Still expecting a jawing match, now that Todd had the violence out of his system, Dean was about to open his mouth when Todd knocked him down again. "He never did go to talkin'," Dean recalled, "and I never did get so tired of being knocked down in my life. Boy, I can talk rings around Todd any time, but I don't want to fight him no more."

Todd ended up catching 100 games for the Royals in 1945 and drove in 70 runs. He was one of the many players who contributed to the team's success - a 95-win season that produced the Royals' third pennant. All but a couple of regulars hit above .270 and all five starting pitchers had winning records. Veterans such as Todd, Gladu and second baseman Salty Parker meshed well with a youngster such as speedy centre-fielder Kermit Kitman, who shared the job with Johnny Corriden. The only real blow to the team came in early August when the Dodgers reclaimed Ed Stevens, arch-supports and all. Stevens was among the I.L.'s top hitters when he left, but his replacement, Howie Schultz, filled in admirably, hitting .338 and producing 28 RBIs in the last month of the season.

Still, the nucleus of the team was the three local players. Bréard excelled again at shortstop and astonished everyone by learning how to switch-hit. He hit .271, 81 points higher than his 1944 average, and drove in 54 runs, displaying a quiet determination as he played through injuries. Gladu led the team with 105 RBIs and a .338 average - second in the I.L. to Baltimore catcher Sherm Lollar. He was the league leader in doubles with 45 and triples with 14, and was called "Monsieur Deux-Buts" (Mr. Double) by his adoring Montreal fans.

Gladu was a serious man who seldom cracked a smile. He devoted most of his energy to hitting. He had tremendous discipline at the plate, rarely swinging at bad pitches, and he was hard on himself when he wasn't swinging the way he felt he should. Jean-Pierre Roy remembers a time when he, Gladu and Bréard were playing winter ball in Cuba and usually met for breakfast each morning. One morning, after a rare game in which Gladu had swung the bat poorly, he was gone by the time his friends arrived for breakfast. When they reached the ball park at noon, they found Gladu already at work,

hitting balls all over the field to kids he had brought along to shag balls for him. Kermit Kitman said he used to marvel at Gladu's hitting ability. "He would hit everything where it was pitched," recalled Kitman. "If it was outside, he'd line it to left-centre. He had a beautiful swing."

If Gladu and Bréard were the quiet ones of the hometown trio, Roy was the livewire. A bachelor during his days with the Royals, Roy had the reputation as a bit of a playboy who could "chanter la pomme," to use a good Quebecois expression that meant he could be pretty charming when he wanted to be. He found the Montreal nightlife tempting. "I liked to go out," admitted Roy. "In those days, Montreal was famous for its nightclubs. Frank Sinatra would come here, so would Dean Martin, Nat King Cole and Lena Horne." Roy said he didn't hang around with many of the other players because he didn't want to get them in trouble. When the Royals were at home, Roy occasionally received morning telephone calls from manager Bruno Betzel on the day he was scheduled to pitch. Roy would reassure his manager, saying, "Bruno, I know I was out late last night and I'm pitching today, but don't worry about it." On one occasion, Roy recalls pitching both ends of a doubleheader after enjoying a late night on the town.

Roy's fondness of the nightlife didn't detract from his pitching. He was far and away the best pitcher in the league, winning a team-record 25 games and topping the league with 139 strikeouts. Roy had a great curve ball, remarkable stamina and a rubber arm, pitching 29 complete games. He also fielded his position well and was a capable switch-hitter. He was the first pitcher in both the minors and majors to reach the 20-win mark in 1945, doing so on August 9. When he won his 24th game a few weeks later, he shattered the Royals' record that Pete Appleton had set in 1935. John Gabbard, Montreal's other right-handed ace, also had a

Jean-Pierre Roy was always ready to pitch, even after a night on the town.

game-winning home run. It naturally won over his tormentors in the stands, but Durrett, still stung by the boos, refused to tip his cap before ducking into the dugout.

The series shifted to Baltimore, where the third game would be played on a Saturday afternoon. A few hours before the game, Roland Gladu was asleep in his hotel room when the phone rang. He answered it groggily and learned that his younger brother, Roger, had been killed in a fire in Montreal the day before. Gladu hung up, took a few minutes to absorb the shock and then called back for details. The fire had started following a factory explosion on the street where Roger Gladu lived. Four people were killed and 50 were injured, including 30 schoolchildren passing by at the time of the explosion. One newspaper account said Gladu was attempting to save some of the children when he was caught in the fire. Despite the painful news, Gladu decided to play the first two games in Baltimore and then return to Montreal for the funeral.

Gladu played a key role in the Royals' 8-1 victory in Game 3, driving in three runs. The next day he had three hits in four at-bats, but Roy, in one of his few bad starts that season, was hammered for 12 second-inning runs as Baltimore romped 19-4. The series was knotted 2-2 and it looked as if the Royals would have to play the fifth game without Gladu. But rain forced the postponement of the series for a couple of days and Gladu was back when it resumed. He scored an important seventh-inning run but the Orioles eked out a win when Sherm Lollar hit a 10th-inning home run against John Gabbard.

Before the next game, with the Royals facing elimination, Roland Gladu vowed to hit a home run in memory of his brother. He wasn't able to make good on the promise, but he was a key player in a thrilling 1-0 victory. Montreal's Ray Hathaway stifled

superlative season, going 20-6, but Roy was unquestionably No. 1 on the stats sheet and in the hearts and minds of the fans.

Roy earned the start against the Baltimore Orioles in mid-September as the Royals opened their quest of the Governor's Cup. Facing Johnny Podgajny, Roy pitched decently but was afforded no support and was a 5-0 loser in front of 17,000 fans at Delorimier Stadium. Red Durrett was the target of the boobirds when he struck out twice with men on base. The fans were still on his back in the second game, especially after he dropped an easy fly ball in left field that led to two Baltimore runs. As fate would have it, Durrett came to bat in the ninth inning with one out and the tying run on base and nailed the third pitch high over the scoreboard for a

Baltimore on two hits, but the Orioles Red Kress had a no-hitter until Howie Schultz poked a one-out single in the ninth inning of the scoreless duel. Gladu was the next batter but was given a semi-intentional walk. Salty Parker followed with a grounder that forced Schultz at third. Al Todd, the next batter, hit a high infield pop-up that looked like an easy third out. But as Orioles second baseman Fred Pfeffer settled under the ball, the hustling Gladu never stopped running from second base. The ball glanced off Pfeffer's glove and Gladu crossed the plate with the only run before Pfeffer could recover and make a play.

More than 22,000 people jammed their way into Delorimier Stadium on a Sunday afternoon to see which team would advance to the Governor's Cup final. Another 10,000 had to be turned away. Roy again hooked up with Johnny Podgajny and pitched well until the fifth, when he allowed a run and was replaced by Gabbard. The Royals nursed a 2-1 lead into the eighth, when Gladu made good on his promise to hit one for his brother, a two-run smash over the scoreboard that sealed the victory for Montreal. It was an emotional post-game celebration for Gladu, who said his brother had always been his biggest fan.

The 1945 I.L. pennant winners. Front row, left to right: Roland Gladu, Salty Parker, Red Durrett, Kermit Kitman and Marcel Dufrèsne (traveling secretary). Middle row, left to right: Johnny Corriden, Gus Brittain, Tom Warren, Bruno Betzel (manager), Jack Banta, John Gabbard, Al Todd, Jean-Pierre Roy, Stan Bréard, Howie Schultz, Roy Nichols, DeWitt Ferrell. Top row, left to right: Lee Hart, Harold Kelleher and William Jenkins.

There wasn't much time to savor the victory, however. The Royals' next opponent was the Newark Bears and Montreal had a few problems, notably its spotty offence and signs of fatigue on the part of ace pitchers Roy and Gabbard. The flaws were much in evidence as the Royals lost the first three games, scoring only five runs and stranding 31 baserunners in the process. But the bats revived in the fourth game, as Red Durrett's two-run homer in the eighth inning produced a 5-4 victory. Roy rebounded to pitch a two-hitter as the Royals won the fifth game 7-2. They returned to Montreal for Game 6, played on a frigid night that forced 15,000 fans at Delorimier to drag out their winter coats. Branch Rickey wired a note of encouragement that arrived just before the game. The note said he'd be on hand for the opening game of the Junior World Series between the Royals and the Louisville Colonels, who had just won the American Association Governor's Cup. But the Royals had two games to win before they could think about that.

Their dreams of a stirring comeback seemed shattered when Newark pounded pitchers Ray Hathaway and John Gabbard for nine runs in the first three innings. But the tenacious Royals cobbled together six runs of their own over the next few innings. Entering the ninth, it was still 10-8 for Newark, who were poised to add another run when Dick Baker led off with a double and tried to advance to third on a fly ball. He came in spikes high, slicing open the pant leg of third baseman Lee Hart. As the umpire called Baker out, Hart pounced on Baker and the benches emptied. Even some fans tried to get into the scrap and police were called onto the field to restore order.

The deficit remained 10-8 as the Royals batted in the ninth. Jean-Pierre Roy, who had delivered key pinch-hits all season, got another, doubling home a run that made it 10-9. When Newark centre-fielder Frank Rabe mishandled a base hit by Tom Warren, Roy romped home with the tying run and Warren went to third on the play. Johnny Corriden capped the comeback by stroking the game-winning single. The team had battled back from a nine-run deficit and a 3-0 disadvantage in the series to force a seventh game. But the deciding game brought nothing but heartbreak as the Royals' bats again turned cold (except for Gladu, who was two-for-three) and Roy had little support in a 5-1 defeat.

Although they had failed to reach the Junior World Series, 1945 had been a memorable year for the Royals. They attracted 397,517 fans, almost doubling their home attendance of 1944. Another 60,000 turned out for the playoff games. The team had won its third pennant and Montreal fans had three of their own to cheer for. Roy once recalled that playing at Delorimier Stadium was like being at a family gathering. Long after he had retired, he could still hear the excited voices in the stands and the cheers of appreciation. The other side to this intimate relationship, however, was that he could also hear the disappointment when he made a mistake and "you could feel they were suffering."

To many, it seemed difficult to beat the season the team had just had. But the Royals' golden years were just beginning. The Dodgers' farm system, started by Larry MacPhail and developed by Branch Rickey, was only now approaching full bloom. And just three weeks after the Royals were eliminated by Newark there was some news that would have a huge impact, not only on the Royals but all of organized baseball. On October 23, 1945, Royals president Hector Racine called a news conference to announce the team had just signed a shortstop named Jack Roosevelt Robinson to play for Montreal in 1946.

The money pitcher. Jean-Pierre Roy got a juicy bounus cheque for winning his 20th game of the season. The team wore satin uniforms in 1945 but abandonned them after the season because the players didn't like them.

When Jackie Robinson became a Montreal Royal, he said: "I'll do my very best to come through in every manner." Archives nationales du Québec.

Jackie

The Courage Not to Fight Back

10

Less than three weeks after the Royals were eliminated from the 1945 playoffs, the club summoned the local media to a news conference at Delorimier Stadium. The purpose of the impromptu gathering wasn't divulged, so there was plenty of speculation among the reporters who straggled into the stadium office on the afternoon of Tuesday, October 23. Some thought club President Hector Racine (back on the job after recovering from a heart attack earlier in the year) would make an announcement concerning the future of manager Bruno Betzel, at odds with the club over his salary. Others suggested that a high-profile personality, possibly even Babe Ruth, was about to be named the Royals manager. Maybe it was to announce that Montreal, because of its strong support of the Royals in 1945, was about to be awarded a major-league franchise.

The reporters stopped their chattering as four well-dressed men swept into the room. Three of them - Racine, Roméo Gauvreau and Dodgers farm chief Branch Rickey Jr., were familiar. The fourth, who became the immediate focus of attention, was a tall, muscular black man introduced as Jack Roosevelt Robinson, the Royals' newest infielder. There was a momentary hush, followed by a tremendous clatter as the reporters dashed for the telephones to relay the incredible news to their editors. They returned to the room a few minutes later while Robinson was posing for photographs,

eager to learn more about this dramatic and unexpected event.

The ceremonial signing in Montreal was the culmination of three years of meticulous and camouflaged manoeuvring by Branch Rickey Sr. The man who had invented the modern farm system, was about to revolutionize baseball once again by breaking the unofficial ban on black players. Rickey had informed the Dodgers ownership of his intention to sign black players when he joined the organization three years earlier, but he had never elaborated.

Baseball people were aware that Rickey was spending thousands of dollars sending scouts such as Clyde Sukeforth throughout North America and Cuba in search of talented black players. But Rickey hid his real intentions, claiming he was about to establish a new Negro League and needed players for the Brooklyn entry - the Brown Dodgers. Rickey concocted this yarn to prevent the controversy and resistance which would have ensued had his plans become public. He was challenging a prejudice that had existed in North American society for generations and had been a part of baseball since the earliest days of organized play.

When the National League was established in 1876, it had no formal policy on race, but there was a "gentlemen's agreement" among its owners not to hire black players. The agreement didn't extend to other leagues, however, and when the American Association was briefly elevated to major-league status in 1884, the team's catcher, Moses Fleetwood Walker, became the first black man to play in the majors. Walker was one of five or six dozen African-Americans who played professional baseball in the 19th century. About half of them played in the organized white leagues.

Many played in the International League in the 1880s and were often treated badly because of their color. Buffalo second baseman Frank Grant was considered to be one of the best players around, but was constantly abused and wore wooden shin guards to protect himself from the stabbing cleats of opposing baserunners. In 1887, Newark had two black players - Fleetwood Walker, who had moved from the American Association, and southpaw George Stovey, whose 35 wins topped the International League.

The I.L. owners soon fell in line with the National League, however, and stopped signing black players, claiming that the white players were refusing to play alongside them. Other leagues followed suit and blacks were effectively eliminated from organized ball by the early 1890s. But black Americans continued to play the game, forming all-black teams that travelled from town to town, entertaining people of both races. In 1920, The Negro Leagues were established, providing black baseball with more structure and organization than the barnstorming circuits.

In the early days of the 20th century, some major-league teams put the "gentlemen's agreement" to the test. In 1901, for example, Baltimore Orioles manager John McGraw signed infielder Charlie Grant, claiming he was an American Indian. Charles Comiskey, owner of the Chicago White Sox wasn't fooled, and he forced McGraw to get rid of Grant. Fifteen years later, Jimmy Claxton, a Canadian from British Columbia, became the first black man to play organized ball in the 20th century, joining the Oakland Oaks of the Pacific Coast League for a few games before his black ancestry was discovered (some accounts have the Oaks passing Claxton off as white, others as a Native American).

The Cincinnati Reds broke new ground in 1911 by signing two Cuban players. But in order to get away with it, they had to certify the men were "genuine Caucasians" of Spanish descent. Several other light-skinned Latin Americans played in the majors and minors over the next three or four decades, including Luis Olmo, with the Royals and Dodgers in 1943, but darker-skinned Latin Americans were still barred.

As black baseball grew in fame and popularity throughout the 1920s and 1930s, and as all-stars from the Negro Leagues started beating major-leaguers in exhibition games, some of the owners of the big-league clubs realized that organized baseball was ignoring a wealth of talent. But with the baseball establishment still opposed to integration, the subject was rarely raised in formal circles. The cause was championed almost exclusively by black sportswriters such as Wendell Smith of the black-weekly Pittsburgh Courier. Pittsburgh was home to two Negro League teams - the Crawfords and the Homestead Grays - and The Courier tried to convince William Benswanger, the owner of the National League Pirates, to hire players from these teams.

Benswanger said he favored integration, and in 1943 he promised the communist newspaper, the Daily Worker, that he would give tryouts to two Negro League stars, catcher Roy Campanella of the Baltimore Elite Giants and pitcher Dave Barnhill of the New York Cubans. But Benswanger eventually cancelled the tryouts because of pressure by baseball commissioner Kenesaw Mountain Landis. He later claimed to have

Commissioner Landis did everything he could to prevent the integration of major-league baseball.

been interested in offering contracts to two of the biggest stars of black baseball - Josh Gibson and Buck Leonard of the Homestead Grays - but was thwarted by Grays owner, Cumberland Posey Jr.

Landis apparently intervened when Clark Griffith of the Washington Senators toyed with the idea of signing black players in the early 1940s. He also stepped in when Bill Veeck, a 29-year-old maverick minor-league team owner, tried to buy the failing Philadelphia Phillies and staff the team exclusively with black players.

Calls for integration, primarily by African-American journalists, led by Wendell Smith, intensified as the war continued in Europe. The contradiction of Americans fighting the racism of Hitler while maintaining

segregation at home was increasingly unacceptable. When Landis died in late 1944, he was replaced by A.B. "Happy" Chandler, who declared, "If a black boy can make it in Okinawa and Guadalcanal, hell, he can make it in baseball," Reporters Smith and Bostic sensed an opportunity. In April of 1945, Bostic showed up at the Dodgers' spring-training camp at Bear Mountain demanding a tryout for Terris McDuffie and David "Showboat" Thomas. Rickey granted the players a tryout but was furious with Bostic, telling him he sympathized with the cause but didn't appreciate his methods.

A week later, Wendell Smith, showed up at the Boston Red Sox camp with three top prospects from the Negro Leagues - outfielder Sam Jethroe and infielders Marvin Williams and Jackie Robinson. The Red Sox had agreed to look at players after some pressure by a local city councillor and a popular newspaper columnist. The players were given a superficial look by a couple of coaches but nothing came of it. Robinson and Jethroe later complained the tryout had been a farce.

While Bostic and Smith were showcasing Negro League players amid growing frustration with the lack of interest, Branch Rickey Sr. forged ahead with his secret plans to sign black players for the Dodgers. He had blasted Bostic at Bear Mountain, not because he disapproved of what the journalist was trying to achieve, but he felt Bostic's zeal might scuttle his strategy. Rickey believed that he needed a trailblazer for the plan to work - one player who would break the ice for the rest, and he was still searching for that man. He wasn't necessarily seeking the best black ball player, but someone who had the right combination of talent and character.

Rickey refused to be rushed. As a member of the Major League Committee on Baseball Integration, formed after the death of Landis, Rickey happily allowed the integration issue to get bogged down by discussion while he moved quietly behind the scenes to make it happen. A few weeks after Wendell Smith brought Jackie Robinson to the Red Sox camp, Rickey started to hear more and more about Robinson from Dodgers scouts, and he decided to find out as much about him as he could.

Robinson was born in Cairo, Ga., on January 31, 1919, to Jerry and Maillie Robinson, sharecroppers who lived in a shack on a plantation. When Jackie was six months old, his father left, leaving behind a wife and five children. About a year later, Maillie decided to move to California, where she found a house in a white neighborhood in Pasadena. Jackie was a lively and slightly mischievous child, who never backed down from the white kids who threw stones at him. When they called him "nigger," he called them "cracker" in return. He became interested in sports at school and was usually the best at whatever he tried. At Pasadena Junior College he emerged as one of the finest athletes in Southern California, playing football, basketball and baseball, and setting a national broad-jump record. When he and a few other black students tried out for the football team at Pasadena, some of the white players staged a boycott and tried to force them to quit. Robinson stood firm, however, and the players eventually ended their holdout.

After junior college Robinson went on to UCLA, then one of the few predominantly white universities which openly recruited black athletes. Robinson became the school's first four-letter man. He was especially adept at football - an All-American at running back - but he was also the best player on his basketball team. Seeing no future for himself in the world of white professional sports, Robinson finished school and entered the army in April, 1942. While there he got a reputation as a troublemaker by fighting to get more seats for black soldiers at the segregated base canteen. He also made a few

enemies when he refused to play for the base football team after being told he'd have to sit out the games against Southern teams.

The camp's baseball team had a few major-leaguers, including the Dodgers Dixie Walker and Pete Reiser, but no blacks were allowed. When Robinson showed up at the field one day he was mockingly told to join the colored team, which didn't exist. Robinson was transferred to Fort Hood, Texas, in early 1944, where he got into more trouble by refusing to go to the back of a military bus. Robinson argued with the driver and was accused of being abusive and using foul language, and the incident was brought to the attention of the Duty Officer. "As serious as the situation was, I had to laugh," Robinson wrote later. "It was so obvious what was happening. I was up against one of those white supremacy characters. Everything would have been all right if I had been a 'yassuh boss' type." The matter was eventually put before a court martial but Robinson was acquitted of all charges and honorably discharged shortly after the hearing.

He turned his attention to baseball, although it had never been his best or favorite sport. He was offered a job with the Kansas City Monarchs of the Negro Leagues for $100 a week, minus meal money, and he accepted. Although Robinson was 26 years old, he was an inexperienced ball player by professional standards. But he played well during the 1945 season, hitting better than .350 and performing solidly at shortstop. He had lightning reflexes and a blinding burst of speed that made him almost unstoppable on the basepaths. Dodgers scouts were also impressed by the intelligence and passion he brought to the game.

As the 1945 season progressed, these same scouts recommended that Rickey consider Robinson as a candidate for the phantom Brown Dodgers. Rickey was impressed with Robinson's credentials as a ball player, and he liked the fact Robinson had played with white players and in front of white crowds while at UCLA. He was also pleased by the reports that Robinson was a serious, intelligent man who didn't smoke, drink or carouse and, like Rickey, he was a devout Methodist. Another plus was that Robinson was engaged to be married to Rachel Isum ,who was from a good family and was planning a nursing career.

Rickey felt that for his plan to work, the trailblazer would have to be beyond reproach in every respect. When he was satisfied that Robinson might fit the bill, he sent Clyde Sukeforth to Chicago to meet with him. Rickey told his trusted scout to watch Robinson play at Comiskey Park, paying particular attention to his throwing arm, and to approach him following the game about the possibility of discussing a career with the Brown Dodgers with Rickey. Sukeforth never saw Robinson in action because the shortstop was sidelined with a bad shoulder. But Rickey still wanted a meeting and he instructed Sukeforth to either bring Robinson to Brooklyn or arrange an appointment for Rickey to meet him in Chicago. Sukeforth was astonished that Rickey was prepared to go to Chicago for a meeting at Robinson's convenience. Although Sukeforth was officially scouting for Rickey's new Negro League, he had started to have some suspicions. "I"m no mind reader, but I was close enough to Rickey to know we weren't doing that," Sukeforth said many years later. He realized that Rickey had something else in mind for Robinson.

Robinson agreed to come to Brooklyn, and the meeting he had with Rickey in the latter's office in August of 1945 has become part of baseball folklore. One Robinson biographer, David Falkner, believes the meeting was really something Rickey staged for public consumption, and that the two men had met a couple of times before Robinson's contract signing. Accounts by the three people present that day - Rickey, Robinson and Sukeforth - indicate that Robinson was shocked to learn Rickey wanted to sign him for the Royals, and not the Brown Dodgers. Robinson was speechless as the Dodgers boss acted out several scenarios to give Robinson a taste of the physical and verbal abuse awaiting him. Rickey apparently assumed the role of a player, spitting racial insults in Robinson's face to test his reactions. After a while Robinson asked: "Are you looking for someone who doesn't have the courage to fight back?" To which Rickey responded: "I'm looking for some one with the courage not to fight back." Sukeforth recalled Robinson pausing for a few moments to consider what had been said. Finally, he declared: "Mr. Rickey, if you want to take this gamble, I promise you there'll be no incident." Robinson signed a contract to play for the Royals. He was to receive a $3,500 signing bonus and a monthly salary of $600.

Rickey had planned to keep the news quiet until he could sign several other players from the Negro Leagues. He had his eye on pitchers John Wright, Roy Partlow, Don Newcombe and catcher Roy Campanella. He hoped to announce these players would soon be joining Robinson in organized baseball, but the approaching municipal election in New York City ruined his plans. Mayor Fiorello La Guardia was an advocate of baseball integration and had set up a committee to study the issue. As the election neared he told Rickey, a committee member, he wanted to announce that, because of the committee's work, black players would soon be signed by major- league teams in New York. Rickey asked La Guardia to delay his news and he immediately contacted Robinson and had him travel to Montreal for a pre-emptive announcement. Rickey wanted to go public before La Guardia could jump on the bandwagon and take the credit for Rickey's work.

While in the army, Lt. Robinson fought for the rights of black soldiers. Courtesy La Presse.

The announcement caught the baseball world by surprise. T.Y. Baird, president of the Kansas City Monarchs, protested the snatching of a player he claimed was his property. Rickey said, in his opinion, the Negro Leagues weren't organized and didn't tender legal contracts. The president of the minor leagues, W.G. Bramham, said there was nothing to prevent Rickey from signing Robinson, but he was obviously unhappy, remarking sarcastically that "we can expect Rickey Temple to be in the course of construction in Harlem soon." Rickey dealt with such barbs by reiterating his moral

disapproval of racial prejudice. He recalled coaching a young black player in college who apparently tried to scratch the blackness off his skin after being refused a room in the team's hotel. But moral concerns aside, Rickey insisted his main objective was to win ball games.

Several major league owners reacted cooly, neither praising nor condemning the move. But Horace Stoneham of the New York Giants vowed he would start scouting the Negro Leagues immediately, now that the ice had been broken. I.L. president Frank

Shaughnessy approved of the experiment, stating that "as long as any fellow's the right type and can make good and get along with other players, he can play ball." Some high-profile baseball personalities disagreed. Pitcher Bob Feller, for one, said he felt Robinson wasn't good enough. Former star Rogers Hornsby said integration wouldn't work because problems would arise with whites and blacks sharing the same clubhouse and staying in the same hotels. Robinson responded to Feller both tactfully and succinctly. "I've played two games against Feller (exhibition games between major and Negro League all-stars), but if you lined up 10 of us (black players), he couldn't pick me out of the bunch." Ironically, Robinson and Feller were both inducted into the Baseball Hall of Fame on the same day, 17 years later.

At the news conference in Montreal, Hector Racine said Robinson came very highly

Cleveland Indian ace Bob Feller thought Robinson would never make it in the big leagues.

recommended by the Dodgers, and that was good enough for him. He also said the signing was "a point of fairness." Farm director Branch Rickey Jr. said he realized there would be a lot of opposition but the Dodgers would stand by their decision. He acknowledged that some players might leave the organization rather than play alongside a black man, but suggested they'd be back "after a year or two in a cotton mill." Rickey Jr. conceded that Robinson would have to handle prejudice but he expressed confidence he would succeed. "Jack Robinson is a fine type of young man - "intelligent and college-bred, and I think he can take it, too," said Rickey Jr. In his 1972 autobiography, I Never Had it Made, Robinson remembers that statement a bit differently, quoting Rickey Jr. as saying "I think he can MAKE it, too." Perhaps it was the way Robinson heard it at the time, preferring to dwell on succeeding as a ball player instead of enduring abuse, but Robinson clearly knew what was at stake. "I realize how much it means to me, to my race and to baseball," he said, "I can only say I'll do my very best to come through in every manner.

The reaction in Montreal was generally positive. One newspaper columnist, Paul Parizeau of Le Canada, said he felt proud that Rickey believed Robinson would be better received in Montreal than in the United States. He said it showed the city was the most democratic place in the world. Parizeau predicted that Robinson would be accepted in Montreal, especially if he played well. Another newspaper provided some evidence Rickey might have been right when he surmised that race might be less of an issue in Montreal. It reported that many people had phoned the newspaper on the night of the news conference, having heard about big news in the Royals' camp. They were only mildly interested to hear it was the signing of a black player and not the awarding of a major-league franchise.

While Robinson was welcome in

Montreal, it wasn't the case in Sanford, Fla., where the Royals had their first southern training camp since before the war. Special arrangements had to be made for Robinson to stay at the private home of a local black family near the ball park because he couldn't stay at the hotel with the rest of the players. The only consolation for Robinson was that he wouldn't be alone because the Dodgers had signed black pitcher John Wright to a minor-league contract. Wright, a quiet right-hander from New Orleans who had pitched well for Pittsburgh's Homestead Grays, was assigned to Montreal, partly to room with Robinson and keep him company, since it seemed unlikely Robinson would be immediately accepted by his new teammates. Wright was sharing in this "noble experiment," as some were calling it, but Robinson was the man everyone was waiting to see - the guy Rickey Sr. insisted would one day be a Brooklyn Dodger.

Jackie and Rachel Robinson were subjected to inhuman treatment on their way to the Royals training camp in the spring of 1946.

When Robinson was a couple of days late arriving at training camp, Rickey attributed the delay to "bad flying weather in the vicinity of New Orleans." But what actually happened was a harbinger of the turbulence that awaited Robinson and his new bride. The couple had boarded a Florida-bound plane in Los Angeles a few days earlier, with a scheduled stopover in New Orleans. While waiting for the connecting flight, they were told they'd have to give up their seats to military personnel, something Robinson later described as a "typical black experience". The promised "brief delay" in New Orleans became a 12-hour wait, but they finally got two seats aboard a plane headed for Pensacola, where they could get a connecting flight to Daytona Beach. At Pensacola, however, they were informed they'd would have to relinquish their seats because the plane was headed for stormy weather and needed to lighten its load. They were appalled when the same seats were given to two white passengers.

The newlyweds ended up taking a bus from Pensacola to Daytona Beach, a trip that took an entire day. Most of the time they were crammed into the back of the bus, where black passengers were ordered to ride. There were so many in this section, people took turns standing so others could sit down for a while. Meanwhile, there were plenty of empty seats up front, in the white section of the bus. When the couple arrived at Daytona Beach - near the Royals' headquarters in Sanford - they were greeted by Wendell Smith. A furious Robinson threatened to abandon the experiment. He'd been on the receiving end of racism before, but he had limited experience with the brutal segregation laws of the South. Rachel, also a Californian, was even less accustomed to such laws. Smith calmed Robinson and convinced him to persevere, but the "noble experiment" was off to a rocky start.

When he faced reporters for the first time in Florida, Robinson said everything was fine and that he was well received by teammates and the people of Sanford. In fact, Robinson and Wright were verbally abused by Sanford residents and virtually ignored by their teammates. One of the few familiar and sympathetic souls Robinson encountered in Florida was Clyde Sukeforth, who introduced Robinson to the Royals' new manager, Clay Hopper. (Bruno Betzel had left the club over a salary dispute and was now managing the Jersey City Giants.) Hopper had followed Rickey to the Dodgers from the Cardinals organization and had done a good job with the Dodgers Southern League team in Mobile, Ala. Hopper, a Mississippi native, had a steady income away from baseball in the cotton industry. He was adamantly opposed to integration, especially in baseball. He had pleaded with Rickey not to force him to manage a team with a black man on it, but Rickey gave him no choice. He also induced Hopper to soften his public stance to the point where Robinson saw no immediate signs of racism in Hopper's manner, even though he knew of the southerner's reputation.

Despite Robinson's positive comments about his acceptance in Florida, it became clear early in spring training that the people of Sanford wouldn't tolerate the presence of Robinson and Wright on the same field as white players. It prompted Rickey to move the Royals' camp alongside the Dodgers at Daytona Beach. The problem wasn't resolved, however, and the Royals had to cancel several spring-training games in Florida, Georgia and

There was never an empty seat in the press box at Delorimier Stadium the season Robinson was with the Royals. Archives nationales du Québec.

Virginia because local segregation laws forbade whites and blacks from playing on the same field. This caused some internal dissent, as several Royals' players became resentful of the disruption seemingly created by Robinson and Wright. The fact he wasn't having a good spring only complicated matters for Robinson. He had developed a sore arm by throwing too hard, determined to disprove scouting reports that were critical of his arm. He also wasn't hitting well at the start. To make matters worse, he was constantly being tested to see how he would stand up to abuse. Rickey had made Robinson promise he would control his volatile temper for the next three years, no matter how intolerable the insult or injustice.

Robinson, a newcomer to second base in 1946, became an all-star at the position.

This was put to the test during an exhibition game between the Royals and the Dodgers. Robinson laid down a bunt and the Dodgers second baseman, Eddie Stanky, who was covering first, tagged him hard in the groin. Kermit Kitman, the Royals centre-fielder that day, remembers that Robinson was angry and in pain, but he didn't react. Stanky, according to Kitman, later apologized for the rough tag, claiming Rickey had told him to do it as a test. (Stanky may not have found the "test" such an onerous task, since he was involved in a plot the following season aimed at keeping Robinson off the Dodgers).

Besides his many other trials, Robinson also had to contend with a new position. He was a shortstop with Kansas City, but now had to learn to play second base because Stan Bréard had a lock on the job at short. Bréard helped him with the transition, as did a utility infielder named Lou Rochelli, who was also in line for the job, a gesture Robinson never forgot. Robinson was a quick learner and, despite his continued problems with the bat, he was starting to impress Hopper with his fielding. He also opened many eyes with his baserunning and intense desire to win.

Hopper was impressed by two incidents in particular. The first occurred during an exhibition game with a minor-league team from Daytona Beach. Robinson was caught in a rundown between first and second. Several players chased Robinson up and down the basepath, but none of them could tag him, and Robinson never let up. He would run right at a player, stop dead and backtrack in a flash. Somehow, Robinson stayed alive and eventually slid safely into second base.

The other incident which won Hopper's admiration was an at-bat against Paul Derringer, a former major-league all-star. Derringer, a Southerner, had approached

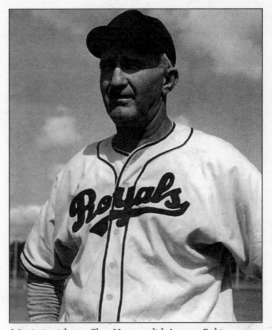

Mississippi-born Clay Hopper didn't want Robinson on the team, but Branch Rickey gave him no choice.

Hopper prior to the game and said, "Tell you what I'm going to do, Clay. I'm going to knock your colored boy down a couple of times and see how much guts he's got." In the first at-bat, Derringer threw at Robinson's head, forcing him to drop face-first into the dirt. Robinson picked himself up without a fuss and dug in again. This time Derringer came inside with a curve that Robinson hit so hard, according to Hopper, "all you could see was the ball flicking the dust where it hit behind the third baseman."

Although Hopper wasn't convinced that his second baseman would be the player Branch Rickey had promised, and he had once said he was glad his father wasn't alive to see him managing a black player, Hopper's opinion would change considerably in 1946. Other doubters would also watch in awe as Robinson emerged as one of the best all-around players in the league. He was an integral man on a Royals team that some baseball historians consider to be one of the best in minor-league history.

11

1946

The Royals Earn Their Crown

Jackie Robinson before the historic 1946 season-opener in Jersey City. The only time his bat was still all day.

Jackie Robinson stepped up to the plate, his knees quaking and his hands so clammy he could barely hold the bat. There was a scattering of applause from the stands but Robinson didn't dare look in that direction, fearing that only the black people in the

stadium would be cheering. He was worried that if he glanced toward the stands, white people would yell racial insults at him. Robinson's wife Rachel paced up and down the aisles, too nervous to remain in her seat. It was the top of the first inning and Robinson was the second man up for the Royals. The lead-off batter, Marvin Rackley, had grounded out and now it was Robinson's turn to face Jersey City Giants left-hander Warren Sandell.

A right-handed batter, Robinson stood with a slightly pigeon-toed stance, his left foot pointing inward. Just under six feet tall and weighing 190 pounds, Robinson had the burly look of a swing-for-the-fences power hitter. But he was patient and selective at the plate, carefully examining Sandell's first five pitches without swinging. With the count 3-and-2, Robinson finally swung and, to the chagrin of some and malicious glee of others, he grounded out to short. A smattering of polite applause acknowledged his efforts as he jogged back to the dugout.

It was April 18, 1946, and Roosevelt Stadium, at the juncture of the Hackensack River and Newark Bay, was jammed to the rafters for the season opener. Opening day was traditionally a major production in Jersey City. Mayor Frank Hague closed the schools and forced city employees to buy tickets so there would be a sellout crowd to cheer on the Giants, the International League farm team of the New York Giants.

This year, more than 50,000 tickets were sold for a stadium that could accommodate only half that many spectators. People were turned away at the gate. In the cramped press box, one reporter likened the scene to a subway car at rush hour. Fans and media had come from all over North America to see Robinson become the first black man to play organized baseball in the 20th century.

Following his first-inning groundout, Robinson next batted in the third inning. The Royals were leading 2-0 and had two baserunners with none out. Robinson had a reputation as a good bunter and the Giants infielders set themselves for that possibility. Robinson rocked them back on their heels, however, by swinging away and connecting with a loud crack. The solid contact felt sweet to Robinson. He knew immediately

that he had hit the ball a long way. He heard an eruption of cheering as the ball cleared the left-field fence, 330 feet away. As he started his jog around the bases, Robinson thought about Rachel, who had suffered with him during these first few months of Rickey's "noble experiment." Then he smiled, realizing what he had just done. He was slapped on the back by manager Clay Hopper as he rounded third base and greeted at home plate by teammate George Shuba, who shook his hand. "That's the way to hit 'em," another teammate said, and all the players on the Montreal bench stood to congratulate Robinson as he came toward the dugout.

There was cheering in the press box as well. Wendell Smith of the Pittsburgh Courier, and Joe Bostic of the Amsterdam

Robinson surprised New Jersey third baseman Larry Miggins by going from second to third on a routine ground-out. Then Robinson worried the Jersey City pitcher so much he was waved home on a balk

News, who both worked for newspapers serving the black community, wore broad smiles. "The thrill ran through us like champagne bubbles, " Smith said. Some white reporters also cheered the home run, but another swore under his breath as the ball cleared the fence. Several reporters looked on glumly as the afternoon progressed and Robinson stole the show.

In the fifth inning, Robinson bunted toward the left side of the infield and beat it out for a base hit. He then stole second base on Jersey City pitcher Phil Oates, showing remarkable speed for a man his size. He scampered with his elbows high and his hands churning in front of his face. He took a daring lead off second base and when teammate Tom Tatum hit a grounder to third Robinson made a break for the base, stopped abruptly, and headed back to second. As soon as Giants third baseman Larry Miggins fired the ball across the diamond to get the runner, Robinson broke for third again and made it safely.

George Shuba congratulates Robinson after his three-run home run in Jersey City. Robinson later confessed he'd been afraid none of his teammates would shake his hand in public.

Robinson then went into what would become a familiar act throughout his Hall-of-Fame career. As Red Durrett, the Royals' next batter, settled into the batter's box,

Robinson took a big lead off third base, drawing a throw from Oates. On the first pitch, Robinson broke for home but stopped halfway and scrambled back to the base. The crowd roared; such daring baserunning was not often seen outside the Negro Leagues. But it was exactly what Rickey wanted Robinson to do. He had told him to "run like lightning and worry the daylights out of the pitchers." Robinson's dancing up and down the basepath so unsettled Oates that the pitcher hesitated in his delivery and Robinson was awarded home plate on a balk. The stadium erupted once more, as fans laughed, screamed and stamped their feet.

In the seventh inning, Robinson singled, stole second and scored on a triple by Johnny "Spider" Jorgensen to give the Royals a 10-1 lead. In the next inning, Robinson reached first on another bunt single - his fourth hit in five at-bats - and advanced to third on a single. Once at third, he "worried the daylights" out of the Giants latest pitcher, Hub Andrews. Like Oates, Andrews was so rattled by Robinson that he balked, and Robinson was waved home. The Royals won 14-1, with Robinson scoring four runs, knocking in three and stealing two bases.

Defensively, he committed a throwing error on a double play but handled everything else hit his way at second base.

Following the smashing debut, Montreal sportswriter Dink Carroll wrote that Robinson "seems to have the same sense for the dramatic that characterized such great athletes as Babe Ruth, Red Grange, Jack Dempsey, Bobby Jones and others of that stamp. The bigger the occasion, the more they rose to it." The New York Times called Robinson's performance a "tremendous feat," considering the circumstances. Joe Bostic wrote that Robinson did everything "but help the ushers seat the crowd." He said the performance proved without a doubt that blacks could play in the major leagues.

The arrival of Robinson only increased the tremendous excitement as the 1946 baseball season got under way. Under restructuring of the minor leagues, the International League was now classified Triple-A, from its previous Double-A status. Like every other club, the Dodgers had a surplus of talent as they made their spring-training cuts, and the Royals were the beneficiaries. This buyers' market was tough on some of the players who'd been with the team during the war; many no longer fit into the organization's plans. The first major casualty for the Royals was Roland Gladu, one of the heroes of 1945. Realizing his future with the Dodgers organization was bleak, because of his age and lack of defensive skills, Gladu jumped to a newly-formed Mexican League run by two millionaire brothers, Jorge and Bernardo Pasquel. The league was aggressive in courting major-league stars and succeeded in landing more than a dozen big-leaguers, including pitchers Sal Maglie of the Giants and the Cardinals Max Lanier.

Most of the Mexican League jumpers, as they came to be known, didn't stay there long because of the adverse playing conditions. Gladu remained for two seasons, hitting .322 both years. He returned to Quebec in 1947, but like the other defectors, he was temporarily banned from organized ball by baseball commissioner Happy Chandler. So Gladu returned to the Provincial League as a player-manager, bringing Maglie, Lanier and other Mexican League stars with him.

Gladu's split with the Dodgers organization occurred at the end of his career. That wasn't the case with Stan Bréard. After unsuccessfully trying to pry Phil Rizzuto loose from the Yankees, the Pasquel brothers were still seeking a quality shortstop. They eventually settled on Bréard - perhaps on the advice of Gladu - and one Wednesday afternoon in mid-May, Bréard failed to report for the Royals' doubleheader against Newark. He was called at home shortly before the first game and complained of illness, although he was vague when asked why he hadn't informed manager Clay Hopper. The Royals were idle the following day, and Bréard showed up at Delorimier Stadium on Friday with another nebulous explanation for his behavior. He was fined $50 but seemed unconcerned and unrepentant for his absence. The Royals were puzzled by Bréard's attitude, until it was reported he was entertaining an offer from the Pasquel brothers. Bréard never confirmed the report but the Dodgers were certain it was accurate. Fearing further raids by the Mexican League, the club filed for a court injunction against the Pasquels. The suit was later dropped when the Pasquel brothers stopped wooing major-league players.

Although Bréard never accepted the Mexican offer, the incident ruined his relationship with the front office and his teammates. He was benched for a few games in favor of Al Campanis, the Royals shortstop in 1943. Disgruntled fans yelled "Bréard, Bréard, Bréard," from the stands, but Campanis did a good job filling in for the home-town favorite. He didn't field as well as Bréard but he was a better hitter. He belted a game-winning grand slam homer one night, while Bréard was still benched. A few days later, Bréard was traded to the San Diego Padres of the Pacific Coast League. He eventually returned to Quebec and played in the Provincial League. But his departure from Montreal was a big disappointment for the fans. With Gladu gone and Jean-Pierre Roy up with the Dodgers, it appeared the three home-brews were gone forever. Not so, as things developed.

Roy had also been in contact with the Pasquel brothers. He had reported to the Dodgers' training camp wearing an expensive watch he'd received from one of the brothers. Roy managed to stick with the Dodgers but was relegated to the bench after a few rocky outings. He asked manager Leo Durocher about his future and was told a spot would open, but he'd have to be patient while Durocher sorted out his staff. Roy was still intrigued by the Pasquels and their up-front offer of $25, 000. He left the Dodgers near the end of May and headed south. When he arrived in Mexico, he was appalled by the chaotic state of the league and he was back in Brooklyn two weeks later. Roy had to return most of the money, but since he had left before playing a game he wasn't subject to the ban on Mexican jumpers, and Branch Rickey allowed him to rejoin Montreal. The Royals were glad to have him back, using him as both a starter and reliever. But he never got along with Clay Hopper, who called him a "French son-of-a-bitch." Roy also wasn't the same pitcher he'd been a year earlier. He returned to the Provincial League in 1947, where he was reunited with former teammates Gladu and Bréard. He made a comeback with the Royals in 1949, but lasted for a half-season before being traded to the Hollywood Stars of the Pacific Coast League.

Despite the loss of two of the three local

The Royals formidable 1946 catching duo of Herman Franks (left) and Dixie Howell.

heroes, the 1946 Royals were shaping up as a formidable squad Many of the players had major-league experience, and several had previously played with Montreal. Baseball scholar Jules Tygiel is convinced Rickey stacked the team to remove some of the pressure from Robinson. He believes the addition of Campanis and the early demotion of 21-year-old George Shuba, despite a strong spring, were examples of Rickey surrounding Robinson with experienced teammates.

By mid-June, the Royals had put together a devastating lineup, anchored by strength up the middle. Two veterans - Homer "Dixie" Howell and Herman Franks - shared the catching duties and provided steady hitting. The middle infielders - Robinson and Campanis - were threats with the bat and became one of the best double-play combinations in the league. Marvin Rackley, a solid hitter and possibly the league's fastest runner, patrolled centre field.

On the corners, the Royals had newcomers

Johnny "Spider" Jorgensen and Lew Riggs at third base, and Les Burge, a familiar face at Delorimier Downs, handled first base. He was a key RBI man, along with returning outfielder Red Durrett, whose two-homer performance in the opener at Jersey City was overshadowed by Robinson's spectacular debut. Tom Tatum and Earl Naylor, who had both seen a bit of playing time with Montreal over the years, were versatile performers who were comfortable at any position in the field and could be dropped into almost any spot in the batting order. The pitching staff was a well-balanced collection of young and experienced arms led by Chet Kehn, Jack Banta and John Gabbard. It was bolstered by newcomers Glen Moulder, Cy Buker and Steve Nagy and further strengthened by the early-season addition of Roy and long-time major-leaguer Curt Davis.

Once the lineup was set, the Royals dominated the league as no team had done

Al Campanis was sent to Montreal to solidify the infield and take some of the pressure off Robinson.

since the 1937 Newark Bears (109 victories). Montreal finished with a team-record 100 wins and captured the pennant by 18 1/2 games. While the club had no 20-game winner, and Hopper considered pitching to be the team's only weakness, Steve Nagy was an impressive 17-4 and Buker, Kehn and Gabbard all posted more than 10 victories. Defensively, the team had the best fielding percentage in the league. But it was an unrelenting offensive attack from every spot in the lineup that set the Royals apart from their rivals.

Robinson won the I.L. batting title with a .349 mark. He also led the league in walks and runs scored and produced 65 RBIs, despite missing almost 30 games because of leg injuries. Skeptics predicted his bat would cool down as the season progressed, but it was obvious by mid-season that Robinson was everything Branch Rickey had promised. "Like plastic and penicillin, Robinson is here to stay," wrote Lloyd McGowan. His superb play (including 40 stolen bases) earned him a spot on the International League all-star team, but surprisingly few votes for the league's Most Valuable Player award. That honor went to Baltimore first baseman Eddie Robinson (.318, with 34 homers and 123 RBIs). Robinson actually came in fourth, behind Newark shortstop Bobby Brown and Montreal's Tom Tatum.

Robinson was far from a one-man-show. Rackley, Tatum, Franks, Riggs and Nagy all joined him on the all-star team. Rackley was the league's leading base-stealer with 65, and posted a .305 batting average. Tatum hit .319 and stole 30 bases. Franks came in at .280, while Riggs, who made a number of game-saving plays at third, hit .303. And Nagy's 17 wins were the best in the League. Naylor, Howell, Campanis and Jorgensen all hit over .290 and power-hitters Burge and Durrett combined for more than 30 homers and almost 200 RBIs.

Marvin Rackley, the only man on the team faster than Robinson, led the league with 65 stolen bases.

a couple of runs you could get better odds on the game." Although gambling wasn't new at the stadium, Racine felt it was getting out of hand. Fans sometimes hollered to players on the field, promising them money if they got a hit or stole a base. It even reached a point where the offer was relayed through the public-address system. Racine put an end to that. He posted undercover agents in the crowd to nab the hard-core gamblers. Despite Racine's best efforts, the gambling likely continued discreetly into the post-season. And most of the betting lines would have favored the Royals to win their second Governor's Cup.

The club's first playoff opponent was the Newark Bears, led by manager George Selkirk (the Canadian-born successor to Babe Ruth as the Yankees right-fielder) and a stocky catcher named Larry "Yogi" Berra. Montreal won the first two games at home - the first on Steve Nagy's strong pitching and three hits by Jackie Robinson, and the second on a ninth-inning suicide-squeeze bunt by Al Campanis. Newark took the next two games, but the Royals won the fifth game 2-1, as Glen Moulder outpitched Vic Raschi and Robinson drove in the winning run.

Because of such offensive fireworks, it wasn't surprising that the Royals attracted more than 400,000 fans to Delorimier Stadium in 1946, surpassing the previous year's attendance. One of the side effects of the larger attendance and increased excitement was a rise in gambling. Hector Racine believed some undesirable characters were hanging out in the stands and that thousands of dollars often changed hands during a game. He was right, although it was hardly a recent development. Montreal lawyer Conrad Shatner remembers attending games in the 1930s with his uncle, a bookie who would take bets during the game. "In those days people used to bet by the inning," Shatner recalls, "Are the Royals going to get any hits, any runs? If the team was down by

The Royals won the series in an exciting, controversy-marred sixth game at Delorimier Stadium, before more than 19,000 fans. Trailing 4-3 in the bottom of the ninth, the Royals had the bases empty with two out when Newark left-hander Herb Karpel thought he had struck out slugger Les Burge on a 2-2 pitch. Umpire Artie Gore called it a ball, angering Karpel, who was even more livid when Burge belted the next pitch over the fence to tie the score. Karpel stormed the plate and was about to jump Gore when he was grabbed by a teammate. Karpel, Selkirk and two other Bears who had stuck their noses into the melee were ejected.

Alex Mustaikis relieved Karpel but Tatum promptly singled and Franks doubled.

Tatum tore around second base and headed for third, where he was waved home by manager Clay Hopper, coaching at third. As the throw arrived just ahead of the runner, it appeared the manager had blown it. But Gore called the runner safe, telling a furious Yogi Berra he had missed the tag. Chaos ensued as players from both teams came off their respective benches and shoved each other while Gore was escorted off the field by police. The brawl didn't change the outcome - the Royals were on their way to the Governor's Cup final against Syracuse.

The Chiefs, who had finished behind the Royals during the regular season, had a reputation for pulling playoff upsets. They shocked the Royals in the opening game of the series but Montreal won the next four to claim its second Governor's Cup of the decade. It was on to Louisville to face the Colonels in the Junior World Series.

The Colonels had won the Series the previous season They had good pitching and defense, but at first glance were no match for the Royals offensively. That seemed evident in the opening game as Les Burge smacked two homers in pacing Montreal to victory. But the next night, Royals were handcuffed on two hits by right-hander Harry Dorish, who held them to two hits, and were overpowered 15-6 in Game 3. One of the problems in Louisville was that team catalyst Jackie Robinson had only one hit in the first three games. The Louisville fans booed him and showered him with a steady barrage of racial insults, such as, "Hey black boy, go back to Canada." Colonels management also apparently had slapped a "negro quota" on tickets, on the premise that there might be clashes in the stands if too may black fans attended the game. The more Robinson struggled at the plate, the louder the abuse, and by the end of the third game Robinson was dying to "go home to Canada."

Throughout the arduous 1946 season the support of Montreal baseball fans was a port in a storm for Robinson. From the moment the Robinsons found an apartment on de Gaspe Street in east-end Montreal - without encountering any racial bias they had anticipated - they felt comfortable and welcome in their new city. Rachel Robinson has often fondly recalled being invited in for tea by the woman who owned the de Gaspe Street apartment when the couple inquired about the vacancy. It was the type of simple courtesy she wasn't used to receiving from white people. The neighbors were friendly and helpful, even though they spoke little English and the Robinsons spoke no French. They took good care of Rachel, who was pregnant with the couple's first child, by running errands for her and giving her post-war ration coupons for butter and sugar.

Reflecting on those days in a 1996 visit to Montreal, Rachel Robinson said, "I think Branch Rickey showed great astuteness in picking Montreal, and a concern for us as people who were launching a social experiment. It gave us a chance to regain the confidence that had been bruised in the South. Jackie also enjoyed the city, even though the intense curiosity of the neighbors sometimes made him feel as if he was living in a fish bowl. A couple of years after leaving Montreal, Robinson told journalist Wendell Smith: "I liked Montreal because it seemed to like me. The people were friendly and gracious. The kids on the streets made a fuss over me and the adults smiled and shook my hand wherever I went."

Because the black community in Montreal was small and somewhat ghettoized at the time, it was rather uncommon for white Montrealers to have black neighbors. There was prejudice in the city, even a certain amount of unofficial segregation, but it was more a problem of neglect than persecution. The Robinsons were a novelty in their neighborhood, seen almost as visitors from another planet, and their skin color didn't go

Illustrated by John Collins.

een—son" is the way it sounded to him, and he liked it - possibly, he mused, because the pronunciation allowed him to pretend he was someone else for a while.

Robinson was also a tremendous drawing card on the road. Black people would travel from all over the United States and Canada to the nearest International League city the Royals were visiting. He was often presented with a gift or an award by an organization for having broken baseball's color barrier. But more often the treatment he received from fans and opposing players was brutal and insulting.

On the field, Robinson was thrown at, spiked and taken out viciously at second base by baserunners. He received death threats in the mail and was abused from the stands, especially in Syracuse and Baltimore. In Syracuse, fans put a black cat on the field yelling, "Here Jackie, here's your cousin." He was often told he couldn't stay in the same

unnoticed. One of the first French words Rachel learned was "noir". But if they weren't quite considered to be one of the family, they were certainly treated as honored guests. The fact the Robinsons were famous and Jackie was helping the local ball club win games, obviously made the reception even more enthusiastic. Robinson was so popular in Montreal, he was often included when players from the hockey Canadiens, the undisputed kings of the local sports scene, made charity appearances.

Robinson was a sensation from the moment he arrived in Montreal, following a tremendous start on the road. Local reporters called him the Dark Dasher and the Colored Comet. He was the favorite of most of the fans, who cheered whenever he came up to the plate and screamed "Allez" when he got on base, urging him to steal second. Robinson enjoyed the way the bilingual announcer at the park would introduce him with a trace of a French accent. "Yakee Rob-

Illustrated by John Collins.

Illustrated by John Collins.

hotel as his teammates and was forced to find a hotel that accepted black people or a room in the private home of a black family. This happened most frequently in Baltimore, the southern-most team in the International League. Montreal third baseman Spider Jorgensen told Robinson biographer David Falkner of a time in Baltimore when an angry mob gathered outside the Montreal clubhouse following a game. They started yelling: "Come out of there, Robinson, you nigger son-of-a-bitch, we'll getcha, we'll getcha." Jorgensen says manager Hopper and the rest of the players left, but he, Marvin Rackley and Tom Tatum stuck around with Robinson until the mob dispersed.

Although it appeared he was taking the abuse and hatred calmly, Robinson was occasionally heard to lament that nobody could understand what he was going through. He was on amicable terms with most of his teammates, but none of them really made any efforts to befriend him or

offer support. Teammates would exchange pleasantries and compliment him when he knocked in a run or made a good play in the field. And they would occasionally stick up for him on the field, but off the diamond he spent a lot of time by himself. Part of this was Robinson's solitary nature; he didn't make friends easily. But it was also because some of his teammates were uncomfortable having a black man on the team. Montrealer Alvin Guttman, an avid Royals' fan, remembers having dinner with a friend at a popular downtown restaurant, the Chic-N-Coop, and spotting a table of Royals' players. His friend approached the players and said he thought Robinson was a great second baseman. "Yeah," one of them replied, "but it's a shame to take a job away from a white man."

The abuse was almost unbearable at times. But Robinson was often able to assert himself without breaking his promise to Rickey. Jean-Pierre Roy remembers a game in Baltimore when Eddie Robinson slammed into Jackie at second base for no reason. Jackie was agile enough to avoid the brunt of

Illustrated by John Collins.

the collision, but he glared at Eddie Robinson and said quietly, "Don't ever do that again." Then, with the Baltimore slugger still on the ground, he brandished the ball menacingly in front of his face as if to say, "The next time I'll put this between your eyes." But for the most part, he had to keep his anger to himself, something that went against the grain of his personality, and it took its toll. He went through a stretch near the end of the season when the stress was so enormous he couldn't eat or sleep. A doctor told him to take a week off and relax, so the next day he and Rachel went on a picnic. But he was back in the lineup the very next day, not wanting to let his detractors claim he was dogging it to protect his league-leading batting average.

Nothing had topped the ill treatment he'd received during the three Junior World Series games in Louisville. Jackie's double-play partner Al Campanis commented after the third game that "Robinson didn't play well down here, but wait till you see him in Montreal, where the fans are his friends." More than 14,000 of Robinson's "friends" showed up at Delorimier Stadium on a near freezing night in early October to support their hero. In a show of disdain for the treatment Robinson had received in Louisville, the fans booed the Colonels when they took the field and booed every time one of the players walked out of the dugout. Robinson was touched by the reaction. "I didn't approve of that kind of retaliation," he wrote later, "but I felt a jubilant sense of gratitude for the way the Canadians expressed their feelings. When fans go to bat for you like that, you feel it would be easy to play for them forever."

Despite the enthusiastic support from the fans, the Royals trailed for much of the game and were behind 5-3 in the ninth with two out and Marvin Rackley on first base. Louisville pitcher Otis Clark courted disaster by walking Robinson and Tom Tatum to load the bases. He was yanked so that left-hander Joe Ostrowski could face Les Burge, a left-handed batter. But Burge also walked, scoring Rackley to make it 5-4. Louisville catcher Fred Walters then tried to pick Tatum off second base and threw wildly, allowing Robinson to race home with the tying run. In the bottom of the 10th, Robinson came to bat with two out and the bases loaded, a perfect scenario to extract a measure of revenge for the mistreatment in Louisville. Robinson did just that, lining a single into left field for a Montreal victory that knotted the series 2-2.

The fifth game was another in which Robinson starred. The Royals took an early three-run lead, only to have Louisville tie it in the seventh. But Robinson scored the go-ahead run in the bottom of the seventh, as he led off with a triple and came in on Lew Riggs' two-out double. In the eighth, Robinson caught the Colonels' defence napping when he dropped a surprise two-out bunt down the third-base line that scored Al Campanis from third with the fifth run in what would be a 5-3 Royals' victory.

A great pitching match-up was in store for Game 6. Young right-hander Harry Dorish got the call for Louisville, while the Royals countered with Curt Davis, 43, the dean of their staff. Davis had appeared in one World Series game in his 12 years in the majors, as a Dodger in 1941, and had lost to the Yankees Red Ruffing. Dorish, who had two-hit the Royals earlier in the series, had won his last eight starts. But the Royals got to him early, with Dixie Howell and Al Campanis each driving in a run in the second inning. From then on the Montreal bats were fairly quiet and it was pitching and defence that enabled the Royals to preserve the 2-0 lead into the ninth inning.

But there was trouble ahead. Walters, the Louisville catcher, doubled to open the ninth and second baseman Chuck Koney

Fans carried Clay Hopper around the field in celebration after the Royals won the 1946 Junior World Series.

got an infield hit, with Walters holding at second. Davis then induced Al Brancato to hit a ball to Robinson who stepped on second and threw to first for a double play. With two outs and a runner at third, the pinch-hitter Otto Denning represented the tying run. The fans got a sinking feeling when Denning pulled a hard smash toward third base. But Lew Riggs, the I.L.'s all-star third baseman, gloved the hot smash and fired to first for the final out. The Royals

had won their first Junior World Series and more than 19,000 fans erupted in celebration.

Police assistance was required to escort players to the clubhouse as fans poured onto the field to mob the players. Fans chanted for manager Clay Hopper to come out on the field and when he did, a group carried him on their shoulders around the park. Then they hollered for Curt Davis and gave him a similar ride. But the loudest cheers were for Jackie Robinson, who had rebounded from a slow start in Louisville to get seven hits in 14 at-bats in the three games in Montreal and had performed brilliantly all season. Robinson emerged and was carried around by the fans as they sang a victory song called "Il a Gagné Ses Épaulettes", meaning "He has earned his stripes." Tears streamed down Robinson's face as he was paraded around the field. Rachel Robinson was so caught up in the emotional tribute to her husband, she waded into the adoring crowd, even though she was eight months pregnant. Fifty years after her husband's debut in Montreal, she still lists the Royals' victory over Louisville as the most exciting end to a baseball season that she ever saw.

After his ceremonial ride, Robinson dried his eyes and returned to the clubhouse to change. He was in a hurry to get to the airport to catch a plane for Detroit, where he was to start a barnstorming tour. But as he came out of the stadium in his street clothes, he was mobbed again by hundreds of people. Robinson had to run down the street to get away from the hordes of admirers, who wanted to touch him and shake his hand. He was rescued by people passing in a car, who stopped and whisked him away. Sam Maltin, a reporter for the Montreal Herald who also wrote stories about Robinson for the Pittsburgh Courier, was in the middle of the mayhem. In the last few months, Maltin and his family had become close with the Robinsons, and he marveled at the adoration his friend inspired. The sight moved him to write a now-famous line about the novelty of a white mob chasing a black man out of love and not hatred. Meanwhile, back in the clubhouse, Clay Hopper, the man who a few months earlier had asked Rickey if "he really thought a nigger was a human being," was telling reporters that Robinson was "a great ball player and a fine gentleman." He also said Robinson was a cinch for the majors.

These chaotic and emotional moments didn't really sink in until Robinson was on the plane heading for Detroit, and a warm feeling came over him. Relating his feelings to Wendell Smith about a year later, Robinson said: "As the plane roared skyward and the lights of Montreal twinkled and winked in the distance, I took one last look at this great city where I had found so much happiness. 'I don't care if I ever get to the majors, I told myself. This is the city for me. This is paradise.'" Rachel Robinson was equally thankful. She felt the season in Montreal had been a good omen for the success of their social experiment. "Thank you Lord for bringing us here and helping us through this season," she said as the plane climbed higher into the sky.

The Royals and their fans missed Jackie Robinson when he moved up to the Dodgers in 1947.

1947-1948
Campy, Chuck and "The Mule"

On September 7, 1947 - the last day of the International League season - the Royals were battling for their third straight pennant. The team had played well for the first half of the season but, lacking the skill and depth of the 1946 squad, had blown an 11 1|2-game, mid-season lead. Now they entered the final day of the schedule a half-game behind the Jersey City Giants, who were to play a single game against Baltimore while the Royals had a doubleheader against the last-place Toronto Maple Leafs. A New Jersey loss would mean the Royals needed only a split with Toronto to win the pennant by a few percentage points. If Jersey City won, however, the Royals would need to win both games to finish in first place.

The team could no longer turn to Jackie Robinson in such crucial moments. Robinson had made the Dodgers out of spring training in 1947, breaking the racial barrier that had existed in the majors for decades. Robinson was now an important part of a Brooklyn club which was heading for its first National League pennant since 1941. The Royals, however, had lost 20 games by a single run in 1947 and missed Robinson's ability to make things happen with a bunt, stolen base, or two-out triple.

Montreal manager Clay Hopper realized he didn't have the same talent he had a year earlier. There had been a lot of pressure on him during the last few weeks of the season. Not only was his team playing poorly, rival clubs seemed to save their best efforts for the

Roy Campanella was a workhorse for the Royals in 1947, catching almost all of the team's games.

Royals. Many clubs were irked by the Royals' recent dominance of the league and disliked Hopper's habit of piling on runs, even when Montreal was way ahead. Giants general manager, Charlie Stoneham (a cousin of New York Giants boss Horace Stoneham) had complained about this after a Sunday game in Jersey City earlier in the season. Hopper, he said, had deliberately tried to humiliate his team in front of its own fans by using trick plays and stealing bases, even though Montreal had a big lead. He insisted

After the glorious championship year of 1946, the next season was frustrating for Hopper and his Royals.

other clubs had experienced the same treatment and were so angry they re-arranged their pitching rotations during the pennant race to help the Giants knock off the Royals and their arrogant manager. Jersey City manager Bruno Betzel wanted to beat his old team so badly he offered to personally add $1,000 to the post-season prize money if his boys could knock off Hopper and the Royals. Betzel's attempt to sweeten the playoff pot was disallowed by league president Shaughnessy.

On the final day of the season, the Giants backed Hopper's boys into a corner by beating Baltimore, thus forcing the Royals to win both games against Toronto. Montreal had a 5-3, ninth-inning lead in the opener, when Maple Leafs third baseman Len Kensecke faced Royals reliever Chet Kehn with two out and two runners on base. Kehn had been a steady pitcher for the Royals over the years, but Kensecke took

him deep for a home run that put Toronto ahead 6-5.

Almost 20,000 fans sat in stunned silence at Delorimier Stadium as Kensecke rounded the bases. Their gloom failed to lift in the bottom of the ninth as the Royals, despite a one-out double by Al Campanis, failed to overcome the deficit. In Jersey City, where the fans had listened in on a radio broadcast of the Royals' game, there was bedlam at Roosevelt Stadium when the Royals' final out was made. Some fans ripped up their seats and threw them onto the field to celebrate the Giants' first pennant since 1939. The Royals won the nightcap against Toronto, but it didn't matter. They had lost the pennant on the last day of the season and were about to enter the playoffs on a sober note. Hopper received a telegram from Branch Rickey consoling him for the loss and complimenting him on his work, despite the outcome. But losing on the last day gave both men an uneasy feeling about the playoffs.

Rickey was right to console Hopper. The team's collapse was not the manager's fault, even if he had antagonized the other clubs. The Royals were never as dominant as their mid-season record seemed to indicate. They were a good squad, winning 93 games and losing only 60, but not nearly as talented as the previous two editions. The club had retained only a handful of the players who had led Montreal to the Junior World Series the previous season. Robinson, "Spider" Jorgensen and Marvin Rackley had all graduated to the Dodgers, and others, including Tom Tatum, Dixie Howell, Steve Nagy and Glen Moulder, had landed jobs with other major-league teams. All-star third baseman Lew Riggs was sent to the St. Paul Saints, the Dodgers farm club in the American Association, and Herman Franks and Les Burge, two of the team's steadiest performers over the last few seasons, retired to take minor-league managing jobs.

There were a lot of holes to fill in 1947. Some of the replacements worked out well - notably, outfielder Dick Whitman and first baseman Ed Stevens, both arriving from Brooklyn, and six-foot-three, 224-pound outfielder Walter Sessi, acquired from the Cardinals organization. This trio led the team offensively, with Stevens, in his third stint with the Royals, pounding 27 home runs and driving in 108 runs. Sessi was outstanding in the outfield, handling 218 chances without an error. On the mound, Ed Heusser, a nine-season major-league veteran, won 19 games for the Royals and Jack Banta, another third-year man with the team, won 15 games and led the league with 199 strikeouts.

Perhaps the steadiest Montreal performer in 1947 was 25-year-old catcher Roy Campanella, one of the original group of players from the Negro Leagues signed by Branch Rickey in 1945. Campanella joined the Royals after spending the 1946 season at Nashua, NH., in the New England League, the only Dodgers' affiliate, besides Montreal and Trois-Rivieres, willing to accept black players. At Nashua, Campanella teamed up with pitcher Don Newcombe, another Negro League alumnus, and player-manager Walter Alston, a tall, powerful man who had once played first base for Clay Hopper in the Cardinals system. Campanella was short and stocky, with amazing strength and durability. He often bragged about catching two doubleheaders one afternoon while playing for the Philadelphia Elite Giants.

Campanella and Newcombe would often hear racial taunts from the stands in the Class-B New England circuit, although it was mild compared to what Robinson was hearing. The even-tempered Campanella

Campanella takes a few cuts at spring training in the Dominican Republic. As a result of Florida's segregation laws, the Dodgers and Royals fled Daytona Beach for the Caribbean after the 1946 season.

didn't let it get to him, but the Nashua general manager, E.J. "Buzzie" Bavasi, was less tolerant. Many years after Campanella's retirement, the catcher told author Roger Kahn about an incident in Lynn, Mass. when an opposing manager referred to him and Newcombe as niggers. "Buzzie jumped him," he recalled, "he was fighting him for what he said...I never did let it peeve me." Campanella was a steadying influence on the younger, less mature Newcombe. Alston had so much confidence in Campanella, he let the catcher run the club whenever he was sick or banished by an umpire.

Campanella caught all but 18 of the Royals' 153 games in 1947, losing 50 pounds in the process. He demonstrated intelligence, leadership and a howitzer arm behind the plate. Offensively, he hit .273 and contributed 13 home runs and 75 RBIs. Many believed Campanella belonged in the major leagues but Rickey, as usual, took no chances, giving him a sampling of Triple-A ball before bringing him up to the Dodgers. In the clubhouse, Campanella was outgoing. He took part in the social life of the team more than Jackie Robinson had done. That was partly because of his personality and also because he carried less of the burden Robinson had shouldered a year earlier. Campanella could relax, something Robinson had never felt he could do. But Campanella also had a serious side. He was often spotted with a Bible tucked under his arm. Years later, in his retirement years, Campanella said his season in Montreal was the turning point of his career, and he lauded the city for the role it had played in the integration of organized baseball.

With players such as Campanella, Stevens, Whitman and Heusser, the Royals should have been a solid threat in the 1947 playoffs. But things went wrong as soon as they took the field in the opening round against the Syracuse Chiefs. They fell behind 6-0 early in the opening game, eventually

Dodger executive Buzzie Bavasi defended Campanella and Newcombe against racial slurs.

closed within a run but couldn't tie it, as Al Campanis, who reached third base late in the game, stood rooted there on a wild pitch to the backstop which should have scored him.

It was a bitter defeat that added to the pessimism of the Montreal fans, already disgruntled by the team's late-season collapse. Attendance for the next game was a respectable 14,000, but it was below the usual turnout for a Royals' playoff game. The Royals fell 2-0 and then lost the first two games in Syracuse, bowing out in a sweep. It was a humiliating way for the defending Junior World Series champs to end a roller-coaster season.

Manager Hopper found the inconsistent, sometimes sloppy play of the Royals hard to swallow following the almost perfect season of a year ago. Before leaving Montreal for his off-season home in Mississippi, Hopper said the team needed to be completely rebuilt because he had some players on the current club who weren't Triple-A calibre. Hopper was trying to send a message to Brooklyn that he needed an injection of talent if things were to improve for 1948.

Hopper wouldn't know whether the Dodgers had heeded his post-season plea until late the following spring. In those days, minor-league managers whose teams were owned by major-league clubs were never sure who they would be getting until the middle of May, when the parent teams were required to trim down to their final rosters. (Nowadays, final rosters must be submitted prior to the start of the season). The Royals were now entering their 10th season in the Dodgers organization, and even the fans were familiar with the process of assembling a team, which could be likened to baking a cake. Start with the basic ingredients: holdovers from the previous season; add a handful of seasoned veterans for flavor and consistency; bake the mix in the spring sunshine for a month; then cover with an icing made from the sweetest ingredients the Dodgers could spare. The first two ingredients were the foundation of the cake, but it was the icing that made the difference.

The possibility of getting a future Dodgers star - a Pete Reiser, Carl Furillo or Jackie Robinson - was always an exciting prospect for Montreal fans. But the excitement was tempered by the realization these players were basically on loan and could be snatched away by the Dodgers at any moment. Montreal writer Mordecai Richler, a Royals' supporter as a young boy, has reminisced how he and his friends avoided becoming too attached to the team's stars. "Ziggy, Yossell and I had learned to love with caution," he once wrote, "If after the first death there is no other, an arguable notion, I do remember that each time one of our heroes abandoned us for Ebbets Field, it

stung us badly. We hated Mr. Rickey for his voracious appetite." Rickey would often come to Montreal to announce these player repatriations in person, jokingly telling assembled reporters that the move was subject to their approval.

But in 1948 all the ingredients were there for a strong team, and Hopper had to be pleased with what Rickey had provided. The first exciting news was that the Dodgers were sending Al Gionfriddo, a hero for Brooklyn in the World Series against the Yankees the previous October. "G.I.", as his teammates called him, made a great running catch in Game 6 that robbed Joe DiMaggio of a home run and preserved a Brooklyn victory. The Yankees went on to win the Series, but the catch would forever stand as a classic. Gionfriddo was a short, speedy outfielder who was sure to get more playing time in Montreal than he had in Brooklyn, despite his World Series stardom. In fact, that 1947 World Series game was his last appearance in the big leagues.

The next piece of good news for the Royals was the arrival of outfielders Marvin Rackley and Duke Snider. Rackley had been outstanding for the Royals in 1946, hitting .305 and leading the league with 65 stolen bases. Snider had been signed by the Dodgers in 1944 out of a Southern California high school and impressed the Dodgers brass from the start. In only 66 games with the St. Paul Saints in 1947, Snider compiled a .316 average with 12 homers and 46 RBIs before finishing the season in Brooklyn.

Snider, who had all-around ability, was a player Hopper had requested from the Dodgers since the first day of spring training, although he must have expected the talented young prospect probably wouldn't be spending much time in Triple-A ball. It was late May before fans at Delorimier Stadium finally got a look at Snider and Rackley. Almost 20,000 were on hand as Snider

Twenty one year old Duke Snider was the Duke of Delorimier, until he became a Dodger in 1948.

introduced himself by belting a home run in each game of a doubleheader. Rackley re-acquainted himself by going three-for-four in the nightcap. The pair were instrumental in Montreal sweeping the twinbill, 8-2 and 13-3.

With Snider, Rackley and Gionfriddo, the Royals obviously had an impressive outfield. The infield was also much improved over the previous season, especially with Jimmy Bloodworth anchoring things at second base. Bloodworth, graying at the temples, was a dapper 30-year-old with lots of major-league experience. At first, Hopper didn't intend to make Bloodworth an everyday player. Leadership, more than RBIs, was expected from him, but he played so well Hopper couldn't keep him out of the lineup. He was also a good influence on rookie Bobby Morgan, still learning the shortstop position.

Another addition was Kevin "Chuck" Connors, a six-foot-five, square-jawed first baseman from Seton Hall University who was a professional basketball player in the off-season and an aspiring actor. (Connors played basketball for Rochester in the NBL, and Boston in the BAA. He gained famed following his athletic endeavors as the star of The Rifleman, a popular television series). Connors wasn't much of a fielder - someone once remarked that he waved at grounders "like a small boy waving at a train." But he could hit with power from the left side of the plate, always an asset at Delorimier Stadium.

At third base the Royals had Lou Welaj, who had played all over the infield in 1947 and brought some speed to the lineup. Most of the catching was handled by Mike Sandlock, who'd been Campanella's back-up in 1947. The job was now his with Campy doing a brief stint at St. Paul (integrating the American Association at Branch Rickey's request) on his way up to the Dodgers.

The pitching aces were Jack Banta, in his fourth season with the club, and Don Newcombe, a phenomenal young fireballer. Newcombe, like Campanella, was one of the players Rickey had signed from the Negro Leagues just after hiring Robinson to play for the Royals. A lanky right-hander, Newcombe had stayed in Nashua a season longer than Campanella trying to improve his control. His main pitch was an explosive fastball, but he also threw a slow, looping curve and a faster, tighter curve, or slider. Although Banta had more victories than Newcombe, and would pitch seven shutouts, the intimidating rookie became Hopper's ace as the season progressed. Hopper often said Newcombe would be the next Dizzy Dean.

The Royals trailed the Newark Bears early in the season but caught them by the second week in June and had a firm grip on first place by the end of the month. Snider, Bloodworth and right-fielder John Simmons, another young Dodgers prospect, were all hitting above .300 and Connors wasn't far behind. Rackley, as it turned out, was recalled to Brooklyn after only a few weeks, but was replaced by Sam Jethroe, an outfielder from the Negro Leagues. A multi-talented player, Jethroe had exceptional speed. In his half-season with Montreal he stole 18 bases, enough to win the league title in a curiously sedentary season. Jethroe saw action in both centre and right field and was moved into the lead-off spot in the batting order.

With the Royals cruising along in first place, the Montreal fans were in fine humor, anxiously awaiting a scheduled exhibition game against the Dodgers during the majors' all-star break. The game was an annual event but it had been ill-fated in recent years. In

Don Newcombe was a young fireballer who gave opposing managers nightmares.

1946, the Dodgers left the field with the score tied because they had to catch a plane. Angry fans booed the Dodgers and bombarded the field with seat cushions. The next year the game was cancelled because of rain, a tremendous disappointment for the thousands of fans who had bought tickets largely for the return of Jackie Robinson. The fans were still hoping to get a look at him in 1948, but the Dodgers committed another public-relations gaffe by resting Robinson after only one inning. The result was more boos and flying seat cushions from the stands. The fans derived some consolation, however, as the home team clobbered a mostly second-string Dodgers squad 15-8.

A month later, the fans were reminded of the Dodgers' omnipotence when the parent club announced it was bringing Duke Snider up to Brooklyn. On the day in May when Snider learned he would be going to Montreal, Branch Rickey had said to him: "Show me some big numbers up there, son. Make me bring you back." In 77 International League games with the Royals, Snider hit .327 with 17 home runs and 77 RBIs The numbers were big enough for Rickey, and the Dodgers made room for the man who would soon be lionized in Brooklyn as the Duke of Flatbush. To replace Snider, the Royals received Dick Whitman. He performed adequately but the team wasn't quite the same without Snider.

The Royals entered the last month of the season with a six-game lead over Newark, but faced the unpleasant prospect of playing 14 doubleheaders in the next 29 days. In those days, minor-league teams had as many as a dozen scheduled doubleheaders, and more were added during the season to make up for rainouts. The nightcap was usually a seven-inning game, but seasons often ended in gruelling doubleheader derbies that left the teams exhausted. The Royals played the first of their string of doubleheaders against Newark and took both games, fattening their first-place lead. It launched a 16-game winning streak that would have locked up the top spot for the Royals had Newark not maintained a torrid pace.

The Royals' winning streak ended during the first game of a doubleheader against Toronto, but they won the seven-inning nightcap 8-0 as Newcombe pitched a no-hitter. The Maple Leafs Vick Barnhart almost ended the no-hit bid with two out in the bottom of the ninth inning, when he hit a line drive that struck Newcombe in the chest. The pitcher momentarily lost sight of the ball and scrambled around looking for it as fans pointed and yelled. He finally located the ball and whipped it to first, getting Barnhart by an eye-lash.

The Royals continued to streak as September neared, sweeping their 17th doubleheader, a league record. (The team stretched it to 19 by the end of the season). Despite a slump that saw Newark cut into Montreal's 16-game lead, the Royals clinched the pennant early in September. They finished with a 94-59 record, beating Newark by more than a dozen games. The players staged a party to mark the team's third pennant in four seasons, but they were so exhausted from all the doubleheaders, it was a low-key celebration.

The brief, late-season slump and the club's overall fatigue had Branch Rickey worried. He had experienced a disappointing season at the box office in Ebbets Field, with the Dodgers out of pennant contention, and he hoped for a little extra revenue from Montreal. The regular-season attendance totals at Delorimier Stadium were good, with more than 477,000 clicks of the turnstiles. It was a club record and one of the best attendance figures in the minor leagues. But Rickey feared a letdown in the playoffs, so he strategically sent a telegram to Buzzie Bavasi, now the Montreal general manager, calling the Royals "a self-sufficient bunch of so-called champions." He said the players were "subconsciously complacent," and that "every mother's son of them should realize that for the past several weeks they've been a sixth-place club." The message was posted in the Royals' clubhouse for motivational purposes. Bavasi sent back a playful reply, informing his boss that the Royals had ended up in first place while the Dodgers were currently in fourth.

Clay Hopper didn't appear to be fazed by Rickey's comments. In a ceremony prior to the last game of the regular season honoring him for being named manager of the I.L. all-star team, Hopper addressed the crowd and boasted the Royals would win the Governor's Cup and the Junior World Series. Hopper had three of his own players selected to the all-star squad. Jack Banta made it as the best right-handed pitcher and the excellent double-play combination of Jimmy Bloodworth and Bobby Morgan were both picked. Although signed as a utility player, Bloodworth had appeared in all but two of the team's games and was voted the league's Most Valuable Player. He hit .294 and drove in 99 runs with 24 home runs, an impressive total for a right-handed batter at Delorimier Stadium.

Bloodworth was expected to be a key figure as the heavily favored Royals faced the Rochester Red Wings in the opening round of the playoffs. The opening game was a match-up between Red Wings left-hander John Mikan and Montreal's ace Don Newcombe. Although Banta (19-9) had the most wins and strikeouts in the league, Newcombe had compiled the best ratio of victories to losses with a 17-6 record. Hopper also regarded the latter as his stopper.

Newcombe was one pitch away from completing a masterful 4-0 shutout of the Red Wings in the opener. He seemed so invincible that many of the more than 18,000 fans at Delorimier Stadium were already happily strolling toward the exits.

But, with two strikes on Hal Rice, Newcombe suddenly unraveled. He threw four straight balls to Rice and loaded the bases by walking Russ Derry and hitting Ed Kazak. That brought up rookie Glenn "Rocky" Nelson, the league's all-star first baseman and a power-hitting, left-handed batter. There was a nervous hush as Nelson dug in, followed by disbelief as he smashed a Newcombe pitch into the gap in left-centre for a bases-clearing triple.

With the Royals' lead sliced to a single run, Hopper walked to the mound and spoke with his unsettled pitcher. Some fans yelled at Hopper to yank Newcombe, while others implored him to keep him in there. Hopper stuck with Newcombe, who made his manager look good by striking out the next batter, Chuck Diering, on three pitches to notch the victory.

The outing was an example of Newcombe's

Al Campanis tries to uncover the Delorimier infield turf he covered as a shortstop for more than a season.

potential, but also an indication that the six-foot-four, 225-pound pitcher still had some things to learn. He was, after all, only 22 years old. "I have to try to get the first ball in there and stay ahead of hitters," he admitted, "I'm trying to improve my curve ball, too." He was soft-spoken and thoughtful off the field, but intimidating while he was on it. Rochester manager Cedric Durst was convinced that Newcombe belonged in the majors, despite his ninth-inning lapse in control in the first game. Durst entertained reporters by describing a nightmare he had following the opening game. In the nightmare, a giant Don Newcombe, with an armful of marble baseballs, had visited Durst's hotel room. "No! No!" Durst shrieked during his dream, "Throw anything you like, but not the fastball, not the fastball." The giant Newcombe then lumbered to the window and fired the marble baseballs down toward the street, creating thunderous explosions that shook the building. Durst said that's when he woke up, trembling.

The Royals went up 2-0 in the series the next night, in a sloppy game that Rochester virtually gave away by committing three errors and walking nine Montreal batters. The Royals outhit the Red Wings 13-9 and won the third game 8-6. Montreal's bats weren't quite as productive at Rochester's Red Wing Stadium, as the team stranded 13 baserunners and lost 5-3. The next game was a rematch between Newcombe and Mikan. Both pitchers were superb, with the only scoring play coming in the first inning. Rochester had runners at first and third with no out when Russ Derry hit a grounder to Chuck Connors at first. Connors elected to concede a run to complete a double play - not a bad decision early in a ball game,

By 1947 the Dodgers had an extensive farm system. Here Clay Hopper (standing at left), Branch Rickey Jr. (seated) and Harold Roettger keep track of things.

but it proved to be the game-winning run and the series was tied 2-2.

Mistakes were the Royals' undoing in Game 5. A base-running blunder by Oscar Grimes, who passed Al Gionfriddo on the bases, cut short an eighth-inning rally. After the Royals moved ahead 5-4 in the ninth on RBI singles by Dick Whitman and Jimmy Bloodworth, they blew the lead in the bottom half of the inning, with Bloodworth's bad throw to first allowing the winning run to score.

The Royals were on the verge of a humiliating defeat to an opponent which had barely made it into the playoffs. But the players responded well to the pressure, with Clarence Podbielan, out-pitched by Bill Reeder in Game 3, winning the re-match.

This set up a dramatic seventh game between Newcombe and Mikan, their third pitching confrontation in the series. A rain postponement provided some extra rest for both pitchers, who went to the mound after four days off. The result was scintillating duel, still scoreless into the ninth inning.

Newcombe set down the Red Wings in the top of the ninth and an equally strong Mikan struck out Sam Jethroe, the Royals lead-off batter in their half of the inning. Branch Rickey, attending this crucial game, slumped in his seat when Jethroe fanned, and he pulled his hat down low over his forehead. Rickey quickly straightened up and tilted his hat back, however, when Mikan promptly yielded his third hit of the day to Dick Whitman, and then walked Oscar Grimes. A single by league MVP, Jimmy Bloodworth, might win the series. Bloodworth did better than that. He connected on a pitch that Mikan had left a little too close to the middle of the plate and lined a home run over the fence in right-centre.

The almost 20,000 fans at Delorimier Stadium started celebrating as soon as the ball left the park. Some of them stormed onto the field, as they had done when the team won the Junior World Series in 1946. Bloodworth was hoisted onto their shoulders before he even had a chance to touch second base. (A technicality the umpires ignored.) It was one of the last games Bloodworth would play at the stadium; a short time later it was announced he'd been hired by the Cincinnati Reds for the following season. Newcombe was the next to be carried on shoulders for a victory lap of the stadium. He had won his second game of the series, giving up only four hits and striking out eight. When the hoopla was over, the erstwhile "subconsciously complacent" Royals set their sights on their next opponent: the Syracuse Chiefs. It would be a rematch of two old rivals - Clay Hopper and Syracuse manager Jewel Ens.

Ens and Hopper had been feuding since the Syracuse manager accused Hopper of throwing at his hitters when the two teams met in the 1946 playoffs. Hopper denied the accusation, but the Syracuse media had vilified him. The acrimony was overshadowed by the excitement of the opening game, a nail-biter in which the lead shifted a number of times. The Royals were leading 4-3 going into the ninth, but Syracuse scored to force extra innings.

A four-run 10th inning by Syracuse seemed to sink the Royals, but a single, a walk and an error loaded the bases for Chuck Connors, who delivered a game-tying grand slam home run off Frank Seward. (It was the fourth grand slam by Connors that season). Bobby Morgan followed with a walk

and, one out later, Cliff Dapper, a faithful Montreal war horse, hit a ball off the top of the fence in right centre to produce the winning run. Dapper had been a Royal on and off since 1942, when he was their 22 year old catcher. Like Bloodworth, he was in his final days as a Royal. He planned to retire at the end of the season to take a managing job in the Southern Association.

More than 21,000 fans crammed into Delorimier Downs the next night and they witnessed another dramatic finish. This time it was Syracuse right-fielder Frank Davis who pulled off the heroics. Batting in the ninth inning with the Chiefs trailing 2-1, he cranked a three-run homer, his record-tying 15th playoff RBI. The Chiefs added an insurance run for a 5-2 victory.

The series moved to Syracuse with Don Newcombe facing Eddie Erautt, a right-hander with a 15-7 regular-season record. during the season. Opposing pitchers often seemed to rise to the challenge of facing Newcombe. Erautt was stingy, allowing only six hits and two runs, both driven in by Sam Jethroe. But the Royals usually didn't need many runs when Newcombe pitched. The powerful right-hander was superb again, yielding a run and four hits for a 2-1 victory. It was Newcombe's third win in four playoff starts, during which he had allowed only 13 hits and five runs.

There were some added fireworks in Newcombe's latest victory. With one out in the ninth, Newcombe buried a slow curve-ball into the shoulder of Syracuse batter Clyde Vollmer. Vollmer wasn't injured, but he glared menacingly at Newcombe before taking his base. Unperturbed, Newcombe quickly got ahead of the next batter, Dick West. The following pitch, however, was up and in, forcing West to hit the dirt. But the ball hit his bat as he was going down and went foul for strike two. An enraged West got to his feet and tore after Newcombe, making an awkward, flying leap at the pitcher. "I intended cutting him with my spikes and stomping on him," West fumed following the game, "I wouldn't waste my fists on him."

Newcombe, more than big enough to defend himself, calmly ducked the flying leap and let the berserk batter sail clear over him. Both clubs poured onto the field at this point, with the Royals closing ranks around Newcombe and several of the Chiefs corralling West and dragging him to the dugout. West was ejected and Syracuse manager Jewel Ens argued that Newcombe should be tossed as well for throwing at his hitters. But the umpires didn't agree, so Newcombe remained in the game and completed his gem by striking out the last two batters.

West was fined $100 for charging the mound but he was unrepentant, saying Newcombe had hit him earlier in the season and he wanted the pitcher to know he couldn't get away with it. But some in the Royals' camp, remembering the disgraceful treatment Jackie Robinson had received in Syracuse, wondered if the attack by West, a native of Louisville, Kentucky, was racially-motivated. Newcombe was still one of only a handful of African-Americans in organized baseball. West denied the attack was motivated by anything other than self-defense, and the matter was dropped. But it seemed to bring the team closer together.

While everyone was still talking about Newcombe, the Royals' other ace, Jack Banta, fashioned a five-hit shutout in a 4-0 fourth-game triumph that gave Montreal a 3-1 series lead. Bobby Morgan's two-run homer in the eighth inning was the clinching blow. Morgan continued to hit in the next game, going four-for-four, with a three-run homer, leading Montreal to a 7-3 win and the team's second Governor's Cup title in three seasons.

Many reporters who had covered the team for years said that this club had better team spirit than the group that had won it all in 1946. But the Royals were a tired bunch following the emotional series with Syracuse and seven games against Rochester. The team got an extra few days of rest before the start of the Junior World Series because the American Association Governor's Cup final was headed for a seventh game between Columbus and the St. Paul Saints, another Dodgers farm club. Not all the players took it easy, however. Chuck Connors took advantage of the break to marry his Montreal girl friend and head to the Laurentian Mountains for a honeymoon.

But the Royals were back to work soon enough as St. Paul won the AA title, setting up a showdown between Brooklyn's two Triple-A farm clubs. As soon as Montreal arrived in St. Paul for the first two games, Clay Hopper decided to try some psychological warfare. He met a St. Paul reporter in the lobby of the hotel where the Royals were staying and and bragged to him that the Royals would win easily, insisting there wasn't one player on the Saints who could make the Montreal team. Hopper even took a few swipes at the the Saints general manager Mel Jones, who had been the Montreal GM before Buzzie Bavasi. Hopper knew the Saints had an inferiority complex when it came to the Royals. They resented Montreal's status as the Dodgers' top farm club, and he knew his comments would get big play in the newspapers. The comments, as expected, angered the Saints and their fans. Hopper had once again antagonized the opposition, turning a friendly rivalry into a grudge match before he'd even unpacked his suitcase.

Hopper's tongue-in-cheek harangue came back to haunt him in the opening game, as Royals ace Don Newcombe had his first bad outing of the post-season. The Montreal batters, meanwhile, were held to five hits by Pat McGlothin, a lanky right-hander with a

The 1948 JWS champs. First row, left to right: Mike Sandlock, Bob Fontaine, Jack Lindsey, Hank Behrman, Joe Tepsic, Al Gionfriddo, Vic Barnhart and Lou Welaj. Second Row: Bobby Morgan, Turk Lown, Art Shallock, John Simmons, Clay Hopper, Maynard DeWitt, Jimmy Bloodworth and Frank Laga. Third Row: Cliff Dapper, George Brown, Walt Sessi, Dan Bankhead, Chuck Connors, Don Newcombe, Clarence Podbielan and Walter Nothe. Courtesy La Presse.

confusing, herky-jerky delivery. The Royals lost 4-0 and appeared jittery during the game - especially sure-handed Bobby Morgan, who bobbled several balls hit his way.

But Hopper was the centre of attention even in defeat. He tried an unorthodox bunt defence during the game and became even less popular with the players and fans of St. Paul. He stationed left-fielder Al Gionfriddo just behind third base, so he could cover while third baseman Lou Welaj played in close to field the bunt. The play earned Hopper a few hoots from the St. Paul fans, who thought he was showing up the Saints by challenging them to hit to the empty field. Hopper looked like a genius, however, when the batter ignored the open field and tried another bunt, popping it up for an easy out.

Hopper and Walter Alston, who had become the Saints manager at the start of the season, were being closely watched by the Dodgers brass. Not only was Branch Rickey on hand for the series, but Walter O'Malley,

one of the team's directors, was also there. Both skippers were aware their performance could lead to the managerial job in Brooklyn, since Leo Durocher had been fired earlier in the season. Hopper didn't hide the fact he wanted the job, and with the big bosses watching, he pulled out all the stops. Alston, on the other hand, was a quiet, methodical manager. A school teacher in the off-season, he took a studious approach to the game. When asked about the controversial bunt play following the game, Alston said he had removed the bunt sign when Gionfriddo was brought in from left field, but the batter had missed the sign. Alston wasn't about to be one-upped by his Montreal rival with Branch Rickey looking on.

In the second game, the Royals looked more like the team Hopper had hyped. Jack Banta pitched a strong game and Montreal broke things open in the ninth inning, scoring four runs on consecutive RBI singles by Cliff Dapper, Sam Jethroe, Banta, and Gionfriddo. The Royals won 7-3 and carried the momentum into Game 3, where they collected 20 hits - three by Bloodworth, who had six RBIs - in a 15-1 rout.

Newcombe was scheduled to pitch the fourth game. He recovered from an unspectacular performance in the series opener and put on a show for 18,000 fans at Delorimier Stadium. He carried a no-hitter into the sixth inning and, staked to a comfortable lead, was able to coast after that in recording an 8-3 win.

With a firm grip on the series, the Royals delivered the knockout punch in the fifth game. Jack Banta, the team's 19-game winner, pitched three-hit, two-run ball before he was lifted in the sixth inning for pinch-hitter Oscar Grimes. The veteran Grimes hit a scorching liner to centre that skipped over ex-Royal Earl Naylor's head and cleaned the bases, putting the game out of reach. The Royals won 7-2 for their second Junior World Series title in three seasons.

More than 11,000 fans who braved the cold, wet weather to support the Royals celebrated the victory, although with less enthusiasm than they displayed in 1946. The Royals had clearly outclassed the Saints, and this series didn't have the emotion of the bitter battle with the Louisville Colonels two years earlier. The 1946 series had also featured the compelling personal triumph of Jackie Robinson, which made the victory even more exciting.

Still, it was a great accomplishment for the Royals. It left no doubt that despite the occasional drawbacks of affiliation with a major-league team (Mr. Rickey's "voracious appetite" being one of them), the steady stream of quality players from the great Dodgers' farm system made baseball a winning proposition in Montreal.

Clay Hopper, meanwhile, left for Mississippi with his second Junior World Series title and a $12,000 contract to manage Montreal in 1949. He was disappointed that he wasn't asked to manage the Dodgers, but consoled himself by saying, "I'll land that Brooklyn job in a year or so." As for his performance with Montreal thus far, he remarked: "I did the best I could and a mule can do no more."

Jackie Robinson's success paved the way for others. Left to right: Robinson, Campanella, Bankhead and Newcombe.

1949-1952

The Emergence of Talkative Tommy

Clay Hopper, the old mule, brought his team back to the Junior World Series the very next year to face the Indianapolis Indians, an affiliate of the American League's Cleveland Indians. Indianapolis was managed by former ironman catcher Al Lopez, who ended a Hall-of-Fame career in the majors in 1947 to take over the American Association team. The Indians had league MVP, third baseman Froilan "Nanny" Fernandez, and Mel Queen, the league's best pitcher. The Royals, who advanced to the JWS by winning the first playoff series 4-0 and the second 4-1, were streaking until they ran into Indianapolis. The Indians won the first two games and had Queen ready for Game 3 at Delorimier Stadium. The Royals countered with their ace, Dan Bankhead (20-6). Another of Branch Rickey's acquisitions from the Negro Leagues, Bankhead had worked through some control problems at St. Paul in 1948 and become the International League's 1949 strikeout leader, dethroning former Royal Jack Banta, who had won the title the previous two seasons before being called up to Brooklyn.

Banta was one of several former Royals contributing to the Dodgers, who were celebrating their second National League pennant in three seasons. Banta had pitched 4 1\3 innings of solid relief on the final day of the season in Philadelphia to help the club clinch the title. The starting pitcher that day was Don Newcombe, who had left Montreal for Brooklyn early in the 1949 season. Luis

Enter talking. "Walkie-Talkie" Tommy Lasorda was an instant favorite with reporters and fans in Montreal

Olmo, a member of the 1943 Montreal squad, had a pinch-hit RBI in the game and the winning run was knocked in by Duke Snider, who'd set the I.L. on fire in the first half of the 1948 season. Other former Royals now in the

Dodgers' starting lineup were second baseman Jackie Robinson (the (MVP Award winner that year), Carl Furillo, one of the league's best outfielders, and Roy Campanella, who was gaining recognition as one of the best catchers in all of baseball. One-time Royals Spider Jorgensen, Dick Whitman and Marvin Rackley bolstered the bench.

As these former Royals prepared for the World Series against the Yankees, Bankhead was trying to get Montreal back into its series. He produced a fine effort, allowing the Indians only five hits in a 3-1 victory. While relieved by the outcome, Hopper was still worried about the anemic output of offensive players such as Sam Jethroe, Chuck Connors and Bobby Morgan. In fact, the entire team was slumping, managing only 12 hits in the first three games of the series, the rest of which would be played at Victory Park, a cozy stadium with ivy running along the outfield fences.

The change of scenery may have helped the Royals, as Connors came alive in Game 4 with a three-run home run, while second baseman Rocky Bridges, a compact, square-jawed scrapper, went three-for-four. Pitcher Clarence Podbielan earned the win with a nifty two-hitter. The series was knotted, but the Royals had their momentum halted the next night by a controversial call by umpire Augie Donatelli. A National League umpire from 1950 until 1973, Donatelli was a respected arbiter in the minor leagues prior to reaching the majors. Some called him the best umpire in the International League in 1949, but he made a questionable call in the 10th inning of Game 5 that cost the Royals the ball game.

It was 4-4 in the 10th - another duel between Bankhead and Queen - when rookie Ronnie Lee relieved Bankhead. He walked Nanny Fernandez, and then surrendered an extra-base hit to Roy Weatherly. Royals right-fielder George Schmees fielded it off

the wall and fired the ball to the infield and Bridges relayed it to catcher Toby Atwell, who was blocking the plate. It was a close play and Fernandez was ruled safe, although he clearly never touched home plate. Donatelli ruled that Atwell had blocked the plate before he had possession of the ball, technically a violation of the rules but one that's rarely called. Furious at losing the game on such a decision, some of the Royals lost their cool and went after Donatelli. They actually managed to to push him around a bit before first-base umpire Pat Padden dragged his colleague into the the Indianapolis dugout, out of harm's way.

The Royals were still livid as they stripped off their uniforms in the clubhouse. They tossed pop bottles into the umpires' dressing room next door. Hopper complained that the Royals were the victims of inconsistent officiating. He argued that Rochester catcher Johnny Bucha had similarly blocked the plate against Al Gionfriddo in the playoffs against Rochester and the Royals outfielder had been called out. League president Shaughnessy met with Donatelli to discuss the call. Donatelli was well prepared for the meeting, reminding Shag he had told him to clamp down on catchers, such as Bucha, who often flagrantly violated the rule. The president had to agree on that point but he advised Donatelli not to be as fastidious in the future. Remarkably, there was no disciplinary action against the Royals who had shoved Donatelli and thrown pop bottles at the umpires' room.

The defeat had the Royals feeling blue as they headed into the sixth game. While they blamed the loss on Donatelli, there were other reasons, which they would have discovered with some soul-searching. Bankhead, while steady, had walked six batters and blown a two-run lead twice. Offensively, Connors drove in three of the four runs. As a team the Royals stranded nine baserunners. So, it was a frustrated bunch of Royals going into the sixth game. Not surprisingly the club was thumped 12-2, a humiliating end to its bid for a second straight Junior World Series' title.

The loss was a disappointment but not entirely unexpected considering the Royals' inconsistent play throughout the season. Although Branch Rickey had predicted the 1949 Royals would win the pennant by 25 games, the team finished in a tie for third place with Jersey City, only a few games ahead of fifth-place Toronto. The Royals took third place by winning a one-game playoff. Since that game was included in regular-season statistics, the Royals Sam Jethroe was able to raise his stolen-base total. He swiped three bases in the game, bringing his 1949 total to 89, two more than Newark's Ed Miller, who had set the modern-day record in 1919.

Jethroe had been a driving force all season. He hit for average and power - 207 hits, a .326 average and 17 home runs - and he brought Montreal fans to their feet every time he got on base. Over the years the Delorimier Downs faithful had acquired a taste for exciting baserunning. They had plenty of exciting speedsters to urge on - Paul Campbell, Claude Corbitt, Jackie Robinson and Marvin Rackley - but Jethroe was probably the fastest of them all. His speed was such a drawing card that Royals' management staged a race between Jethroe and U.S. Olympic sprinter Barney Ewell prior to a game at Delorimier Stadium. From a standing start, Jethroe won the 75-yard dash by a few yards, although Ewell won a rematch later in the season. Jethroe's speed and talent were undeniable, but there didn't seem to be any room for him in Brooklyn now that Duke Snider had nailed down the centre-field job, so the Dodgers sold him to the Boston Braves at the end of the 1949 season.

Connors also had a good year in 1949 and the Royals were glad to have him back after it seemed he might make the Dodgers as a backup to Gil Hodges. Connors certainly was not your typical ball player. He would often raise eyebrows in the clubhouse by delivering lines from Shakespeare, as he'd heard them performed on stage by John Gielgud and Maurice Evans. Not to be mistaken for a high-brow, however, Connors was also known to goose opposing players who crossed his path at first base. He would do almost anything for a laugh - from sitting on first base during rain delays, paddling an imaginary canoe with a bat, to hitting a home run and running the bases backwards. Despite his frequent clowning he was intense at the plate and hated to strike out. He once stormed back to the dugout in a rage after a called third strike and asked a teammate what he thought of the call. "It was a strike," stated the teammate. Connors promptly grabbed him by the throat and tossed him against the dugout wall.

It was Connors' wisecracking, not his temper, that sometimes landed him in trouble with Branch Rickey. Connors was famous in baseball circles for his booming rendition of "Casey at the Bat." Rave reviews for his skit earned him a part in a Dodgers variety show in spring training of 1949. Connors only had a small part, but after he took the stage he threw away the script and improvised his way into a major role. His most memorable line was a dig at Rickey, nicknamed "El Cheapo" by the New York press. Connors remarked that "Mr Rickey's got a lot of money and he's got a lot of ballplayers, but he never lets them get together."

Shortly after delivering the sarcastic comments, Connors was on the receiving end of a shot - not from Rickey, but from a baseball. He lost sight of a ball thrown his way during infield practice and took it smack in the mouth. He was knocked cold for several minutes and when he woke up he required five stitches to close a deep gash on his lip. Although his clumsiness in the field may have hurt Connors' chances of making

Towering Chuck Connors was a big target at first base.

the Dodgers, and his wisecracking may not have endeared him to Rickey, he was a welcome sight in Montreal.

Another godsend for the Royals in 1949

was Bobby Morgan, one of the Dodgers' final cuts. Many believed Morgan had a good shot at making the Dodgers in 1949 as a backup to third baseman Billy Cox. But Morgan hit meekly in spring training and limped around on a bad ankle for much of the camp. He was sent to Montreal and Hopper was instructed to play him at third base, since Jackie Robinson and Pee-Wee Reese seemed to be fixtures in their middle infield positions. Hopper obeyed the directions for a while but shifted Morgan back to shortstop when it was evident that Rocky Bridges was better at second base than at short. Morgan won the batting title with a .337 average and was named the league MVP. He was regarded as the best defensive shortstop in the league, with the possible exception of Buffalo's Billy De Mars. Morgan and Bridges became a cohesive combination. Morgan was more graceful but Bridges was an effective performer, usually with a trademark wad of gum and chewing tobacco crammed into his cheek.

On the mound, Bankhead was Hopper's main weapon in 1949, but he was supported by the bespectacled, bridge-playing Clyde King, who was 17-7. There was also a whiff of nostalgia for Montreal fans when Jean-Pierre Roy came up from the Provincial League to again play for the Royals. But he wasn't nearly the pitcher he'd been a few years earlier and Montreal eventually sold him to the Hollywood Stars of the Pacific Coast League. While there, Roy, who loved to sing, did some crooning in night clubs. That pastime ended a short while later, when Stars manager Fred Haney caught Roy performing after curfew and he banished him to Oklahoma. Haney explained he had sent Roy there because it was the name of the song the pitcher was singing when Haney caught his night-club gig.

Optimism had reigned for the 1949 Royals when they came out of spring training. Branch Rickey predicted a runaway pennant and Clay Hopper was quoted in a

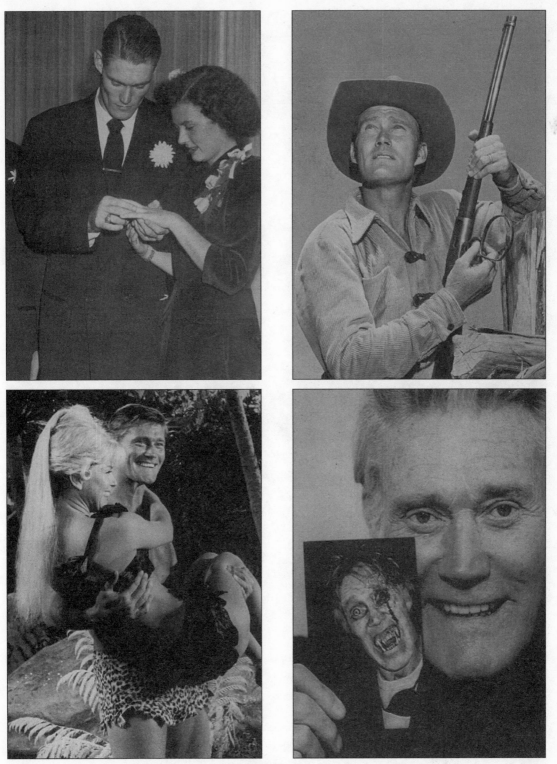

The many sides of Chuck Connors (from top left, clockwise): Connors getting married in Montreal in 1948; in the hit TV series The Rifleman; in monster make up; and sweeping Doris Day off her feet.

Walter Alston, a schoolteacher in the off-season, was a thoughtful, studious manager.

newspaper as echoing his boss's sentiments. But Hopper later denied making such a claim: "Ah never did say any such thang," he drawled. The season had barely started when Hopper realized he didn't have the same type of personnel he'd had in 1946 or 1948. As the season progressed, he occasionally sensed a lack of commitment in some of his players. Once, in early August, after the team had just dipped into fifth place, Hopper blasted his troops for a lack of effort. The incident caused some dissension in the ranks, and for the first time Hopper was challenged by some of his players. The problem was serious enough for Rickey to personally intervene. He met with the players prior to a game and told them that he had no intention of replacing Hopper before the end of the season.

Things seemed to stabilize during the playoffs with word out of Brooklyn that Hopper would be returning as manager in 1950. It was a shock when Buzzie Bavasi announced at spring training in 1950 that Rickey had changed his mind: Hopper and St. Paul manager Walter Alston would be swapping jobs. It was not an especially popular decision. Hopper was on good terms with many of the reporters who covered the team, especially the English-speaking ones with whom he occasionally played golf. And the Montreal fans appreciated the way Hopper would turn his runners loose on the basepaths, or "take the halter off", as he called it. The fact he didn't always play the percentages endeared him to local baseball fans who, in the words of sportswriter Baz O'Meara, liked "color, dash and competitiveness" in their managers. But Hopper was decidedly unpopular with some of the French-speaking reporters who covered the team. That wasn't surprising, since Hopper had once called Jean-Pierre Roy "a French son-of-a-bitch."

Many predicted that Alston, "a colorless pedagogue" in the words of O'Meara, would

be a flop in Montreal. He had a good record as a Triple-A manager, having led the Saints to the Junior World Series in his first season and a pennant the following year. But his accomplishments weren't as impressive as Hopper's. In four seasons as manager of the Royals, Hopper compiled a 371-243 record, a .604 winning percentage He had won two pennants, three Governor's Cups and reached the Junior World Series three times in four seasons, winning twice. True, he had a lot of talent to work with in Montreal, especially in 1946 and 1948, but he had also brought a less-talented group all the way to the Junior World Series in 1949. Some of Hopper's supporters contended their man was still in line for the manager's job in Brooklyn. But it seemed clear that Branch Rickey had simply decided Alston was major-league material and Hopper was not.

Alston's first season as the Royals skipper in 1950 didn't generate much excitement. The team finished in second place with 86 wins, a slight improvement over the previous year, but it was overshadowed by an opening-round playoff elimination against the Baltimore Orioles.

Individually, Rocky Bridges had another superb year, this time at shortstop replacing Morgan, who was finally a Dodger. And Don Thompson, dealt to Montreal when the Boston Braves acquired Sam Jethroe, was impressive in the outfield. It was an off-year for Chuck Connors, who played much of the season with a sore hand that hampered his swing. On the bright side, George Shuba landed back in Montreal near the end of the season. He'd been with the club at the start of 1946 and hit seven early-season home runs before he was demoted. Following a brief stint in the majors, the Dodgers returned him to Montreal, where he quickly resumed his long-ball hitting and fine outfield play.

The 1950 season also afforded Montreal

"Yes, that boy has it," said Branch Rickey when he saw Carl Erskine pitch for Montreal in 1950.

fans a glimpse of future Dodgers ace Carl Erskine, who appeared in 18 games for the Royals, producing a 10-6 record and pitching well enough to warrant a visit by Rickey. "The Deacon" arrived in Montreal in early August to assess Erskine in a game against Jersey City. Once Rickey settled into a seat behind home plate, alongside Roméo Gauvreau, he launched into one of his typical stream-of-consciousness monologues, overheard by Lloyd McGowan. "Judas Priest, here comes trouble. . . good grief, the bases are loaded. . .I hope Mr. Alston leaves Erskine in. This is what I flew miles to see. Will our boy have the heart to throw the change-up to those gentlemen? Ah, he fooled Blaylock with a change-of-pace, the best in the entire Brooklyn organization. . .Yes that boy has it." Erskine won the game 3-1, giving up only five hits, and the performance earned him a trip to Brooklyn. The fans, realizing from past experience what a visit from Rickey meant, didn't have

to wait for the official announcement. One of them yelled, "Goodbye, Erskine," as the winning pitcher walked off the field.

Erskine wasn't the only pitching arrival in Montreal in 1950. Unlike Erskine, who was merely passing through, this pitcher would spend nine seasons with the team, winning more than 100 games. Tommy Lasorda, a talkative southpaw from Norristown, Pa., owned a good sinking curve, but little else in his pitching repertoire. He was a fearless competitor, however, and he turned more than a few heads in 1950 by pitching a one-hitter in the playoffs against Baltimore, a few days before turning 23. The lone hit in his 5-0 victory was a topped infield chopper which the runner barely beat out.

Lasorda was delighted to be in the Dodgers' organization, the team for which his childhood hero, Van Lingle Mungo, had once pitched. Signed by the Philadelphia Phillies, Lasorda was languishing in the Class-C Canadian-American League, pitching for Schenectady, when his break came. He was having a yo-yo year, but whenever Lasorda faced Trois-Rivieres, the Dodgers' affiliate in the Class C league, he was Mungo reincarnated. This caught the eye of the Trois-Rivieres manager, former Dodgers and Royals pitcher Ed Head. At the end of the 1948 season the Phillies didn't protect Lasorda from the draft and the Dodgers signed him, on Head's recommendation. Lasorda's association with the Dodgers continues to this day.

The arrival of Lasorda and "Shotgun" Shuba bolstered the 1951 Royals, who felt the repercussions of off-season changes. For the first time in the last 10 years, the Royals were part of a Dodgers' organization which wasn't run by Branch Rickey. Shortly after the 1950 season concluded Rickey lost a board-room battle to Walter O'Malley, a Dodgers shareholder and director. Rickey left Brooklyn to become the general manager of

Lasorda had a good curveball, tremendous confidence and a ferocious desire to win.

the Pittsburgh Pirates. Royals general manager Buzzie Bavasi was called to Brooklyn to work with O'Malley, and his Montreal post was filled by Major Guy Moreau, a Quebecer who had previously been the team's business manager. The emergence of O'Malley would dramatically affect the organization down the road, but little changed in the first few years. Brooklyn still had one of baseball's most extensive farm systems and, for now, Montreal remained the main beneficiary.

The International League itself was going through significant change. Concerned by a continual decline in box-office receipts for the Newark Bears, the New York Yankees had sold their top farm team to the Chicago Cubs following the 1949 season. The Cubs transferred the team to Springfield, Mass., the first new IL franchise since 1937. The Bears had been one of the most successful teams in league history and the Royals' long-time nemesis. Their departure was linked to the increased availability of television. Many New Jersey baseball fans could now follow the three major- league clubs in nearby New York from the comfort of their living rooms, causing diminished interest in the local minor-league teams. The Jersey City Giants were also struggling, and the parent New York Giants moved the club to Ottawa following the 1950 season, giving the league a third Canadian franchise.

But with all the changes, Montreal continued to be the team to beat as the 1951 season opened. The Royals had a core of good, experienced players such as Al Gionfriddo, Toby Atwell, George Shuba and Clarence Podbielan. Also, Bobby Morgan was back, shipped by the Dodgers to get more playing time following a disappointing year as a utility infielder with Brooklyn, where he hit only .226 in 199 at-bats. Replacing Morgan on the Dodgers' bench was the scrappy Rocky Bridges, whom the Dodgers hoped would add hustle and grit.

Junior Gilliam, another Dodger acquisition from the Negro Leagues was a major asset for the Royals.

The most important development for the 1951 Royals, however, was a deal engineered by Fresco Thompson, a former player and manager in Montreal who was now in the Dodgers' front office. Thompson bought two young ball players from the Baltimore Elite Giants of the Negro Leagues: pitcher Joe Black and second baseman-outfielder Jim "Junior" Gilliam. A smooth fielder and a switch- hitter, Gilliam fit right into the Royals' lineup at second base, occasionally playing the outfield. The versatile Black helped the pitching staff as both a starter and reliever. And in yet another example of extensive Dodgers' recruitment and their ability to scout and sign black players, a 30-year-old Cuban third baseman named Hector Rodriguez was delivered to Montreal, where he would make a significant contribution.

Gilliam made an immediate impact, collecting six RBIs in the season-opening 15-7 win against Baltimore. It was a harbinger of things to come for Gilliam, who went on to hit .287 and lead the league in runs scored with 117. Rodriguez, meanwhile, hit .302 and led the league with 26 stolen bases. He was named the International League's rookie of the year, an award introduced a season earlier. Gilliam and Rodriguez both made the I.L. all-star team, as did Bobby Morgan and left-hander Chris Van Cuyk, whose brother Johnny had also pitched for the Royals. Steeped and well-balanced in starting pitching, the 1951 Royals had five pitchers win 10 or more games - lefties Lasorda, Van Cuyk and Mal Mallette and righties Bob Alexander and Jim Hughes. Alexander's 15 wins topped the staff.

The Royals won 95 games in 1951, coasting to the pennant by an 11-game margin. It was the fifth time in the last seven seasons that the club had posted a winning percentage above .600. Montreal opened the playoffs against Buffalo, a team that had barely finished above .500. The Royals won the first two games 7-0 and 5-0, but the third game was error-filled, disgusting Fresco Thompson, in attendance to monitor things for the Dodgers. Thompson left the ball park early, saying the sloppy encounter reminded him of "the married men against the single men at the annual office picnic. All that was missing was the keg of beer on third base."

The Royals stumbled to a 7-6 win and then polished off the Bisons in the fourth game. Lasorda, a fierce competitor, was among a number of Royals who were shocked at how meekly the Bisons had submitted. Lasorda couldn't believe his ears when he heard some Buffalo players discussing their plans for the off-season in the middle of a game. The Royals expected much more resistance from the Syracuse Chiefs, who had a reputation for playing well in the playoffs, but that series was also a rout, as the Royals won in five games. Solid pitching and a barrage of home runs by Gilliam, Shuba, and late-season addition Bert Hass accounted for Montreal's success. Haas

Scrappy Rocky Bridges (right, with Kermit Wahl) always had a wad of chewing tobacco in his cheek

was with the Royals as far back as 1939, and he had played against them - for the Columbus Red Birds - in the 1941 Junior World Series. The Royals scooped him up as a 37-year-old free agent, after he had accumulated several years of big-league service.

Riding a wave, the Royals entered the Junior World Series for the fourth time in the last six seasons. Their opponent was the Milwaukee Brewers, who had defeated the St. Paul Saints in six games for the American Association Governors' Cup. Managed by the legendary Charlie Grimm, a major leaguer, either as a player or manager, for most of the previous 35 years, the Brewers loomed as a formidable opponent. A farm team of the

National League's Boston Braves, the Brewers had only one fewer regular-season win than Montreal, and they had a statistical advantage in other areas. They had a pair of 15-game winners in Ernie Johnson and Murray Wall, sound defence and plenty of power from first baseman George Crowe, who led the league with 119 RBIs, and MVP catcher Al Unser, a .293 hitter with 17 homers. Three other Brewers, including former Royal Gene Mauch, were .300 hitters.

The Royals won two of the first three games in the series but lost the next three, after the scene shifted to Milwaukee. Montreal grabbed a 10-2 lead in the next game and seemed a cinch to prolong the series. But the pitching staff collapsed and the Royals went down to an ignominious 13-10 defeat, losing the Junior World Series in six games.

The netting above the right field scoreboard stopped some home runs from landing on the factory roof.

In 1952, the Royals bounced back, winning their second straight pennant, and matching their 95 victories of the previous year. And they did it without the benefit of many holdovers from 1951. Bobby Morgan, George Shuba, Toby Atwell and Hector Rodriguez had all graduated to the majors - Shuba and Morgan to the Dodgers and Rodriguez and Atwell to the White Sox and Cubs respectively. But, as usual, the Dodgers sent some quality replacements. The first player to come over in 1952 turned out to be one of the best acquisitions in Royals'

history. His name was Glenn Richard "Rocky" Nelson, a first baseman whom the Dodgers had obtained in the off-season. Nelson enjoyed great success in the International League while playing for Rochester, but he had struggled in his major-league stints. A power-hitting, left-handed batter, Nelson seemed tailor-made for the Royals, who needed a first baseman in the mould of Les Burge, Jack Graham and Chuck Connors - predecessors with the power to pull the ball over the short right-field fence at Delorimier Stadium. It wasn't to be, however - at least, not at first. Nelson broke his ankle early in the season and was sidelined for the rest of the year.

Some of the slack was picked up by "Junior" Gilliam, returning for his second season. He hit .301, led the league in runs scored and stolen bases and capped a sensational year by winning the league's Most Valuable Player award. The Royals also had splendid performances from lanky centre-fielder Carmen Mauro, who'd played sporadically for the Cubs in recent seasons, catcher Tim Thompson and third baseman Don Hoak, a sensational fielder and fiery competitor. Lasorda was the main man on the mound with a 14-5 record. He was supported by Mal Mallette, Ed Roebuck and 19-year old left-hander Johnny Podres.

The only team with better offensive

statistics in 1952 was the Rochester Red Wings, led by player-manager Harry "The Hat" Walker, who had beat the Royals with a timely home run in the 1941 Junior World Series. Walker had moved on from the Cardinals' Columbus affiliate to a decent big-league career with the parent club. But now he was back in the minors, still able to hit the ball with authority. The Royals got past Toronto in seven games in the opening round of the playoffs but Walker's Red Wings then knocked off Montreal in six games to advance to the Junior World Series.

In the off season, there was a threat of further changes to the International League landscape. The lowly St. Louis Browns of the American League had just completed their seventh straight losing season, going an abysmal 64-90. Fan interest was understandably lagging despite a number of stunts by team owner Bill Veeck - such as sending midget Eddie Gaedel to bat as a pinch-hitter.

By the end of the 1952 season, a discouraged Veeck was ready to sell the Browns, and the city of Baltimore expressed immediate interest. A handful of other cities considered making a bid for the team, including Montreal, but the Orioles were favored to land the franchise. For a while, it appeared that Baltimore would be leaving the International League for the majors as early as 1953, a prospect that disheartened I.L. officials, since Jersey City and Newark had already disbanded. Many believed the league would be in serious difficulty if another large-market team left. But the American League refused to approve the transfer of the Browns to Baltimore and the team stayed in St. Louis for another season. The Orioles also stayed put.

Veeck's money troubles meant he had to cancel some of the deals he had made following the 1952 season, including the one which brought Tommy Lasorda, the

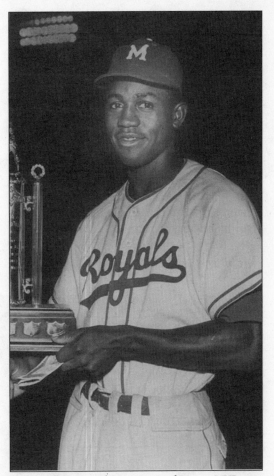

Junior Gilliam won the International League MVP award in 1952, after an outstanding season

Royals' best pitcher, to his club. Lasorda was a loyal Dodger, but after three seasons and a 35-17 record with the Royals, he was itching to get a crack at the majors. He was crushed when Veeck's deal fell apart and he was returned to the Dodgers, who again assigned him to Montreal.

Lasorda, who never had much of a fastball, was constantly experimenting with new pitches to complement his above-average curve. He played with a loads of enthusiasm and emotion, delivering his pitches with a high leg-kick. Lasorda was a battler, a characteristic that probably stemmed from his teenage years, when he was regarded as a good boxer. He often brought his fighting skills to the baseball diamond. Lasorda got into a lot of fights in his early days - and not always against players on opposing teams. In his first year of pro ball, at the Class-D level, he attacked his own shortstop after the infielder booted an easy grounder. Lasorda never again attacked a teammate but he continued to engage in scraps with opposing batters, largely because of his willingness to deck them whenever he deemed it necessary. His reputation around the league was that he'd send his own grandmother sprawling to the dirt if he was mad enough.

Lasorda was also an expert bench jockey, fond of teasing and practical jokes, such as sending unsuspecting batboys to the hardware store to buy a pitching rubber or a batter's box. He was an instant hit with the fans and media in Montreal. Reporters called him "Talkative Tom", "Walkie-Talkie Tommy" and "The Loquacious Lasorda". You always knew when Tommy had arrived at the ball park. He was a more subdued Lasorda when he reported to the Royals in 1953, his failed shot at the big time still an open wound. But he promised to help the Royals go all the way to the Junior World Series again, and he kept his word.

The 1951 Montreal Royals won the pennant and the Governor's Cup, but their celebrating ended when they lost the Junior World Series to Gene Mauch and the Milwaukee Brewers.

1953-1954
Storm Clouds on the Horizon

14

As one of his players once noted, Walter Alston wasn't the type of manager to frown "when he can muster a smile." But Alston wasn't smiling heading into the 1953 season. He was bemoaning the loss of several key players to the big leagues, wondering aloud how he would fill the gaps their departures had created. No more Carmen Mauro in centre field. No more Jim Pendleton (a .291 hitter in 1952) at shortstop, and most important, no more Junior Gilliam at second base. Gilliam had graduated to Brooklyn, where he was impressive enough to bump Jackie Robinson into left field.

As usual, the Dodgers provided a few new players to fill the cavities, and Alston had another good team. The best of the 1953 crop was a Cuban-born player who was coming off a starring role in the Cuban League. Edmundo Amoros, nicknamed "Sandy" because of his resemblance to a

Sandy Amoros, (left) supplied the offence while fellow Cuban Chico Fernandez brought a steady glove to shortstop for the Royals. Courtesy La Presse.

boxer named Sandy Saddler, was a compact speedster who, in the opinion of Dodgers scout Al Campanis, had the potential to be the fastest man in baseball. Amoros wasn't a good base-stealer but he could fly around the diamond and get to balls in the outfield that no one else could reach. He was another swift Montreal centre fielder in the tradition of Jimmy Ripple, Marvin Rackley, Sam Jethroe, and Duke Snider. Amoros opened the season as the lead-off batter but hit so well with men on base Alston soon moved him to the third spot. He was a sensation from his opening-game, six-for-six debut to the last few weeks of the season, when he fashioned a 25-game hitting streak.

Amoros wasn't the only Cuban to join the team that season. Humberto "Chico" Fernandez landed the starting job at shortstop. The two spent a lot of time together, isolated by their inability to speak English. They didn't understand much of what was happened around them, especially when they first arrived. But Alston found ways to make things easier for them. He devised a special, simpler set of signs for the Cubans that required less explanation than the system used by the rest of the team. The club's travelling secretary, Rocky Brisebois, was assigned to stay close to Amoros and Fernandez, making sure they found their way to the ball park each day and ate properly in restaurants. Thus far, the only thing Amoros knew how to order was apple pie and ice cream.

Although Fernandez would smile and nod in agreement at whatever Alston said, the manager was never sure how much the slender 21-year-old understood. Alston was fairly certain that Amoros didn't comprehend a thing. It didn't help that Amoros was prone to the occasional lapse in concentration, sometimes missing a sign or forgetting how many outs there were. Alston would grumble mildly when Amoros would fail to bunt or get doubled off base when he forgot the number of outs. But, in general, Alston didn't have much to gripe about with Amoros, who won the batting title in his rookie season, posting a .353 average with 23 homers and 100 RBIs.

The only player on the team to top Amoros in homers and RBIs in 1953 was first baseman Rocky Nelson. Healthy again after missing the previous season with a broken ankle, Nelson hit .308, blasting 34 home runs and producing a league-leading 136 RBIs. He won the league MVP award and helped Alston forget about the loss of the previous season's MVP - second baseman Junior Gilliam.

The 1953 season again featured a season-long tussle between the Royals and Harry "The Hat" Walker's Rochester Red Wings. A year earlier, Montreal had won the IL pennant but the spoils went to Rochester, which finished in second place and went on to win the Governor's Cup and Junior World Series. The tables were turned in

Rocky Nelson emerged as one of the league's best RBI men, driving in 136 runs in 1953.

1953. The Red Wings won the pennant, but the Royals, finishing second, were playoff winners and represented the International League in the Junior World Series. Amoros, Nelson and Tommy Lasorda (17-8) were the stars but Don Hoak, Tim Thompson, Ed Roebuck and Ken Lehman were crucial to the team's success. Hoak, a terrific defensive third baseman, chipped in with the bat, hitting .269. Thompson, a second-year catcher with the team, hit .293 and drove in 59 runs. Roebuck and Lehman won 15 and 13 games respectively.

Infielder Stan Rojek and outfielder Dick Whitman, a couple of old Royals' hands now well into their thirties, defied their age and knocked in more than 30 runs each. Also contributing in 1953 was Dick Williams, a utility player who'd spent part of the last two seasons with the Dodgers. He played in 66 games for the Royals and hit .278. Years later, like Gene Mauch, who had played for the Royals in the 1940s, Williams would return to Montreal as manager of the major-league Expos.

The 1953 Royals were more than respectable. Their .274 team batting average was second only to Rochester. They had the best fielding percentage in the league and, with Lasorda, Lehman and Roebuck, one of the top pitching staffs. Facing Buffalo in the first IL playoff round, the Royals stumbled in the opener, losing 3-2 in front of 5,000 fans who sat at Delorimier Stadium in winter coats. Montreal tied the series with a 1-0 victory, scoring when Buffalo's Ed Harrist floated a knuckleball to the backstop for a wild pitch. This time, only 3,800 fans showed up to watch Glenn Mickens and Ken Lehman combine on a three-hitter.

Lehman saved an 8-5 triumph in Game 3 in Buffalo, and things looked even rosier for the Royals when Hamp Coleman recorded a 2-1 win in the next game. Buffalo cut into the 3-1 series lead, however, winning Game 5 by capitalizing on a throwing error by Montreal second baseman Roy Hartsfield. The Royals returned to Montreal and another sparse crowd of about 6,000 turned out on a cool night at Delorimier. They were rewarded for their patronage as Lasorda, who'd lost the opening game of the series, pitched a four-hitter and Rocky Nelson slammed a two-run homer in a 7-0, series-winning triumph.

But the Royals now had to get past the Rochester Red Wings, last year's Junior World Series' winner and this season's regular-season champ in the I.L. The Red Wings were poised for a repeat. They boasted several .300 hitters, including outfielders Tommy Burgess, Allie Clark, Wally Moon and first baseman Charlie Kress, the team's big power threat. Outfielder-manager Walker, with a .303 batting average, was still a tough out.

Rochester won 97 games in cruising to the pennant but needed seven games to subdue the fourth-place Baltimore Orioles in the opening playoff round.

The Red Wings showed even less spark against Montreal. Nelson homered in the first game, and then contributed to a 15-hit attack for an 11-7 win in Game 2. Hamp Coleman made it a 3-0 series lead with a five-hitter, leaving Lasorda the chance to wrap up the series at Delorimier. Pitching in front of 9,150 fans, the first decent Montreal crowd of the playoffs, Lasorda didn't have his best stuff. But he was his usual bulldog self, and the Royals were only trailing 2-1 when they batted in the sixth inning.

Don Hoak started a rally with a double and scored the tying run on Sandy Amoros' single. Later in the inning, with the bases loaded, Ken Wood hit a shallow fly ball into centre field that Vern Benson, the Rochester second baseman, caught with his back to home plate. Amoros took advantage of Benson's awkward position, tagged up and barreled home with the go-ahead run. It would prove to be the winning run when Lasorda slammed the door, giving Montreal a series sweep and its fifth Governor's Cup in eight seasons.

The next challenge, a familiar one for Royals' supporters, was the Junior World Series. The Royals had played in the JWS five times previously, winning twice (1946, 1948) and losing three times (1941,1949 and 1951). The latest opponent was the Kansas City Blues, who had finished second in the American Association and boasted some future major leaguers, such as AA batting champ Vic Power, Bill "Moose Skowron, Elston Howard, Bob Cerv and Alex Grammas. Skowron and Howard would become important players on the powerful New York Yankees teams of the 1950s and early 1960s. The Royals-Blues' match-up was especially interesting because the parent

Pitcher Ed Roebuck (centre) is congratulated by Walter Alston (left) and third baseman Don Hoak after a big win over Kansas City in the 1953 Junior World Series.

clubs, the Yankees and Dodgers, were again clashing in the World Series.

The Junior World Series opened on Friday, October 2. The same day, the Dodgers were trying to rebound from losing the first two World Series games at Yankee Stadium. It turned out to be a good day for the Dodgers organization. Former Royals Carl Erskine and Roy Campanella combined to lift the Dodgers to a 3-2 win - Erskine by striking out 14 batters, and Campanella with a tie-breaking homer in the eighth inning. The Royals, meanwhile, clobbered the Blues 10-0 in front of almost 9,000 fans at Delorimier Stadium. The next day, another former Royal, Duke Snider, hit two doubles

and a home run to lead the Dodgers to another win, knotting their series at two. In the Junior Series, Montreal held its end up by beating the Blues 6-2, as Hamp Coleman continued to pitch well and Rocky Nelson went four-for-four with his fourth homer of the playoffs. Both the parent Dodgers and the affiliate Royals had produced two victories in their respective series. But only the Royals would keep winning.

Montreal made it eight straight playoff victories, winning the third game 5-3, another solid performance by Lasorda. Blues manager Harry Craft sent nothing but right-handed batters against Lasorda but it didn't faze the stubborn southpaw. Rocky Nelson

The 1953 I.L. Governors' Cup and Junior World Series Champions. Front row, left to right: Sandy Amoros, Glenn Mickens, Chico Fernandez, Ken Lehman, Art Fabbro, Rocky Nelson and Stan Rojek. Second row, left to right: Ed Roebuck, Gil Mills, Tim Thompson, Walter Alston, Frank Marchio, Tom Lasorda, Earl Mossor. Back Row, left to right: Ernie Cook (trainer), Hamp Coleman, Ernie Yellen, Roy Hartsfield, Dick Whitman, Don Hoak, Al Epperley, Robert Ludwick, Bob Alexander, Ken Wood, Rocky Brisebois (traveling secretary)

continued to be a playoff hero, driving in three runs. The Royals were hot but baseball fever obviously wasn't contagious. A Delorimier Stadium crowd of just over 5,000 watched Game 3 on a cold, bleak night. Attendance had also been disappointing for the second game, which had to compete for attention with a televised World Series game and the National Hockey League all-star game, played at the Montreal Forum.

The series shifted to Kansas City, where the Royals had a temporary lapse, losing 4-3. But they steamrolled the Blues 7-2 to capture the Junior World Series in five games. Hamp Coleman beat the Blues for the second time in the series and all but one Montreal player got a hit in the game. Leading the way offensively were Dick Whitman - re-acquired by Montreal near the end of the season - with a homer and three RBIs, and Sandy Amoros, who also homered.

While this third Junior World Series'

championship in eight seasons brought deep satisfaction for Royals' management, the end-of-season post mortem raised some troubling questions. Since the end of World War II, the Royals had consistently been the league-leader in attendance, often drawing close to a half-million spectators during the regular season, a total that usually exceeded 600,000 including playoff games. Those days were definitely over. The Royals had surrendered their attendance crown to the Toronto Maple Leafs in 1952. Then, in 1953, they failed to reach the 300,000 mark for the first time since the post-war boom in minor-league baseball attendance. The low playoff attendance was especially alarming because the team was performing so well. Were Montrealers losing interest in baseball?

Everyone seemed to have a theory to explain the no-shows. One hypothesis was that fans, spoiled by the team's success, were now taking the team for granted. Another theory suggested the fans were bored because they no longer had a hero such as Jackie Robinson, or entertaining performers such as Sam Jethroe, Jean-Pierre Roy and Chuck Connors. The Montreal front office acknowledged that recent editions of the team had not been the most colorful, but it argued that the Royals had reached the Junior World Series twice in the last three seasons, so management must be doing something right.

But the problem extended beyond the Royals. Attendance was down throughout the minor leagues, in part because of increased availability of major-league baseball telecasts. That had already contributed to the demise of the International League's New Jersey teams. Other minor-league, and even some major-league clubs, were starting to feel the pinch. But television was only part of the story. As the post-war economic boom took hold, more and more people moved from the city to the suburbs and spent less time downtown, where the ballparks were located. Attending a game became a chore for many people, especially since the stadiums built in the 1920s and 1930s usually had little or no parking. Also, there were increasingly more things to do than go to a ball game, as more and more families bought cars, television sets and weekend homes in the country.

There was also an increase in the popularity of other sports - especially football - which either lured some fans from baseball or at least divided their loyalties. In Montreal, the Canadian Football League's Alouettes, whose season started in mid-summer, were gaining in popularity. That meant less space for the Royals on the sports pages and yet another competitor for a consumer's loose change. Besides, the Royals were never No. 1 in the hearts and minds of Montreal sports fans. The city was, and still is, passionate for the NHL's Canadiens. Although the baseball and hockey schedules

overlapped for only a few weeks, and the beloved Canadiens weren't in direct competition with the Royals, they where the undisputed champions in fan interest.

Even in Brooklyn, where the Dodgers were worshipped, there were troubling signs. Team owner Walter O'Malley expressed his concern about a new race track near Ebbets Field, which he claimed "will kill baseball in Brooklyn." A story surfaced in some newspapers that the Dodgers' owner was so pessimistic about the team's future in Brooklyn, he was considering moving the Dodgers to Montreal (ironic since the Royals were having their own problems). In hindsight, the story may have been a mistake, a gross exaggeration or the first hint of disenchantment with Brooklyn, which would eventually lead O'Malley to move the Dodgers to Los Angeles. The yarn also may have been a seed planted by O'Malley in his secret plan to extricate himself from Brooklyn and head west, where there was oodles of money to be made.

While some people in Montreal were worrying about the Royals' slide in popularity, others were discussing the possibility of landing a major-league franchise for the city. The idea had been a topic of conversation and speculation for at least 10 years. Proponents of such a project contended that Montreal was a large city for a minor- league venue, and it represented a larger market than a number of major-league cities. Among International League franchises, only Baltimore was comparable to Montreal in city population.

The notion gained momentum throughout 1953, and midway through the season Montreal entered the competition to land Bill Veeck's troubled St. Louis Browns. The favorite was Baltimore, which had been trying to get back into the majors since it was squeezed out of the American League in 1902 to make room for the New York

Yankees (then called the Highlanders). The city had almost won the Browns' franchise following the 1952 season but the American League owners failed to approve the transfer. Now Baltimore was again in the hunt, joined by Montreal and Toronto.

Montreal's city council passed a motion to buy the Royals' name, territorial rights and Delorimier Stadium from the Dodgers, who had bought the ball park in 1945, and to lease the park to the Browns if they chose to come to Montreal. Buzzie Bavasi of the Dodgers met city councillors and told them the Dodgers were willing to sell for about $2.3 million. The council found the price a bit steep and didn't pursue the matter. As things turned out, the Browns' franchise went to Baltimore, as expected.

But the mere fact O'Malley was willing to sell the Royals hammered home the point that the team was not a sacred cow within the Dodgers organization. The declining attendance was not going unnoticed. It was also clear the Dodgers' owner wasn't as attached to the Montreal operation as Branch Rickey had been. While running the Dodgers between 1942 and 1950, Rickey had visited Montreal several times a year. The visits were often bad news because they usually meant he'd be taking the Royals best player back to Brooklyn with him. But Rickey's presence demonstrated the important place the Royals held in the Dodgers chain. Perhaps Rickey was also showing his gratitude for the role Montreal had played in the launching of Jackie Robinson's career. O'Malley, on the other hand, rarely visited Montreal and seemed ambivalent about the city and the team. By now, he was preoccupied with the need for a new stadium in Brooklyn, and may have seen the sale of the Royals as a way to help finance the project.

While Montreal, Baltimore and Toronto were competing to fill the American League vacancy, the International League braced itself for the loss of one of these key franchises. The league needed to maintain its eight-member operation, so when it lost Baltimore it quickly invited the city of Richmond, Va., to join the I.L ranks. Richmond had been in the league many years earlier but, like the Royals, had folded following the 1917 season.

Replacing the Orioles was only one of the league's problems. Something had to be done about the disastrous Springfield Cubs. The Cubs had been the league's doormat for the last three seasons, a performance that soured the fans. In 1953, the Cubs attracted fewer than 100,000 spectators. It was obvious the team had to go and it was also apparent that the best replacement was in Havana, Cuba.

In the years prior to the Communist takeover in 1959, Cuba was an exotic travel destination for tourists, who enjoyed the white beaches, sport fishing and lively casinos and nightclubs. Baseball was a popular sport in Cuba and the country was an important winter baseball spot, where major-leaguers could get some off-season playing time. The game had been popular in the country for generations and a number of Cubans had made it to the major leagues, several via Montreal. Teams from Havana had also competed in leagues in Florida.

Roberto Madura, a local promoter with ties to major-league baseball, lobbied the I.L to admit the Havana Sugar Kings for the 1954 season, and the league's owners agreed. The owners were concerned about the increase in travel costs, since each team would make two trips per season to Havana. But Madura agreed to pay the other clubs $60,000 each to offset the extra expenses. Thus, the I.L. had responded to a crisis of dwindling attendance and the loss of a major franchise by making its organization even more international. The 1954 configuration was truly Pan-American, with franchises in Montreal, Toronto, Ottawa, Syracuse, Buffalo, Rochester, Richmond and

Being hired as Dodger manager was O.K. by Walter Alston, and great for Dodger owner Walter O'Malley.

Havana. And the Sugar Kings further enhanced the international flavor of the league with a roster comprised largely of Latin-American players.

While the 1954 season featured the arrival of new teams, it was an old team, the Toronto Maple Leafs, which pulled away from the pack and won the pennant. Toronto hadn't won a pennant since 1943 and it had made the playoffs only three times in the ensuing years. Led by manager Luke Sewell, a former big-league catcher and manager, and MVP Elston Howard, who would become the New York Yankees first black player, the team won 97 games, nine more than the second-place Royals. Howard wasn't the only reason for the Leafs' success. Three former Royals - Sam Jethroe, Hector Rodriguez and Ed Stevens also had excellent seasons.

A squabble in Brooklyn's front office in the off-season resulted in new managers in both Brooklyn and Montreal for the 1954 season. Dodgers manager Chuck Dressen

wanted a new, multi-year contract and he had his wife write a strongly worded letter to O'Malley, pleading his case. O'Malley wasn't amused by the tactic and he fired Dressen. His logical replacement was Walter Alston, the dean of the Dodgers' minor-league system. In four years with the Royals, Alston had won two pennants, finished second twice and brought the team to the Junior World Series twice, where he had both a win and a loss.

Alston had been a conservative, by-the-book skipper in a city that craved a bit of flair from its managers. As a result, he was respected but not overly popular with Montreal fans, and his departure wasn't mourned as Clay Hopper's had been. It undoubtedly surprised many Royals' fans when Alston, described by The Montreal Star's Lloyd McGowan as "The Man Nobody Knows," went on to manage the Dodgers for 23 seasons. His players would have been less surprised, however. They knew that his soft-spoken exterior belied an inner toughness, which surfaced whenever he wanted to get his point across. Lasorda, for one, could recall Alston getting so irate one night he flipped over a table and sent the team's post-game meal crashing to the clubhouse floor. "Walter always knew how to get my attention," Lasorda wrote, years later.

Replacing Alston in the Delorimier Stadium dugout was former Royals' pitcher Max Macon, who'd been in the Dodgers' system as a minor-league player and manager since retiring from the Royals in the early 1940s. Macon was more talkative than Alston, and his first move endeared him to reporters and fans alike. He brought in Homer "Dixie" Howell as his catcher and coach. The two were old friends and Howell had been a key part of the great 1946 Royals team that won the Junior World Series. Like Macon, Howell had spent the last few years playing and managing in the minor leagues. At 34, Howell was a team leader from the start, belting a three-run homer in the home-opener against Syracuse. He was a workhorse in 1954, catching 107 games and upgrading Montreal's offence by hitting .305 with 13 home runs and 57 RBIs.

The team received another superlative performance from first-baseman Rocky Nelson, the 1953 league MVP. Nelson won the home-run title with 31, drove in 105 runs and hit .311. Early in the season, Nelson had a brief tryout with the Cleveland Indians, but was released after failing to get a hit in four at-bats. He returned to the Dodgers and was again assigned to Montreal. He was disappointed that the Indians hadn't given him a full shot, but if he had to play in the minors, he reasoned, it might as well be in Montreal.

Nelson was not especially big but he had a quick swing, with lots of wrist action. He tried to meet each pitch in front of the plate, so he could pull the ball as much as possible. He was a tough competitor with a square jaw and a determined squint to his eyes. Like many players, he chewed tobacco, sometimes enjoying a chaw off the field. On the team's visits to Havana, Nelson was often spotted with a wad of tobacco in one cheek and a Cuban cigar in the other. Nelson never made it big in the majors, but he was one of the best players in International League history. He was at his prime in his years with the Royals. In 1954, he was the team's only star after Sandy Amoros was snapped up by the Dodgers in mid-July.

With Nelson leading the way offensively and Lasorda (14-5) contributing on the mound, the Royals put up a good fight in the 1954 playoffs before being eliminated in the Governor's Cup final in seven games by the Syracuse Chiefs. Despite the respectable showing, president Hector Racine was in a gloomy mood. The Royals had lost more than $50,000, he said, making 1954 the most financially disappointing season in his

two decades with the club. Racine said the team wasn't in trouble, since the Dodgers made money on other ventures at Delorimier Stadium, such as the building's roller-skating rink, the concession stands and rental fees for other sporting events (although the CFL Alouettes were about to leave Delorimier for Molson Stadium.). Still, the Dodgers were worried about declining attendance in Montreal.

There were also questions about the fate of manager Max Macon. Rumors of his departure started as soon as the Royals lost against Syracuse. Macon had done a decent job, even dusting off his 39-year-old pitching arm for a few mound appearances. But the buzz was the Dodgers would replace him in the off-season and transfer him elsewhere in the organization. The rumors must have been agonizing for Macon because he knew his team might have fared better had Bavasi given him a free hand in the handling of a 19-year-old rookie from Puerto Rico named Roberto Clemente.

Clemente, a Dodgers' discovery, could run, hit, field, throw and thrill a crowd. Some players called him a showboat, but the fans loved his performance and most predicted he would become a big-league star. After Clemente went three-for-four in the Royals' 1954 home-opener, Lloyd McGowan wrote an open letter to Buzzie Bavasi, telling him, "the fans thank you for Roberto Clemente, who should be a very popular player here." But after the opening game Clemente was used sparingly, usually as a pinch-hitter or pinch-runner. He would appear in a game, ignite the crowd with a triple or a great catch in the outfield and then disappear from the Royals' lineup for days, even weeks. He was once benched after hitting three triples in a game. "I was confused and almost mad enough to go home," Clemente recalled later. Macon told reporters that the outfielder, although talented, was young and inexperienced and not ready to play every day. To which Clemente responded: "Mr. Macon does not like me."

This was frustrating for many Montreal fans, who were eager for a new hero, a dynamic performer in the image of Jackie Robinson. They felt Clemente could be that person. Near the end of July, Clemente won the first game of a doubleheader with a 10th-inning homer against the Havana Sugar Kings. He doubled in his first at-bat in the second game and was intentionally walked his next time up. There was a small crowd of about 4,000 at the stadium that night, but they made plenty of noise, cheering Clemente enthusiastically. An International League official attending the game remarked: "The Montreal fans have a new idol, a new star." The only hitch was this new idol was spending most of his time on the bench. Didn't the Dodgers realize how good Clemente was?

The answer was unequivocally affirmative. The Dodgers knew they had someone special in Clemente, but they

Future superstar Roberto Clemente, upset about being benched in Montreal, almost went home to Puerto Rico.

wanted to keep it a secret from other organizations. Buzzie Bavasi realized he owned a future major-league star and he longed for the day Clemente would be joining Duke Snider and Carl Furillo in the Dodgers outfield. But the Dodgers had a dilemma. They were loaded with stars at

almost every position, and with Jackie Robinson now in the outfield, there was no immediate place for Clemente on the roster. This was a problem because the Dodgers had given the youngster a $10,000 signing bonus and, in those days, a bonus of more than $4,000 required a club to keep the signed player on its major-league roster for at least a season. If a team failed to do that, the player couldn't be protected in the annual draft.

Since Clemente wasn't quite ready to crack the Dodgers' lineup and Bavasi wasn't willing to leave one of his current players unprotected, he decided to take an enormous risk. He left Clemente off the Dodgers' roster and tried to hide him in Montreal, where he hoped no one would notice him. Macon was instructed to restrict Clemente's playing time and use him only against the best International League pitchers. Bavasi wanted to keep the future star's numbers as unimpressive as possible. Clemente appeared in less than two-thirds of the Royals' games, averaging fewer than two at-bats per game and his batting average was only .257. On paper, he didn't look like much of a major-league prospect.

As the season ended, and the Dodgers

sent Clemente home to Puerto Rico to play winter ball, it seemed that Bavasi's ruse might have worked. But there was one baseball executive who was not fooled by the smokescreen. Branch Rickey Sr., the Pittsburgh Pirates' boss, legendary for never forgetting the name of a talented prospect, had heard of Clemente. He sent trusted scout Clyde Sukeforth to have a look. When Rickey received Sukeforth's report, he ignored the skewed statistics and, with the first shot at a draft pick because of the Pirates' last-place finish in 1954, he drafted Clemente from under Bavasi's nose.

Clemente, of course, went on to a brilliant major-league career and was inducted into the Baseball Hall of Fame in early 1973, just 11 weeks after he was killed in a plane crash while flying to Nicaragua with supplies for earthquake victims.

Former Montreal Royals at Dodger training camp in 1955. Top row, left to right: Walter Alston, Gino Cimoli, Bert Hamric, Carl Furillo, Jim Hughes, Glenn Cox, Duke Snider, Walter Moryn, Dixie Howell, Ed Roebuck, Joe Black, Sandy Amoros, Robert Milliken, Chico Fernandez, Tim Thompson, Roy Campanella, Chuck Templeton and Johnny Podres. Front row, left to right: Don Newcombe, Norm Larker, George Shuba, Don Hoak, Junior Gilliam, Carl Erskine, Tom Lasorda, Jackie Robinson. Courtesy Alvin Guttman.

1955-1957
Rocky and His Friends

Rumors of Max Macon's demise were not exaggerated. It was announced prior to the 1955 season that Greg Mulleavy, a 49-year-old Dodgers scout, would be taking over as Montreal manager. A white-haired, grandfatherly type with a slight paunch, Mulleavy maintained that any ballplayer could improve if he worked hard enough. He was also a firm believer in establishing a good rapport with his players. In 1935, as a player with the Buffalo Bisons, he was voted the club's most popular player. But Mulleavy also knew that a manager needed talented players to produce a winner, which is why his first order of business as Montreal manager was to badger the Dodgers about a young pitching prospect named Don Drysdale. An 18-year-old right-hander from the Class-C California State League, Drysdale was a blue-chipper with a good chance of making the Dodgers before his 20th birthday. He was six foot six and armed with a blazing fastball, which he wasn't afraid to throw close to a batter's chin.

Mulleavy wasn't the only manager in the Dodgers' chain who wanted the young smoke-thrower. Tommy Holmes, a former Newark Bear who became a star outfielder with the National League's Boston Braves, was now managing the Dodgers' Double-A squad at Fort Worth and he, too, coveted Drysdale. The two managers made their respective pleas to Dodgers vice-president Fresco Thompson, who decided Mulleavy could have Drysdale, as long as he kept him in the starting rotation.

Top prospect Don Drysdale had managers within the Dodger organization competing for his services.

Thompson wanted the young pitcher to get plenty of work. He warned Mulleavy that the Royals would lose Drysdale if he didn't take his regular turn in the rotation. Drysdale joined a veteran pitching staff that included Ken Lehman, Glenn Cox, Glenn Mickens and the dean, Tommy Lasorda.

Rocky Nelson reached new heights in 1955, winning the Triple Crown and the MVP.

Lasorda had been recalled by the Dodgers in mid-1954, but saw almost no action. He felt betrayed by his old friend Walter Alston and complained about not getting an opportunity to prove himself. Alston candidly told Lasorda he was in Brooklyn for his enthusiasm, not his talent. The Dodgers were in a pennant race (which they ended up losing to the Giants) and Alston thought Lasorda's non-stop cheering and bench-jockeying would help the club in its stretch drive. Lasorda was crushed to hear this, and for the first time in his career he seriously wondered whether he would ever make it in the majors.

Lasorda had another fling with the Dodgers in 1955, but he was cut to make room for Sandy Koufax, a 19 year-old "bonus baby" who was struggling to find the strike zone and should probably have been pitching regularly in the minors. But as they had done with Roberto Clemente, the Dodgers signed Koufax for a bonus of more than $4,000 and had to keep him on the major-league roster for a season, or risk losing him in the draft. Perhaps because the Pirates had snatched Clemente under similar circumstances, Bavasi decided to keep Koufax with Brooklyn. It meant that Lasorda was sent to Montreal for the sixth straight season. Years later, Lasorda would relate that it took one of the greatest pitchers of all time to knock him off the Dodgers. Lasorda was angry when it happened, but he maintained a positive attitude. He'd lost none of his swagger when he reported to the Royals, several weeks into the season. "Don't worry fellas," he crowed, "the Warren Spahn of the International League has just returned."

With Lasorda back, the Royals had a valued veteran to help compensate for the loss of Sandy Amoros, Dixie Howell and Ed Roebuck, all summoned by the Dodgers. Now 27, Lasorda was taking an interest in the development of the younger players, and the Royals had several in 1955. Besides Drysdale, whom Lasorda immediately took under his wing, there were Charlie Neal, Jim Williams and Clyde Parris. Neal was a second baseman, a position played by three different players in 1954. Williams, a Toronto native, won a starting job in the outfield, alongside proven performers Gino Cimoli and Bobby Wilson. Parris, who inherited the third-base job, had won the Eastern League batting title in 1954, hitting .313 for Elmira. At shortstop, Chico

Manager Greg Mulleavy (right) with Walter Alston.

Fernandez was back after a good season in the field and at the plate. Dick Teed, the Montreal catcher in 1951 was again in Royals blue, platooning with newcomer Johnny Bucha, a tough, wily warhorse. Relentless Rocky Nelson was back at first base.

The International League also did some shuffling in 1955. The Ottawa franchise folded after finishing in last place and attracting fewer than 94, 000 fans. Coincidentally, some shifting in the American Association provided the I.L. with a replacement for Ottawa. The St. Louis Cardinals moved their AA team, the Columbus Red Birds, to Omaha, and Columbus switched to the I.L. The team was competitive in its first year but the 1955 season featured another battle between the Royals and the Maple Leafs.

The Leafs still relied on former Royals Sam Jethroe and Hector Rodriguez, but also had a speedy outfielder named Archie Wilson, who was among the league's best run-producers. On the mound, ace right-hander Jack Crimian had a season that earned him the league's Most Valuable Pitcher award. Montreal and Toronto took turns leading the pack in 1955, with the Havana Sugar Kings close behind. In early August, during one of the few spells when the Royals were in third place, they faced the Leafs in consecutive doubleheaders in Montreal. The Royals won all for games to vault back into first and create some momentum for the last month of the season.

Lasorda won the third game of that series with his best outing of the season. Since returning from the Dodgers, the "Warren Spahn of the International league" had not pitched like Spahn, the Milwaukee Braves gifted southpaw. He hadn't even pitched like

a vintage Tommy Lasorda. He had suffered through a miserable 2-7 season heading into the Toronto series, although his last few starts were encouraging.

Lasorda attributed his change in fortune to an incident a few weeks earlier, when he, Drysdale, Bucha and infielder Wally "Buckshot" Fiala were strolling down a street in Buffalo. Lasorda, still seeking his first win of the season, was shuffling along despondently when he was hit smack on the head by a load of pigeon droppings. "Why me?" he moaned. But he won his next couple of starts and was convinced the Buffalo incident heralded a change in his luck. In the series against Toronto he tossed a complete game, allowing two runs on four hits, while striking out seven and walking

The 1955 I.L pennant winners. Front row, left to right: Rocky Nelson, Don Drysdale, Wade Browning, Greg Mulleavy (manager), Wally Fiala, Clyde Parris and Jim Williams. Second Row, left to right: Dave Lambton (trainer), Bobby Lachance (clubhouse boy), Johnny Bucha, Ken Lehman, Joe Staneck, Dick Teed, Tom Lasorda, Bobby Wilson and Bob Watt (asst. general manager). Third row, left to right: Pete Wojey, Glenn Mickens, Gino Cimoli, Bob Addis, Glenn Cox, Chico Fernandez and Charlie Neal.

only two batters. When he won six of his next seven decisions, it seemed that 'Walkie-Talkie Tommy" was again cock-of-the-walk.

Lasorda's hot pitching was timely in a tight pennant race between the Royals and the Leafs. So was a seven-game Royals' winning streak in the closing days of the season. The streak pushed the Royals into first place by a half-game with only a doubleheader against Rochester left to play. The Leafs also ended the season with a doubleheader - against Buffalo. Lasorda shut out the Red Wings with a five-hitter in the first game, as Bobby Wilson and Charlie Neal sparked the offence in a 6-0 win. The performance allowed Lasorda to finish the regular season with a winning 9-8 record. But Toronto kept pace, winning the first game of its twinbill against Buffalo, to the chagrin of more than 8,000 fans at Delorimier, who followed the result on the scoreboard.

Mulleavy had no choice but to have Ken Lehman pitch the nightcap. He would have saved his ace for the opening game of the playoffs had Toronto lost. It was the right move. Lehman was sharp and he held a 4-1 lead with one out and a runner on in the ninth. Consecutive walks loaded the bases, a development that coincided with news from Toronto that the Maple Leafs had completed a doubleheader sweep. The Maple Leafs were now even with the Royals and the pennant rested on Lehman's next few pitches.

Mulleavy strolled to the mound, spoke with his left-hander, who had already won 21 games, and decided to stick with him. A run-scoring groundout cut Montreal's lead to 4-2, but Lehman induced Rochester centre-fielder Jack "Ozark" Brandt to lift a fly ball to right that landed in Bobby Wilson's mitt. The Royals threw their gloves in the air in both relief and celebration and rushed to congratulate Lehman, whose 22 victories made him the winningest pitcher in the International League for the second straight season. The Royals had claimed their eighth pennant with a nine-game, season-ending winning streak.

Rocky Nelson was three-for-five in the doubleheader with a double and two runs scored - just another day at the office for the man who was easily the best player in the league in 1955. Nelson was voted Most Valuable Player, the first repeat winner in league history (he also won in 1953). He also became the first Montreal Royal, and only the third player in I.L. history, to win the Triple Crown. Nelson led the league in batting average (.364), home runs (37) and RBIs (130). He played in every game and had the third-best fielding percentage among regular first basemen. Regarded as one of the best sluggers ever to play in the I.L., Nelson was a popular topic of conversation among league managers. They were baffled as to how to pitch to him and even more mystified that he was still playing in the minor leagues.

Since 1949, Nelson, a native of Portsmouth, Ohio, had been given tryouts by the Cardinals, Pirates, White Sox, Indians and Dodgers, but failed to stick with a team for more than half a season. Some felt that because he was a slow starter, managers lost patience with him and returned him to the minors before he hit his stride. Reggie Otero, manager of the Havana Sugar Kings, saw Nelson clobber major-league pitchers while playing winter ball in Cuba. He contended that all Nelson needed was a big-league manager with enough patience to let Nelson get comfortable. Dixie Walker, the former Dodgers star who had replaced his brother Harry as manager at Rochester, also thought major-league managers were too hasty with Nelson. "If he had the confidence in the majors that he has here, you would have to rank him with the greatest," said Walker. But with five trials and his 30th birthday behind him, it was starting to look as if Nelson might never make it.

He did finally catch on in the majors, however, following two more failed attempts with the Dodgers and Cardinals and another stint in the International League (where, in 1958, as a Toronto Maple Leaf he won his third MVP and his second Triple Crown). But when he did arrive, with the Pittsburgh Pirates from 1959 through 1961, it was as a substitute player. He had a couple of good seasons, hitting .291 and .300, but never approached his Triple-A success.

There were, however, some memorable moments with the Pirates. Nelson was the first baseman on the May night in 1959 when Pittsburgh left-hander Harvey Haddix lost his perfect-game bid in the 13th inning. Nelson couldn't come up with third baseman - and former Royal - Don Hoak's errant throw after fielding Felix Mantilla's grounder. In 1960, Nelson belted a two-run homer off the Yankees Bob Turley in the first inning of the seventh game of the World Series. That wasn't quite as dramatic as teammate Bill Mazeroski's game-winning homer leading off the bottom of the ninth. But it was that type of power that the Royals had come to expect from Nelson, on whom the club relied heavily as it headed into the first round of the 1955 Governor's Cup playoffs against the Rochester Red Wings.

One player the Royals wouldn't be able to count on was rookie pitcher Don Drysdale, sidelined with a sore arm for the rest of the season. In contrast to Lasorda, Drysdale had a great start but slumped in the second half to finish with an 11-11 record. His quick temper was partly responsible for his slide. Following a mid-season game in Buffalo, a frustrated Drysdale punched a Coke machine and broke a bone in his throwing hand. He continued to pitch but the injury bothered him for the rest of the season.

It wasn't Drysdale's only outburst in his season with Montreal. During the first game of a doubleheader in Havana, teammate

Drysdale was a big kid with a powerful arm.

Chico Fernandez failed to take out the Sugar Kings shortstop to break up a double play. The Royals lost the game 1-0 and Drysdale, the starting pitcher, stormed into the clubhouse, picked up a chair and was about to heave it against the wall when Mulleavy told him to calm down. "What will it prove?" asked the manager. "The ball game's over." (Although Mulleavy must have known how the young pitcher felt, since he himself once remarked that, "Chico plays as Chico feels.")

Lasorda, never shy about expressing his own anger, told Mulleavy to let Drysdale throw the chair, if it would make the kid feel better. Mulleavy relented and Drysdale sent the chair crashing through the clubhouse wall. Lasorda pitched the second half of the twinbill, lost 1-0 and, taking his own advice, hurled a chair through the same wall Drysdale had assaulted a few hours earlier.

Venting one's emotions wasn't the only thing the young pitcher learned from an old pro that season. In his memoirs, written in 1990, Drysdale recalled learning how to throw a spitball while on another Montreal road trip to Havana. Emilio Cueche, a pitcher for the Sugar Kings, was having a good outing and the Royals were convinced he was throwing spitters. Drysdale's teammates told him he had no choice but to retaliate, and catcher Johnny Bucha gave him a crash course on spitballs in the dugout between innings. Drysdale wasn't subtle about it. He simply put his fingers in his mouth, smeared the ball with saliva and fired. Suddenly, the Havana batters started to strike out on pitches that seemed to dive right under their bats. By the end of the regular season, Drysdale had mastered the spitball but was still learning how to pace himself through a long schedule. His arm was hurting, so he returned home to California prior to the playoffs.

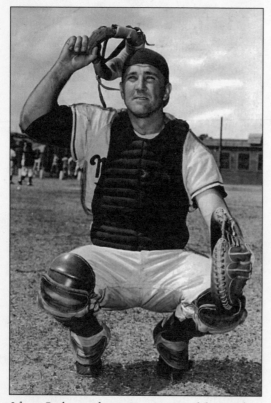

Johnny Bucha, a wily veteran, gave Drysdale a crash course in throwing spitballs.

Drysdale didn't miss much. The Royals were pathetic against the Rochester Red Wings and were eliminated in five games. The third game of the series featured a bench-clearing brawl that started when Lasorda applied a gung-ho tag on Rochester's Howie Phillips as the pair collided during a rundown. The third game was probably the turning point. Trailing by two runs in the ninth, the Royals had a chance to do some damage when Rocky Nelson came up with two runners on and nobody out. He worked a 3-and-0 count and Mulleavy, going against the odds, let him swing away at the next pitch, even though Clyde Parris, the team's next-best RBI man, was in the on-deck circle. Nelson swung at a lousy pitch and hit a weak ground ball off the end of his bat for a rally-killing double play.

Montreal's dismal playoff performance was baffling, given the team's tremendous offensive power. Besides Nelson, the league batting champ, Jimmy Williams, Bobby Wilson, Gino Cimoli and Chico Fernandez had all hit better than .300. Parris, Wilson and Cimoli had each driven in more than 80 runs. Charlie Neal not only formed a slick double-play duo with Fernandez, he contributed 19 homers and 75 RBIs. It was a good, balanced club which, for an inexplicable reason, had choked in the playoffs. Or maybe it was simply due for a cold spell following a nine-game winning streak.

The turnstile count was also disappointing in 1955. The Royals attracted just over 200,000 fans, 10,000 more than in 1954, but a far cry from the good old days. General manager Guy Moreau had tried some promotions to lure people into the stands, one of them offering fans $1,500 worth of prizes. The gimmick attracted only 2,473 people.

The parent Dodgers finally won a World Series in 1955, beating the despised Yankees after losing five times to them since 1941. But the club had attendance problems of its own and team president Walter O'Malley announced near the end of the season that Brooklyn would play seven of its home games at Jersey City's Roosevelt Stadium in 1956. O'Malley explained that attendance had lagged at Ebbets Field for the last two seasons and the team badly needed a new, modern stadium with parking facilities. O'Malley was impressed by the new Municipal Stadium in Milwaukee, where the Braves played, and he urged the city of New York to build a similar park in Brooklyn.

O'Malley wasn't the only New York owner having box-office blues. Giants owner Horace Stoneham was apparently unhappy with declining revenues and said to be pondering a transfer of his team to Minneapolis. It was a rumor reminiscent of the far-fetched story which had surfaced a few years earlier about O'Malley possibly moving the Dodgers to Montreal. That was obviously an attempt to put some heat on the city of New York for a new ball park. The Giants-to Minneapolis tale - they owned an American Association team in that city - also seemed to be a pressure tactic. The club's lease on the Polo Grounds was to expire soon and it was seeking a new deal. But the story did stoke the fire. If both the Dodgers and Giants bemoaned the declining fan support, maybe New York could no longer support three major-league baseball teams.

While there was franchise stability in the

1955 pocket schedule.

majors in 1956, the International League had to shift a team to another city. Syracuse had drawn only 85,191 fans in 1955, despite almost making the playoffs. So it was farewell to the Chiefs and hello to the Miami Marlins. The owners of the new Miami franchise hired Bill Veeck to help run the team, and the famed baseball maverick created an immediate stir by signing legendary pitcher Satchel Paige. Paige, by most accounts, had started his career in the Negro Leagues in 1926 and was one of the most widely known personalities in the game. Many observers believe he would have been among the top pitchers in baseball history if the majors had lifted the color barrier sooner. Paige had always been evasive about his age, but he was probably into his forties when Veeck first hired him to pitch for the Cleveland Indians in 1948. Now Paige was beyond 50, and Miami fans greeted him warmly when Veeck introduced him during a special ceremony. Paige was brought to the field by helicopter and escorted to the bullpen, where a rocking chair awaited him. But he did more than rock that season. He appeared in 37 games, winning 11 and losing four, and compiling a miniscule 1.86 ERA. Amazingly, the venerable Paige pitched two more seasons for the Marlins, winning 10 games each year and posting a sub-3.00 ERA.

The lacklustre Royals could have used

some of the Paige pizzazz in 1956. They finished in fourth place and exited quickly in the playoffs. The team was even worse in 1957, spending most of the season in last place, eventually finishing there, 20 1|2 games out of first place. It was the Royals' worst consecutive seasons since 1939 and 1940, the first years of the club's association with the Dodgers. The last time the Royals had finished in the cellar was in 1907, when they were playing at Atwater Park.

There were myriad reasons for the decline, most of them related to personnel changes. After winning the pennant in 1955, many of the Royals' best players were grabbed by the Dodgers. Rocky Nelson, Charlie Neal, Chico Fernandez, Gino Cimoli, Don Drysdale and Ken Lehman were all moved up to Brooklyn in 1956. And after six seasons in Montreal, Tommy Lasorda was sold to the Kansas City Athletics of the American League.

Lasorda was a loyal Dodgers employee and he was disappointed at leaving the organization. But he wanted another chance to hit the big time, and this was it. He didn't have much success with his new team, however. Lasorda lost his first four decisions and was traded to the New York Yankees. The Yankees then sent him to the Denver Bears of the American Association, a demotion that seemed to further dim his dream of making it to "The Show."

The Dodgers shipped some young prospects to the Royals to plug the big holes

Manager Greg Mulleavy (left) approves of second baseman Sparky Anderson's familiar-looking haircut.

left by the departures of Lasorda, Nelson and a handful of others. But the crop of would-be Dodgers wasn't as bountiful as other years. The best of the lot were catcher John Roseboro, being groomed to take over for Roy Campanella, and Jim Gentile, a 40 home-run man from the Texas League. Roseboro hit 32 home runs and drove in 95 runs in the season-and a-half he played for the Royals. Gentile, the six-foot-four, 215-pound, left-hand-hitting first baseman, hammered 24 home runs and drove in 90 runs in 1957.

Veterans such as Clyde Parris, Jim Williams and Bobby Wilson continued to play well for Montreal. And George Shuba was back hitting home runs. But that couldn't compensate for a shaky pitching staff, which had been decimated by the Dodgers. Besides Lehman and Drysdale, pitchers recalled by Brooklyn in the last two seasons included Pete Wojey and Roger Craig. By 1957 the team's only bright spots on the mound were a stocky New Brunswick native, Billy Harris, and Rene Valdes, a willowy Cuban.

With such a shredded roster, Greg Mulleavy needed a miracle to survive as manager. It wasn't to be. In the middle of June, 1957, with the Royals dead last, Mulleavy was fired and replaced by Al Campanis, the former Royals shortstop who was now a Dodgers scout. Mulleavy was philosophical about the move, saying the team had lost 15 games by one run and wasn't as bad is it appeared.

The Campanis appointment was only temporary. When he left the team to go on a scouting assignment for Brooklyn a few weeks later, Campanis left Al Ronning in charge of the team. The Dodgers didn't seem to have a new Montreal manager high on their list of priorities, but by the end of the month, Tommy Holmes was hired for the position. Holmes was a former manager of the Dodgers farm team at Fort Worth. He had

played against the Royals a decade earlier, as an outfielder with Newark, before reaching the majors and becoming a .302 career hitter in 11 seasons with the Boston Braves. In 1945, Holmes set a modern-day National League record with a 37-game hitting streak, a mark that stood until Cincinnati's Pete Rose hit safely in 44 straight games in 1978. Holmes mounted no such streak managing the Royals and his contract wasn't renewed at the end of the 1957 season.

Much had also been happening in the Royals' administrative offices in the 1956-57 period. The franchise suffered a tremendous loss prior to the 1956 season when club president Hector Racine died. He was an instrumental figure for more than 20 years, guiding the Royals through the lean days of the Depression and finding it a niche in the Brooklyn organization. On the day he completed the deal with Larry MacPhail for the Dodgers to buy the Royals, Racine declared it was a great day for baseball in Montreal, and the next 10 years proved him right. The Royals won seven pennants, six Governors' Cups and three Junior World Series titles under Racine's presidency.

At one time, Racine had immersed himself in almost every aspect of the team's operation, even dropping by Montreal sandlots in search of local talent. But he kept a lower profile after suffering a heart attack in the spring of 1945. A few days before the home-opener that year, Racine was in hospital but he telephoned Marcel Dufrésne, the Royals traveling secretary, to wish the team luck. He broke down and sobbed on the phone as he told Dufrésne how much he missed the team and wished he could attend the game. Racine was back on the job later that season, in time to announce the team's signing of Jackie Robinson. He supported the move wholeheartedly, making it clear to fans and players that the Royals felt the addition of Robinson was not only good for the team, it was also "a point of fairness."

"Butch" Bouchard became president of the Royals after an all-star career with the Montreal Canadiens

Lucien Beauregard and Col. Roméo Gauvreau stayed on in key executive posts following Racine's death, and Rene Lemyre became the new general manager, replacing Guy Moreau. Former Montreal Canadiens captain and star defenceman Emile "Butch" Bouchard joined the board of directors and was eventually named Racine's successor as president.

In 1956, early in Bouchard's tenure, the Dodgers sold Delorimier Stadium to a real-estate company, Sherbrun Investments, and leased the park until the end of the 1960 season. Buzzie Bavasi said the Dodgers made the deal because they were under the impression the city of Montreal would be building a new ballpark. Bavasi wouldn't say who had provided him with such information. The city had backed away from buying the stadium a few years earlier and had no plans to build a new one - at least none it had made public. The city could have used a new park because Delorimier Downs was showing its age and had an acute shortage of parking facilities.

Many people feared the sale of the stadium was a preamble to Brooklyn pulling the plug on the Royals. But Bavasi vowed that wasn't true. He said the organization would build a new park in Montreal if the leasing deal for Delorimier Stadium fell through. He envisaged a smaller park with a seating capacity of between 12,000-14,000, roughly half the capacity of Delorimier. Bavasi believed attendance levels in Montreal would never again approach the levels of 1946-1949. His opinion was based on the general decline in baseball attendance, but he also felt Montrealers had become blasé about the Royals. "I think the Montreal fans may have been spoiled by a succession of fine ball clubs," said, Bavasi. "It wouldn't be the first time it has happened."

Whether complacency was a contributing factor, it was undeniable that the Royals had peaked in popularity, at least in terms of attendance. There had been a steady decline since 1949, some of it attributable to the fact more and more of the team's games were available on radio. When only 265 people showed up for a game in September, 1957, it was a clear sign that something was wrong. Asked if he thought Montreal attendance would improve, Bavasi cryptically replied that, if it did "it would make a big change in our present plans." He didn't elaborate but the comment seemed ominous.

At the end of the 1956 season, O'Malley bought the Los Angeles Angels of the Pacific Coast League. By this time he was having no luck convincing the city of New York to build him a new stadium and was seriously considering moving the Dodgers to Los Angeles. City councillors in Los Angeles were offering land for a lavish ball park and other perks that made the deal difficult to refuse. By acquiring the PCL Angels, O'Malley also gained the territorial rights necessary for the Dodgers' move. When news of the purchase was announced during spring training in 1957, many Dodgers were convinced it would be their last season in Brooklyn. The news raised some concern in Montreal, but Bavasi insisted that neither the acquisition of the Class AAA Angels, nor a Dodgers' move to the West Coast, would affect the the future of the Royals.

In early October, 1957, while the Milwaukee Braves were in the process of beating the Yankees in the World Series, Walter O'Malley announced that the Dodgers were moving to Los Angeles for the 1958 season. The rumors that had been circulating for months had come true, breaking the hearts of thousands of loyal Brooklyn fans. The announcement came two months after Horace Stoneham had shocked the baseball world by announcing he was taking his New York Giants to San Fransisco. It was no coincidence that both teams were leaving at the same time. O'Malley had convinced Stoneham the West Coast was baseball's promised land, and it would be easier if both teams moved there.

Despite Bavasi's assurances the Royals would continue as the Dodgers' premier farm team, there was plenty of uncertainty as the 1958 season approached. Would the Dodgers still be interested in having their top farm team clear across the continent? Would St. Paul, somewhat closer, now become the top farm club? And what would happen to the Los Angeles Angels, the organization's third Triple-A team, now that the parent club was moving to the West Coast?

Royals' president Emile Bouchard tried to put a positive spin on things, saying the Dodgers' move to Los Angeles meant the Angels would probably be sold and the organization would return to operating only two Triple-A teams: Montreal and St. Paul. He was confident Montreal would still receive the Dodgers' best minor-league talent. But that confidence would be shaken in the months to come.

16

1958
Once More, With Feeling

Now that the Dodgers were based in Los Angeles, they could no longer operate a minor-league team in the same market. But instead of selling the Pacific Coast League's Los Angeles Angels, as Emile Bouchard had wishfully predicted, the Dodgers decided to move the franchise to Spokane, Washington. Air travel was less efficient in those days, and since clubs liked to have their top minor-league prospects close at hand, the location of a farm team was important. Montreal was easily accessible for the Brooklyn Dodgers, but not so convenient when the team moved to Los Angeles. At least, not as handy as Spokane. There was no official announcement, but it seemed clear the Royals' reign as the No. 1 Dodgers farm club was about to end. It was a blow Bouchard had feared, despite his outward optimism, and one that he had tried to prevent.

Sometime in 1957, when rumblings grew stronger that Walter O'Malley was moving the Dodgers to the West Coast, Bouchard, backed by an anonymous group of "local sportsmen," had made an unsuccessful bid to buy the Royals. The plan was to have local ownership for the team, but maintain its status as the Dodgers' main farm club. O'Malley rejected the offer without much thought. What was striking about the proposal was that it was similar to the deal the Royals struck with the Dodgers for the 1939 season, an arrangement that was scrapped after one year. Hector Racine, the Royals' long-serving president, believed the

You couldn't tell the players without a program in 1958.

only way for the team to be successful was to be taken over by a major-league organization, and he convinced the Dodgers to buy the Royals for the 1940 season. Now, 17 years later, a group of "local sportsmen" wanted to revert to a working agreement. It showed that, like 1939, there was some uncertainty in Montreal about the Royals' future. And it was also a clear indication of how things had changed in the International League.

In the 30 years since the Royals had re-entered the I. L., teams owned by major-league organizations - Montreal, Newark, Jersey City and Rochester - had dominated the league, winning the pennant 22 times. But by 1957, with the New Jersey teams gone and the Rochester franchise no longer the property of the Cardinals, Montreal was the only league member still owned by a major-league organization. Six teams had working agreements with a big-league club, and the Toronto Maple Leafs, who had won the pennant three of the last four seasons, had no major-league connection. The "local sportsmen" obviously felt the Royals had no future in the Dodgers' organization now that they were based in Los Angeles and had added Spokane, Wash., as a Triple-A affiliate.

The first inkling that the Spokane Indians might soon be eclipsing the Royals in the Dodgers' farm structure was when the parent club sent Jim Gentile, Montreal's home-run and RBI leader in 1957, to Spokane for the 1958 season. Maury Wills, a promising infielder and gifted base-stealer, ended up in Spokane, rather than Montreal, for a final tune-up before joining the Dodgers. Wills would have been perfectly suited for Montreal, as a successor to Jackie Robinson, Marvin Rackley and Sam Jethroe, players who had aroused the passions of the Montreal crowd with their tremendous speed. As a Dodger in 1961, Wills stole 104 bases - the first modern-era player to top the century mark. He might have been a wonderful tonic for the ennui that had seemingly set in at Delorimier Downs.

Still, the Royals wouldn't really feel the repercussions of Spokane's arrival for another year. They assembled a promising club in 1958. Sparky Anderson was back after a season with the Los Angeles Angels of the Pacific Coast League, and the Royals hoped for a repeat of 1956, when he played a slick second base and hit .298. Catcher Dick Teed, who had played for Montreal in 1955,

also returned. Veteran right-hander Babe Birrer joined the Royals from Los Angeles, lending some experience to a shaky staff. But the most important acquisitions from the Angels were manager Clay Bryant, who succeeded Tommy Holmes as the Royals manager, and old pal Tommy Lasorda, the winningest pitcher in the team's history.

After being traded from Kansas City to the Yankees, and playing for their American Association affiliate, Lasorda asked the Yankees to return him to the Dodgers organization, where he felt his career options would be better. The Yankees obliged and the Dodgers welcomed their prodigal son by placing him with the Angels for the 1957 season. In Los Angeles, Lasorda was reunited with Bryant, his skipper in A-ball a decade earlier at Greenville, S. C. But it wasn't a joyous reunion. Although the Dodgers rated Bryant as a strong developer of young talent, Lasorda regarded him as the worst manager he'd ever played for.

Lasorda's animosity toward Bryant put him in a delicate spot at the end of the season, when a player-coach job opened up with the Royals. Coming off a 7-10 season for the Angels, Lasorda, now 30, was pondering his future and the Montreal job looked like a good career move. The only drawback was working for Bryant, whom he likened to a dictator. He could have pitched for Spokane in 1958, but Lasorda preferred the Montreal job and decided he could put aside his personal feelings about Bryant. He asked Al Campanis to put in a good word to Buzzie Bavasi and the Dodgers general manager hired him, adding the duties of travelling secretary.

Bryant, who was 46 when he assumed the reins in Montreal, didn't have an easy-going personality. He was a big, lean, stone-faced man, whose expression was stern, even when he smiled. That was in striking contrast to Mulleavy, his predecessor. Bryant

Bryant and Lasorda smiled – but only for the camera.

philosophy entering the 1958 season. He had resigned himself to the fact he would probably never be a major-league pitcher. "If you don't like my suit, I can buy a new one," he remarked. "But if you don't like my fastball, there's nothing I can do about it." He seemed to have acquired a certain maturity in the two years since he left the Royals. In the past, the bantam rooster had always felt confident about going head-to-head with any batter, a battle he often won in his previous seasons with the Royals. Lasorda now had a different approach. "In a large park like this (Delorimier Stadium), all you need is control and a good team behind you," he explained after pitching a one-hit, late-April shutout against Miami.

Lasorda got off to a tremendous start in 1958, compiling a streak of 31 scoreless innings before the season was a month old. The International League record was 54, set in 1916 by spitball specialist Urban Shocker, playing for Toronto. During the scoreless streak, Lasorda's wife Jo, back home with her parents in South Carolina expecting the couple's second child, went into labor and Tommy was summoned to join her. But he was scheduled to pitch that night against the Maple Leafs and, hoping to keep his streak alive, he elected to stay with the team. The couple's son, Tom Jr. - nicknamed "Spunky" - was born shortly before game time, and the new father handed out cigars before trying for his fourth straight shutout, a bid that ended in the fifth inning.

The streak of 31 scoreless innings was just one of Lasorda's accomplishments in 1958. He led the league in wins, innings pitched and complete games. And with five shutouts, an ERA of 2.50 and an 18-6 record, he was an easy winner of the league's Most Valuable Pitcher award. Ironically, the best season of his career had come after he had all but forsaken his dream of pitching in the big leagues. In August, the team staged a Tommy Lasorda Night at Delorimier Stadium,

detested defeat and was known to take things out on his players, sometimes making them sit silently in the clubhouse and stare at the ground after a loss. He also had a sarcastic tongue, which he'd unleashed when things weren't going well. But when the team won, he lavished praise on his players and made sure they got credit for their accomplishments.

Sparky Anderson said Bryant ran a ball club like a general handles his troops in an army regiment. Lasorda, meanwhile, said he was most bothered by Bryant's lack of communication with his players. He would sometimes ignore a player if he met him in an elevator or hotel lobby. But communication, of course, was Lasorda's forte, and as Bryant's coach he became the liason between the manager and the players.

As a pitcher, Lasorda had a fresh

showering him with a number of gifts, including a car.

Lasorda was the anchor of a good Royals pitching staff in 1958. Birrer, who like Lasorda joined the Royals from the Los Angeles Angels, was a pleasant surprise, posting a 12-5 record and 2.36 ERA, one of the lowest in the league. Rookie Bob Giallombardo also won 12 games, while Billy Harris and Rene Valdes, two of the few bright spots on the 1957 team, combined for 19 wins. It was especially satisfying for Harris, whose promising career was sidetracked in 1956, after he and teammates Bob Walz and Dixie Howell were arrested following a nightclub brawl in Miami. Their manager, Greg Mulleavy, bailed them out of jail, but they were in the Dodgers' doghouse for a while. Howell, a player-coach, was fired after the incident, but Harris persevered and was now a key man in the Montreal rotation.

A familiar figure returned to the Royals outfield, as the Dodgers returned Sandy Amoros to Montreal. He had been a hero in the 1955 World Series' triumph over the Yankees with a game-saving catch in Game 7. But Amoros hadn't played well after that moment of glory and the Dodgers had apparently given up on him. The Royals were pleased to have him back. They also had a warm welcome for third baseman Clyde Parris, International League batting champion in 1956 who was sidelined for most of 1957 with a broken elbow.

Complementing these seasoned veterans were solid roster additions such as switch-hitting centre-fielder Solomon "Solly" Drake, who led the Pacific Coast League with 36 stolen bases while with Portland in 1957. There was Bob Lennon, a left-handed, long-ball hitter who smacked an astounding 64 home runs in the Southern Association in 1954. Jim Koranda, a long-serving Dodgers' farmhand, arrived to play first base.

Some people were still fretting about the failures of 1957, the Royals' worst season since 1939. Others worried about the team's future in Montreal and still couldn't quite get used to the Dodgers operating out of Los Angeles instead of Brooklyn. But the Royals relegated these issues to the back-burner by reeling off 12 wins in their first 15 games, the best start in franchise history.

The 12th victory came in the 1958 home-opener at Delorimier, against Miami Marlins pitcher and future major-league player and manager Dallas Green. The early-season success seemed to arouse the dormant Delorimier patrons. They cheered lustily, not realizing at the time they were witnessing the last home-opener the Royals would ever win and the start of the last good season the storied franchise would ever have.

As the 1958 season unfolded, it became another race between the Royals and the Toronto Maple Leafs, the regular-season champion in three of the previous four seasons. The Leafs were owned by millionaire Jack Kent Cooke, who spent his money

Lasorda showing why he was on his was to becoming the winningest pitcher in Royals history.

liberally, buying the best players he could find. "Whatever is worth buying in the pitching or power line will find its way to Toronto", he boasted. In 1956, Cooke snapped up Luke Easter (whose given name was Luscious), a proven power hitter with the Cleveland Indians. Cooke was also quick to sign Rocky Nelson in 1957, after Nelson had failed to stick with either the Dodgers or the Cardinals the previous season. Many accused Cooke of buying pennants for Toronto, a charge to which he pleaded guilty, especially when his purchases performed well. Easter dominated the league's power statistics in 1956 and 1957, with Nelson close behind. It surprised no one that the Leafs were well positioned for their third straight pennant. But it was astonishing that the Royals were in a position to dethrone them.

Montreal led the league by five games at the end of May, slumped briefly in June, but still held a slender lead by the start of July. The Royals maintained the lead into September, despite a string of injuries, which at one point in August had reduced the roster to 16 healthy players. They had a three-game lead over Toronto heading to Rochester for their last five games of the season. The Royals swept a Friday doubleheader, 2-0 and 3-0, and the second game, a four-hit gem by Billy Harris, clinched the pennant. It was the ninth - and last - pennant in the team's history. A proud Clay Bryant, who was tossed into the shower, said his men had won the title with sheer determination. The team's 90-63 record marked the ninth time the Royals had reached the 90-win plateau since joining the Dodgers' organization almost 20 years earlier.

Lasorda and the pitching staff had performed well, but they had ample support from the Royals' bats. Solly Drake put together a 26-game hitting streak in mid-summer and was among the league's batting leaders all season, finishing fourth with a .301 average. That was one point higher than teammate Clyde Parris, who contributed 93

RBIs. Jim Koranda hit 20 home runs, drove in 83 runs and filled in at several positions, including catcher. Sandy Amoros, despite an off-year in average, produced 16 homers and 63 RBIs. The Royals' middle-infield combination of Sparky Anderson and Bobby Dolan shone both offensively and defensively.

Noted more for their tenacity than their overall skills, the 1958 Royals now prepared to start the playoff round against Columbus, a club managed by former Montreal and Brooklyn pitcher Clyde King. The Jets were a .500 team which had narrowly grabbed the final I.L. playoff spot. But they borrowed some of the Royals' tenacity in a quirky, high-scoring series, which had Columbus holding a 3-2 lead heading into Game 6 at Delorimier Stadium.

The reliable Lasorda came through in the sixth game, holding off the Jets until his teammates exploded for eight sixth-inning runs for a 12-2 victory, highlighted by Clyde Parris' homer and four RBIs. Billy Harris pitched the deciding game in front of a Montreal crowd of just under 11,000, the largest to date. Despite working with only two day's rest, Harris yielded four singles as the Royals romped 11-0 to win a series in which they averaged more than seven runs a game but also allowed an average of almost five runs.

The Governor's Cup final opened in Montreal with the Royals facing Toronto ace Bob Tiefenauer, second to Lasorda in wins in 1958, but the league ERA leader with a remarkable 1.89. Rain delayed the opener for two days, but it wasn't enough to induce Bryant to go with his ace Lasorda against Tiefenauer. Lasorda was given an extra day of rest while Bob Giallombardo started the opener. He was removed in the fourth inning and Tiefenauer held a 3-0 lead into the eighth, when the Royals tied it. Bob Lennon then hit a solo homer in the ninth for a Montreal victory.

The well-rested Lasorda started Game 2 and was yanked in the first inning, as former Royal Rocky Nelson's three-run homer helped stake the Leafs to a 6-0 lead. The Royals stormed back, led by Bob Lennon's two homers, and vaulted into a 9-7 lead. Toronto pulled even in the ninth, before Jim Koranda ended what one reporter called a "thrill-a-minute marathon" with a home run in the bottom of the 11th inning, lifting Montreal to a 10-9 victory and a 2-0 series lead.

Not only did the Royals lose the third game at Maple Leaf Stadium, but outfielder Sandy Amoros passed out in the dugout and was rushed to the hospital with a severe case of pneumonia that sidelined him for the rest of the playoffs. His replacement was Tommy Davis, a promising young player with limited Triple-A experience.

Bob Giallombardo's two-hit, 5-0 victory in Game 4 moved the Royals within a game of a Junior World Series' berth. Victory seemed at hand when the Royals scored six first-inning runs in the fifth game. But Billy Harris, who had won his last 10 pitching decisions for the Royals, was unsettled by Rocky Nelson's homer in the second inning and never recovered. He was shelled in the fourth inning and the Leafs eventually took an 8-7 lead. The gritty Royals responded with four runs in the eighth, as Sparky Anderson doubled home the tying run and Tommy Davis singled in the go-ahead run. Montreal held on to win 10-9 and were off to the Junior World Series for the seventh time in 18 seasons.

The Royals' pugnacious play had earned them league-wide respect. True, they didn't have any superstars but, as The Gazette's

Dink Carroll observed, "there wasn't a loafer on the club." Veteran catcher Dick Teed was especially impressed by the club's ability to cope with injuries and slumps. "I've never played on a team where the guys have picked each other up like they do on this one," he said. Despite their exciting, scrappy play, the Royals still had trouble attracting fans. Attendance was up only marginally over 1957, when the Royals were the worst team in the league.

Such indifference to the Royals' last-to-first revival was another sign the team might be living on borrowed time. There was still a core of loyal supporters, and it must have crossed their minds that Montreal's 1958 Junior World Series appearance might be its last. If there was any consolation, it appeared that the team had a good chance of winning its fourth JWS crown. The rival Minneapolis Millers had no overpowering pitchers, no .300 hitters and were coming off a third-place finish in the American Association with a so-so 81-72 record. On the plus side, the Millers had good defense, a low team ERA and their manager-second baseman, Gene Mauch, had won the American Association Manager-of-the-Year award. Also, the Millers had momentum, winning their last seven playoff games, including a four-game sweep of Denver in the previous round.

The Millers' streak reached eight games when Al Schroll outpitched Tommy Lasorda in front of 8,791 spectators at Delorimier Stadium, for a 6-2 win in the JWS opener. The next game was frustrating for the Royals. They stranded 14 baserunners and failed time and again in the clutch. They paraded five pitchers to the mound and lost 7-2.

Lucky Numbers

1 — One Year's supply of Pal Hollow Ground Blades, courtesy of Pal Blades Corporation Limited.
2 — A Presto lighter courtesy of L. E. Waterman Pen Co.
3 — A beautiful Rhinestone jewellery created by Jay Kel Ltd., famous for hand set originals in precious sterling silver.
4 — A $5.00 dollar coupon in merchandise courtesy of IGA stores.
 Prizes are to be claimed at the cigarette counter in the main lobby.

A 46039

Numéros Gagnants

1 — Un approvisionnement d'un an de Lames Concave Pal, gracieuseté de Pal Blades Corporation Limited.
2 — Un briquet Presto, courtoisie de L. E. Waterman Pen Co.
3 — Un joli set de pierres de Rhin créé par Jay Kel Ltd., renommé pour ses sets originaux faits à la main en précieux argent sterling.
4 — Un coupon d'une valeur de $5.00 dollars en merchandises, courtoisie des magasins IGA.
 Les prix doivent être réclamés au kiosque des cigarettes situé dans le lobby principal.

Check your ticket stub!

The 1958 Royals were the last good team the franchise would have. First row, left to right: Bobby Dolan, Tommy Davis, Charlie Rabe, Sandy Amoros, Bob Lennon and Jim Koranda. Second row, left to right: Jackie Collum, Sparky Anderson, Billy Harris, Marty Devlin, Clay Bryant (manager), Tom Lasorda, Dan Gatta and Clyde Parris. Third row, left to right: Yvon Dunn (trainer), John Jancse, Bob Giallombardo, Harry Schwegman, Solly Drake, Dick Teed, Bob Darnell, Dick Gray and Rene Valdes.

With only one more chance to win at Delorimier before the series shifted to Minneapolis, the Royals staged an eighth-inning rally that sliced the Millers' lead to 3-2. With the tying run at third base, Bobby Dolan missed a squeeze-bunt attempt and Dick Teed was trapped in a rundown between third and home. In the ninth inning, Jim Koranda lofted a two-out fly ball that looked, for a moment, like a game-tying home run. But Millers left-fielder Stu Locklin made a one-handed catch against the wall and the Royals faced a 3-0 series deficit. Only the 1937 Newark Bears had ever overcome such a disadvantage to win a Junior World Series.

The first game in Minneapolis, in front of 7,072 fans, started promisingly for the Royals. They scored the first run of the game in the top of the second, but didn't muster a hit against Tom Borland the rest of the way. The Millers supported their pitcher with seven runs for their 11th straight victory and the Junior World Series championship.

The 1958 Royals had been impressive with their spirit and hustle but, as Dink Carroll noted, "somewhere along the line the spark had gone out." Pitching and hitting had collapsed and Clay Bryant had no explanation, other than to point out that the team had been involved in so many close, emotional games, they were physically and emotionally exhausted by the start of the Junior World Series. It was a humiliating loss for the team in four straight games, and it stung all the more when the secretary of the eight-member American Association, still basking in the Millers' triumph, asked rhetorically, "Do you think the Royals could have finished ninth in our league?"

1959-1960
Turning Out the Lights

17

As the 1959 Royals took shape, it was growing apparent that the team wouldn't be making a Junior World Series appearance in the near future. The Dodgers were obviously intent on boosting the Spokane affiliate, at the expense of Montreal. That seemed evident when Tommy Davis, a talented prospect who had filled in capably for Sandy Amoros during the Royals' 1958 playoff run, was sent to Spokane, as was Montreal's best young pitcher, Bob Giallombardo. Davis blossomed at Spokane, winning the 1959 Pacific Coast League batting championship with a .345 average.

Not only did the Royals have to compete for players with the new kid on the block - the Indians - they had to contend with their kid brother, the St. Paul Saints. The Saints had recently built a $2 million stadium that hadn't cost the Dodgers a dime, a feat the parent team felt should not go unrewarded. So the Saints were given shortstop Bobby Dolan and first baseman Jim Koranda, two of Montreal's better players during the 1958 season.

With the departure of Koranda, Dolan and the latter's double-play partner Sparky Anderson, who had won a spot with Philadelphia Phillies, the Royals were left with a skeleton for 1959. The team had some steady veterans - Bob Lennon, Clyde Parris, Sandy Amoros, Dick Teed and Tommy Lasorda - but was short on young, dynamic talent. Even the usually upbeat Lasorda, back in his triple-role of player, coach and

traveling secretary, wasn't too optimistic about the team's chances. In fact, for a while it seemed he, too, would be heading west, as the manager in Spokane. He had also been considered as a possible replacement for departing Montreal general manager René Lemyre. But Clay Bryant wanted to keep Lasorda as his right-hand man, despite their differences, and the Dodgers obliged.

On opening day in Montreal, as Bryant used the public-address system at Delorimier Stadium to introduce the players to the 5,800 fans, he paused when he got to Lasorda. "And now...," he began ceremoniously, ".....the man of many jobs - pitcher, assistant coach, road secretary, trainer, bat boy, you name it.....here he is... Tom Lasorda." The crowd clapped and whistled as Lasorda jogged out to stand beside his teammates. His smile widened as the ovation continued, and he doffed his cap to the crowd. As his teammates teased him about the reception, Lasorda shrugged his shoulders, as if to say, "I can't help it if they love me."

The warm feelings of opening day quickly chilled, however as the 1959 season turned dreary for the Royals, a bitter pill for the fans who were excited by the pennant race a year earlier. This time, the Royals were out of contention early, not even a playoff threat. The team's ineptness brought out the snarly side of Clay Bryant, a notorious sorehead when it came to losing. After one of the team's few early-season wins, a 5-3 decision

Once considered a state-of-the-art ballpark, Delorimier Stadium was reduced to rubble after the Royals folded.

over the Miami Marlins, Bryant didn't even pretend to be encouraged. "I looked at the scoreboard and saw that we had five runs, then I asked somebody to read the name on my uniform," he said with a sneer. "I couldn't believe it when he said 'Montreal'."

Bryant's sour attitude occasionally made him some enemies, not the least of which was I.L. president Frank Shaughnessy, a bit of a poor loser himself in his managerial days. Shag had once praised Bryant as the type of hard-headed manager the game needed, but the two had a tiff at the end of the 1958 season, when Bryant publicly complained the league president had failed to congratulate him on the Royals' pennant victory. Shaughnessy and Bryant traded barbs for much of the 1959 season.

Lasorda was the team's best pitcher in 1959, with a 12-8 record. Lennon, Parris and Amoros all performed well, but the club ended up in seventh place with a 72-82 record. The attendance - 135, 340 - was the lowest in the league and the Royals' worst mark in almost 20 years. Interest in Triple-A baseball had apparently reached rock bottom in Montreal, and the idea of seeking a major-league franchise resurfaced. Except this time the discussions weren't about joining the National or American League but a new league being proposed by Branch Rickey.

The Continental League was the brainchild of Rickey, now retired from the Pittsburgh Pirates, and a group of business people led by Bill Shea of New York. Rickey, 77, was still an innovator and he thought it was time for major-league baseball to spread to new parts of the continent. Shea wanted a team in New York to replace the Giants and Dodgers, but felt he had little chance of convincing the National League to expand there. Both the National and American Leagues had been comprised of eight teams since the start of the century, and didn't appear too interested in expansion. Besides New York, several places wanted a major-league franchise - Montreal, Toronto, Houston, Denver, Dallas-Fort Worth, Atlanta, Buffalo and Minneapolis-St. Paul - and regarded a new league as their only hope.

In Montreal, a group of investors pursued a franchise after Dodgers owner Walter O'Malley offered to sell them the Royals at an affordable price. The group asked the city and provincial governments to lend their support by building a new stadium, capable of housing a major-league team. The potential investors also claimed that Jackie Robinson, who had retired from the Dodgers, had agreed to be the team's manager. The Montreal bid had barely got off the ground when it received news that the proposed Continental League had collapsed. The major leagues, worried about new competition, suddenly agreed to expand their ranks, effectively shooting down the new league. The American League announced the addition of two new franchises for the 1961 season - the Los Angeles (later California) Angels and the Washington Senators. The old Senators had recently become the Minnesota Twins. The National League admitted the Houston Colt .45s (later the Astros) and the New York Mets for the 1962 season.

As the major leagues were being pushed into expansion by Bill Shea and his Continental League, the International League had some problems of its own in 1960, starting with Havana. A few years earlier, Fidel Castro had intensified the

battle to overthrow the Batista regime and with the resulting increase in fighting around Cuba's capital city, armed soldiers began boarding the buses of visiting International League teams. Some clubs threatened to stop travelling to Cuba, but in 1958 Frank Shaughnessy visited the country and convinced the teams there was no danger. Still, it was unnerving as the revolution descended from the hills and moved closer to Havana. Gunfire could often be heard as teams were playing in the city's Gran Stadium.

When Castro took power in 1959, counter-revolutionaries prolonged the battle and relations with the United States became hostile. But the new Cuban leader vowed to maintain the Sugar Kings in Havana and he kept his promise. The team stayed in Havana and, led by star pitcher Mike Cuellar and manager Preston Gomez, finished third in the regular season and went on to win the Junior World Series by beating the Minneapolis Millers in seven games. Because of bad weather in Minnesota, five of the seven games were played in Havana, where 100, 000 fans turned out, the largest playoff attendance for one team in International League history.

Castro, a former pitcher, was an avid baseball fan. He had a special seat installed along the first-base line at Gran Stadium and he would watch games from his perch above the Havana dugout, surrounded by armed soldiers and body guards. One story had Castro jumping onto the field one afternoon to berate a Havana pitcher who was an officer in the Cuban army. The unfortunate player was being shelled by the Buffalo Bisons, so Castro called time, as if he were the manager, walked briskly to the mound, screamed at the pitcher and slapped him twice before storming back to his seat. Witnessing this, the visiting Buffalo players dropped to the floor of their dugout.

Despite Castro's promise to keep the Sugar Kings in Havana, "even if I have to pitch myself," it was obvious that things were deteriorating as the 1960 season progressed. There were more accounts of violence and stories about fans, fuelled by rum and the revolutionary spirit, firing shots into the air to celebrate victories. A couple of times the bullets actually grazed players. Also, the Cuban nationalization of American oil refineries, banks and sugar mills, made it less politically acceptable for American baseball teams to play there. The Havana franchise lost an influential supporter with the retirement of Frank Shaughnessy in 1960, after more than 20 years as I.L. president. On July 13, 1960, the new president of the International League, Thomas H. Richardson, moved the Havana franchise to Jersey City. He hoped that area could again be a viable minor-league market, now that there were no longer three major-league teams in New York City.

But once the Cuban crisis was resolved, the league seemed in danger of losing one of its older and more established franchises: the Montreal Royals. The Dodgers continued to strip the Royals for parts in 1960, sending Billy Harris, one of the team's steadiest pitchers over the last three seasons, to Spokane, along with top shortstop prospect Earl Robinson and second baseman Curt Roberts. Roberts had been acquired from Richmond early in 1959 and ended up hitting .296 in 128 games for the Royals. Ed Rakow, a young right-hander who had won nine games for Montreal in 1959, went up to Los Angeles briefly before joining the growing gang of ex-Royals in Spokane. Sandy Amoros had a last fling with the Dodgers in early 1960, but was then traded to the Detroit Tigers

Not surprisingly, it was a great season for the Spokane Indians. They won the Pacific Coast League pennant, thanks to the work of the former Royals and the Dodgers' top prospects. Speedy outfielder Willie Davis was the best of them all, winning the batting title, stolen-base crown and the league's MVP award.

By contrast, it was the worst of times for the Royals, as they suffered through their poorest season since rejoining the league in 1928. The club started well, arriving in Montreal for the home- opener in third place, only a half-game behind the Rochester Red Wings. The Montreal sports pages were filled with news about the Montreal Canadiens winning a record fifth consecutive Stanley Cup, so there was little mention of the Royals' return. Still, the opener drew 8,725 fans, a decent turnout by recent standards. They watched passively as the Royals were defeated 8-2 by Mike Cuellar and the soon-to-be-extinct Havana Sugar Kings. From then on, things worsened for the Royals. They dropped their next six games to go 0-7 on their first home stand and proceeded to lose on the road, extending their losing streak to 14 games.

Montreal general manager Fernand Dubois desperately sought ways to maintain fan interest during the slump. He had joined the club in the 1930s, managing a hot-dog concession with his wife, and had risen steadily through the ranks. He was an energetic type with a dashing, Cesar Romero moustache. Dubois had a flair for promotions, although his schemes didn't always work. Once, he organized a mass wedding ceremony at the stadium for 100 couples. Montreal Mayor Camillien Houde was on hand as the happy couples assembled in the infield on a blisteringly hot July day. Everything was proceeding as planned until a bunch of brides and grooms, forced to stand in the blazing sun, started to keel over. They flopped by the dozens and Mayor Houde, baffled by what was happening, called for ambulances and had a number of the fainters carted away to the hospital.

For the 1960 home-opener against Havana, Dubois had tried to boost attendance by inviting Fidel Castro to throw out the first ball. Castro sent his regrets, however, citing a previous engagement. Now with the team on an abysmal losing streak, Dubois came up with another stunt: he vowed not to shave until the team won a game. When the Royals finally ended the 14-game skid by winning the first game of a doubleheader against Buffalo, Dubois, looking a bit like Castro himself by this time, had his whiskers shaved by a barber at home plate between games. The Royals promptly lost the nightcap and went on another losing streak.

By the the first week of June the last-place Royals had won only two of their last 27 games and the effects of the poor showing were being felt at the turnstiles. The club had one of its best days in early July, sweeping a Sunday doubleheader against Columbus, but only 4,794 fans were at Delorimier Downs to share in such a rare event.

A few Royals were productive, notably first baseman Joe Altobelli, outfielder Gordie Windhorn and pitcher Ron Perranoski. But Windhorn quit at mid-season to oversee an investment he'd made in a bowling alley. Perranoski, a promising youngster from the Cubs organization (who years later would later become Tom Lasorda's pitching coach with the Dodgers), was sent to Spokane near the end of the season to help the Indians clinch the PCL pennant. The transfer of Perranoski was further evidence the Royals were on the point of extinction as a Dodgers farm team.

Among the number of Royals who were struggling in 1960 was old reliable, Tommy Lasorda. News about the Continental League had again raised his hopes about playing at the major-league level, and its collapse was another disappointment. He wasn't pitching well and his already strained relationship with Clay Bryant further deteriorated as the

G.M. Fernand Dubois came up with contests to keep the fans interested. This one involved a prize of $10,000 if the ball went through a hole in the outfield fence.

team stumbled and the manager steamed. The inevitable clash came in late June when Lasorda approached Bryant on behalf of a player who wanted a raise. Bryant refused and Lasorda relayed the bad news. The battle was on when Bryant charged that Lasorda had already promised the raise, thus undermining his authority as manager.

A few nights later, Bryant summoned Lasorda to his office. General manager Fernand Dubois, who was with Bryant, told Lasorda the Dodgers believed he was a disruptive influence on the team, so he was being given his unconditional release. Lasorda, who considered himself to be the most loyal of Dodger employees, couldn't believe his ears. Uncharacteristically quiet at first, he sprang to his feet once the shock wore off and lunged at Bryant, whom he blamed for branding him as a troublemaker. Dubois separated the two and let Lasorda telephone Dodgers general manager Buzzie Bavasi to give his side of the story. Bavasi admitted the issue had been exaggerated, but told Lasorda he couldn't possibly return to the Royals after the blowup with Bryant. He offered Lasorda a job as a scout and, realizing it was his only option, the longest-serving Montreal Royals player turned in his glove, ending his playing career.

Lasorda had at least gone out in grand style. A few nights earlier, he was being lashed by the Buffalo Bisons. They had loaded the bases with none out and Bryant was on the top step of the dugout, poised to remove Lasorda. Realizing this would likely be his last game as a player, Lasorda wanted to walk off the field at the end of an inning, rather than on the end of Bryant's hook. He turned his back on home plate, gazed into

Joe Altobelli was one of the few bright spots on the team in 1960, but few fans came out to see him play.

the sky and prayed for something - anything - to get him out of the jam.

The next batter hit a screaming line drive that handcuffed Royals third baseman George Risley. But the ball caromed off his glove and shortstop Jerry Snyder made a diving, backhanded catch for the out. He then flipped the ball to second, where the runner was caught off base, and the second baseman relayed it to first base, where another runner had strayed. With head high, Lasorda walked off the mound, escaping his final jam with a bases-loaded triple play.

It was a fitting way for Lasorda to leave the Royals after spending parts of nine season with the team and compiling an impressive 107-57 record. He was the winningest pitcher in Royals' history and one of the team's most popular players. After several years in the Dodgers farm system as scout, coach and manager, Lasorda almost returned to Montreal to manage the Expos in 1975, but opted to remain with the Dodgers as third-base coach and he succeeded Walter

Gordie Windhorn was playing well until he decided to leave the team before the end of the season.

Alston as the team's manager a year later, remaining in that capacity until he stepped down following a 1996 heart attack.

With Lasorda out of the picture, the rest of the 1960 season became a death watch for the team's small band of supporters. Dubois begged Buzzie Bavasi for new players, to no avail. He also hounded him for details about a telegram Bavasi had sent in December of 1959 that mentioned a new municipal stadium in Montreal and a 20-year lease for the Royals. Bavasi was evasive about the telegram. Nor was it ever clear how he got the notion the city of Montreal had agreed to build a ball park - although there was no doubt that Delorimier Stadium was a dinosaur in an era of classy, bowl-style stadiums.

Dubois tried to establish a syndicate of local businessmen to study the possibility of building a new ball park, but there wasn't much interest. The Dodgers had until October 31 to renew the lease on Delorimier Stadium, but they were mum about their plans. By mid-September, with attendance at a post-1928 low of 130,000, and Dubois unable to extract any information from the Dodgers regarding the club's future, he announced he was leaving at the end of the season to run a local sports centre.

At the ball park, there was an air of resignation. Alvin Guttman, who had watched games at Delorimier from the early days of the stadium's history, attended a 1960 game and observed, "I could see the demise coming. I felt that the whole thing was falling apart."

The Royals' last home game - on September 7, 1960 - was like a wake. Only 1,016 fans were on hand as Montreal lost 7-4 against the Buffalo Bisons, who were helped by a two-run homer by former Royal Bobby Morgan. The ninth-inning blow was somehow fitting, in that it was a bittersweet

Tom Lasorda never forgot his nine seasons in Montreal. "I loved that place, the people. I enjoyed every year I was there. Every time I go back to Montreal I feel good. There are still a lot of people who remember me."

reminder of better days. After the game Dubois moved through the press box with team president Emile Bouchard. They shook hands with reporters, apologized for the horrible season and spoke frankly about the team's bleak future.

A few weeks later, the Dodgers made the expected announcement: they were discontinuing their Montreal operation and the franchise was up for sale. The Dodgers said the decision was based on sharp financial losses in recent years, although it was obvious they had been gradually abandoning the Royals since leaving Brooklyn for Los Angeles. Walter O'Malley was never keen about having three Triple-A farm teams, and the Royals had become the least useful affiliate. In the ensuing weeks, there were rumors of potential local buyers for the Royals, but nothing materialized. Before the year had ended, the International League took over the franchise and transferred it to Syracuse.

There were many eulogies for the Royals - and for baseball in the city - after the last out had been recorded at Delorimier Stadium in the 1960 season. But for Lloyd McGowan, who had covered the Royals with wit and joy since the historic home-opener in 1928, this wasn't a requiem. "Baseball isn't dead in Montreal," he assured the mourners. " It's just taking a recess."

Gene Mauch, an ex-Royal, was hired to manage the Montreal Expos, before the team even had a logo.

One last look at a classic ballpark. Delorimier Downs on a warm summer night.

Extra Innings
Putting it all Together

18

This book would not have been possible without the diligent, perceptive and entertaining reporting of the many Montreal sportswriters who followed the Royals day-in-day-out, season after season, from the earliest days in 1890 to the club's demise 70 years later. These reporters left behind what amounts to a daily record of several thousand Royals games. I am grateful to those who covered the team's Atwater Park years in anonymity (before the invention of the by-line), and to their successors whose

Lloyd "Mickey" McGowan, the dean of the Royals' press corps, captured the fun of baseball in his reporting. Courtesy Don McGowan.

Dink Carroll provided invaluable insights for thousands of Montreal sports fans who read his stories everyday.

names became well-known to the city's sports fans. I am especially indebted to two members of the Royals' press corps who, unfortunately, are no longer with us: Lloyd "Mickey" McGowan of the Montreal Star and Dink Carroll of the (Montreal) Gazette.

McGowan was a hard-living, cigar-smoking night-owl who covered the club from the inauguration of Delorimier Stadium, in 1928, to the final out 33 years later. He had an unparalleled talent for making his readers feel as if they were watching the action themselves while he occasionally leaned over to make an observation or whisper the latest baseball gossip in their ear. Carroll, a former McGill University football player and media man for the Royals' arch rivals, the Toronto Maple Leafs, joined the Gazette in the mid-1940's. A quiet man, he didn't often socialize with his hard-drinking colleagues, and contributed literary reviews to the Saturday edition of the Gazette—in addition to his usual write-up of a baseball, hockey or football game and his "Playing the Field" sports column. If McGowan was a Runyon-esque caricaturist, Carroll was a studious observer who paid attention to every detail. Had they been a broadcasting team, Carroll would have done the play-by-play, McGowan the color commentary, and it would have been a wonderful show. Their energy and skill, along with that of their colleagues, allowed me feel as if I was covering the Royals myself through their stories, even though I was only a year old when the team folded.

It would also have been impossible to write a history of the Royals without the help of the many former players, managers, team executives and nostalgic former fans who shared their memories with me and, in some cases, lent me their cherished Royals souvenirs to be reproduced in this book. I thank them all.

Thanks to Robert Matheson and Brodie Snyder who provided valuable siggestions. And a special thanks to Terry Scott, a sportswriter in the tradition of McGowan and Carroll, who edited the manuscript with insight, precision, creativity and humor. He improved the book considerably.

I'd also like to thank Mary Hughson, for her wonderful design and desk-top publishing skills. Mary's talent, professionalism and sheer hard work gave the book the exact look and feel I always hoped it would have.

Finally, I would like to express my sincere appreciation to Terry Mosher, the manager of the team, who supported the project from the very beginning and guided it through every slump and streak and showed a skilled and steady hand in managing a rookie. You were right, Terry; somehow it all got done!

William Brown
August 1996

Royals Statistics

INTERNATIONAL LEAGUE AWARDS

BATTING CHAMPIONS

1904: Joe Yeager (.332)
1908: Jimmy "Sheriff" Jones (.309)
1916: James Smythe (.344)
1946: Jackie Robinson (.349)
1949: Bobby Morgan (.337)*
1953: Sandy Amoros (.353)
1955: Rocky Nelson (.364)**
1956: Clyde Parris (.321)
* Won Most Valuable Player Award (MVP)
** Won Triple Crown and MVP

HOME RUN CHAMPIONS

1915: Lucky Whiteman (14)
1917: H.R. Damrau (16)
1942: Les Burge (28)
1954: Rocky Nelson (31)
1955: Rocky Nelson (37)*
1960: Joe Altobelli (31)
*Won Triple Crown and MVP

RBI LEADERS (first awarded 1925)

1953: Rocky Nelson (136)
1955: Rocky Nelson (130)*
1960: Joe Altobelli (105)
*Won Triple Crown and MVP

STOLEN BASE LEADERS

1911: Ward Miller (63)
1930: Henry "Hinkey" Haines (45)
1934: Harvey Walker (33)
1941: Paul Campbell (24)
1946: Marvin Rackley (65)
1948: Sam Jethroe (18)*
1949: Sam Jethroe (89)
1951: Hector Rodriguez (26)
1952: Jim Gilliam (18)**
*Tied with John Welaj of Toronto Maple Leafs
** Won MVP

PITCHERS—Most Wins

1916: Leon Cadore (25)
1929: Elon "Chief" Hogsett (22)
1935: Pete Appleton (23)
1945: Jean-Pierre Roy (25)
1946: Steve Nagy (17)
1948: Jack Banta (19—tied Reeder, Rochester)
1954: Ed Roebuck and Ken Lehman (18)
1955: Ken Lehman (22)
1958: Tommy Lasorda (18)*
*Won Most Valuable Pitcher Award

PITCHERS—Most strikeouts

1945: Jean-Pierre Roy (139)
1947: Jack Banta (199)
1948: Jack Banta (193)
1949: Dan Bankhead (176)

PITCHERS—Best winning percentage

1930: Roy Buckalew (13-4, .765)
1935: Pete Appleton (23-9, .719)
1945: Les Webber (11-3, .786)
1946: Steve Nagy (17-4, .810)
1947: Ed Heusser (19-3, .864)
1948: Don Newcombe (17-6, .739)
1951: Mal Mallette (10-2, .833)
1952: Mal Mallette (13-2, .867)

PITCHERS—Lowest ERA

1945: Les Webber (1.88)

MOST VALUABLE PLAYER

(First awarded 1932. Voted on by IL sportswriters.)

1948: Jimmy Bloodworth, 2B
(.294, 24 HR, 99 RBI, .976 Fielding
Percentage; second in league).

1949: Bobby Morgan, SS
(.337, 19 HR, 112 RBI)*

1952: Jim Gilliam, 2B-OF
(.301, 9 HR, 112 RBI)**

1953: Rocky Nelson, 1B
(.308, 34 HR, 136 RBI)***

1955: Rocky Nelson, 1B
(.364, 37 HR, 130 RBI)****

* Won batting title

** Won stolen base title

*** Won RBI title

**** Won Triple Crown

ROOKIE OF THE YEAR

(First awarded 1950. Voted on by IL sportswriters.)

1951: Hector Rodriguez, 3B
(.302, 8 HR, 95 RBI, 26 stolen bases)*

1956: Fred Kipp, P
(20-7, 127 strikeouts, 3.33 ERA)

* Won stolen base title

MOST VALUABLE PITCHER

(First awarded 1953. Voted on by IL sportswriters.)

1958: Tommy Lasorda (18-6, 2.50 ERA)

MONTREAL ROYALS IN THE MAJOR LEAGUE BASEBALL HALL OF FAME

Walter Alston (manager, 1950-1953)

Ed Barrow (manager, 1904, 1910)

Roy Campanella (1947)

Roberto Clemente (1954)

Jocko Conlan (1931-1932)

Don Drysdale (1955)

Burleigh Grimes (manager, 1939)

Waite Hoyt (1917)

Rabbit Maranville (manager, 1937-1938)

Jackie Robinson (1946)

Duke Snider (1948)

I. L. PENNANT-WINNING SEASONS FOR MONTREAL ROYALS

YEAR	RECORD	PCT.
1898*	64-48	.586
1935	92- 62	.597
1945	95-58	.621
1946	100-54	.649
1948	94-59	.614
1951	95-59	.617
1952	95-56	.629
1955	95-59	.617
1958	90-63	.588

*IL temporarily known as Eastern League.

MONTREAL ROYALS POST-SEASON RECORDS – GOVERNORS' CUP

1935: ROYALS over Buffalo 4 games to 2. Syracuse over ROYALS 4 games to 3.
1937: Baltimore over ROYALS 4 games to 1.
1941: ROYALS over Buffalo 4 games to 3. ROYALS over Newark 4 games to 3.
(Won Governors' Cup.)
1942: Syracuse over ROYALS 4 games to 1.
1943: Toronto over ROYALS 4 games to 0.
1945: ROYALS over Baltimore 4 games to 3. Newark over ROYALS 4 games to 3.
1946: ROYALS over Newark 4 games to 2. ROYALS over Syracuse 4 games to 1.
(Won Governors' Cup and Junior World Series.)
1947: Syracuse over ROYALS 4 games to 0.
1948: ROYALS over Rochester 4 games to 3. ROYALS over Syracuse 4 games to 1.
(Won Governors' Cup and Junior World Series.)
1949: ROYALS over Rochester 4 games to 0. ROYALS overt Buffalo 4 games to 0.
(Won Governors' Cup.)
1950: Baltimore over ROYALS 4 games to 3.
1951: ROYALS over Buffalo 4 games to 0.

ROYALS over Syracuse 4 games to 1.
(Won Governors' Cup.)
1952: ROYALS over Toronto 4 games to 3.
Rochester over ROYALS 4 games to 2.
1953: ROYALS over Buffalo 4 games to 2.
ROYALS over Rochester 4 games to 0.
(Won Governors' Cup and Junior World Series.)
1954: ROYALS over Rochester 4 games to 2.
Syracuse over ROYALS 4 games to 3.
1955: Rochester over ROYALS 4 games to 1.
1956: Toronto over ROYALS 4 games to 1.
1958: ROYALS over Columbus 4 games to 3.
ROYALS over Toronto 4 gamed to 1.
(Won Governors' Cup.)

MONTREAL ROYALS JUNIOR WORLD SERIES APPEARANCES

1941: Columbus over ROYALS 4 games to 2.
1946: ROYALS over Louisville 4 games to 2.
1948: ROYALS over St. Paul 4 games to 1.
1949: Indianapolis over ROYALS 4 games to 2.
1951: Milwaukee over ROYALS 4 games to 2.
1953: ROYALS over Kansas City 4 games to 1.
1958: Minneapolis over ROYALS 4 games to 0.

MONTREAL ROYALS RECORD

YEAR	RECORD	PCT	FINISH
1897*	49-76	.392	Seventh
1898	68-48	.586	First
1899	62-51	.549	Second
1900	54-72	.429	Seventh
1901	65-67	.492	Sixth
1902	59-77	.434	Sixth
1903**	37-95	.280	Seventh
1904	67-62	.519	Fifth
1905	56-80	.412	Sixth
1906	57-83	.407	Seventh
1907	46-85	.351	Eighth
1908	64-75	.461	Fifth
1909	68-83	.450	Sixth
1910	71-80	.470	Fifth
1911	72-80	.474	Fifth
1912	71-81	.467	Sixth
1913	74-77	.490	Fifth
1914	60-89	.403	Seventh
1915	67-70	.489	Fifth
1916	75-64	.539	Third
1917	56-94	.373	Seventh
1928	84-84	.500	Fifth
1929	88-79	.527	Fourth
1930	96-72	.571	Third
1931	85-80	.515	Fourth
1932	90-78	.536	Fourth
1933	81-84	.490	Sixth
1934	73-77	.487	Sixth
1935	92-62	.597	First
1936	71-81	.467	Sixth
1937	82-67	.550	Second
1938	69-84	.451	Sixth
1939	64-88	.421	Seventh
1940	80-80	.500	Fifth
1941	90-64	.584	Second
1942	82-71	.536	Second
1943	76-76	.500	Fourth
1944	73-80	.477	Sixth
1945	95-58	.621	First
1946	100-54	.649	First
1947	93-60	.608	Second
1948	94-59	.614	First
1949	84-70	.545	Third
1950	86-67	.562	Second
1951	95-59	.617	First
1952	95-56	.629	First
1953	89-63	.586	Second
1954	88-66	.571	Second
1955	95-59	.617	First
1956	80-72	.526	Fourth
1957	68-86	.442	Eighth
1958	90-63	.588	First
1959	72-82	.468	Sixth
1960	62-92	.403	Eighth

*Team started season in Rochester
**Team started season in Worcester

MONTREAL ROYALS
MANAGERS

1897	George Weidman* Charles Dooley*		1934	Oscar Roettger* Frank Shaughnessy
1898	Charles Dooley*		1935	Frank Shaughnessy
1899	Charles Dooley*		1936	Frank Shaughnessy Harry Smythe*
1900	Charles Dooley*		1937	Walter "Rabbit" Maranville
1901	Charles Dooley*		1938	Walter "Rabbit" Maranville Alex Hooks*
1902	Charles Dooley*			
1903	Eugene DeMontreville*		1939	Burleigh Grimes
1904	Charles Atherton* Edward Barrow		1940	Clyde Sukeforth
1905	James Bannon*		1941	Clyde Sukeforth
1906	James Bannon* Malachi Kittridge*		1942	Clyde Sukeforth
			1943	Lafayette "Fresco" Thompson
1907	Malachi Kittridge* James Morgan*		1944	Bruno Betzel
1908	James "Doc" Casey*		1945	Bruno Betzel
1909	James "Doc" Casey*		1946	Clay Hopper
1910	Edward Barrow		1947	Clay Hopper
1911	Edward McCafferty		1948	Clay Hopper
1912	William Lush* William "Kitty" Bransfield*		1949	Clay Hopper
			1950	Walter Alston
1913	William "Kitty" Bransfield*		1951	Walter Alston
1914	William "Kitty" Bransfield* Daniel Howley*		1952	Walter Alston
			1953	Walter Alston
1915	Daniel Howley*		1954	Max Macon
1916	Daniel Howley*		1955	Greg Mulleavy
1917	Daniel Howley*		1956	Greg Mulleavy
1928	George Stallings Edward Holly		1957	Greg Mulleavy Al Campanis Al Ronning Tommy Holmes
1929	Edward Holly			
1930	Edward Holly			
1931	Edward Holly		1958	Clay Bryant
1932	Edward Holly Walter "Doc" Gautreau*		1959	Clay Bryant
			1960	Clay Bryant
1933	Walter "Doc" Gautreau* Oscar Roettger*			

* Player-Manager

Bibliography

BOOKS

ALLEN, Maury: *Jackie Robinson, A Life Remembered.* Franklin Watts. New York, 1987.

ALSTON, Walter and BURICK, Si; *Alston and The Dodgers.* Doubleday & Company, 1966.

BENSON, Michael: *Ballparks of North America: A Comprehensive Guide to Baseball Grounds, Yards and Stadiums 1845 to Present.* McFarland and Company Inc. Jefferson, N.C., 1989.

BLOUIN, Jean: Roland Beaupre: *Monsieur Baseball se Raconte.* Les Presses Libres. Montreal, 1980.

CAMPANELLA, Roy: *It's Good To Be Alive.* Little, Brown & Company. Boston, 1959.

CLIFTON, Merritt: *The Quebec Provincial League: Disorganized Baseball.* Samisdat.

DRYSDALE, Don with VERDI, Bob: *Once a Bum, Always a Dodger.* St. Martin's Press. New York, 1990.

FALKNER, David: *Great Time Coming.* Simon and Schuster. New York, 1995.

FOX, Larry: *Last to First: The Story of The Mets.* Associated Features Inc., Harper and Row Publishers. New York, 1970.

GOSSELIN, Gérard: *The Montreal Royals Since 1890* . Montreal, circa 1948.

HUMBER, William: *Diamonds of The North: A Concise History of Baseball in Canada.* Oxford University Press. Don Mills, Ontario, 1995.

JEDWAB, JACK: *Jackie Robinson's Unforgettable Season of Baseball In Montreal.* Les Editions Images. Montreal, 1996.

JENKINS, Kathleen: *Montreal: Island City of The St. Lawrence.* Doubleday & Company, Inc. Garden City, New York, 1966.

KAHN, Roger: *The Boys of Summer.* Signet. New York, 1973

KENDALL, Brian: *Great Moments In Canadian Baseball.* Lester Publishing Limited. Toronto, 1995.

KOPPETT, Leonard: *The Man in The Dugout.* Crown Publishers Inc. New York, 1993.

LASORDA, Tommy and FISHER, David: *The Artful Dodger.* Arbor House. New York, 1988.

O'NEAL, Bill: *The International League.* Eakin Press. Austin, Texas, 1992.

O'NEAL, Bill: *The Pacific Coast League.* Eakin Press. Austin, Texas, 1990.

O'NEAL, Bill: *The American Association.* Eakin Press. Austin, Texas, 1991.

PARADIS, Jean-Marc: *100 Ans de Baseball a Trois Rivieres.* Trois Rivieres, 1989.

RILEY, Dan (Editor): *The Dodgers Reader.* Houghton Mifflin Company. New York, 1992. Excerpts consulted are from:
   –*New York City Baseball: 1947-1957* by Harvey Frommer.
   –*Bums: An Oral History of the Brooklyn Dodgers* by Peter Golenbock.
   –*The Dodgers Move West* by Neil J. Sullivan.
   –*Nice Guys Finish Last* by Leo Durocher.

ROBINSON, Jackie: *I Never Had it Made* (As told to Alfred Duckett). The Ecco Press. Hopewell, New Jersey, 1972.

ROWAN, Carl T. with ROBINSON, Jackie: *Wait Till Next Year: The Story of Jackie Robinson.* Randon House. New York, 1960.

SNIDER, Duke, with GILBERT, Bill: *The Duke of Flatbush.* Kensington Publishing Corp. New York, 1988.

SUGAR, Bert Randolph: *Baseball's 50 Greatest Games.* JG Press, 1986.

TYGIEL, Jules: *Baseball's Great Experiment: Jackie Robinson and His Legacy.* Oxford University Press. New York, 1983.

WAGENHEIM, Kal: *Clemente.* Praeger Publishing, 1973.

ARTICLES

BEAUCHAMP, Jacques: "Sparky Anderson Est L'Inspiration No.1 Des Royaux. "*Montreal Royals Programme, 1959.*

CHAMPAGNE, Gérard: "Les Superstitions Parmi Les Jouers du Montreal. " *Montreal Royals Programme, 1958.*

FISHER, Red: "Man of Many Jobs. " *Montreal Royals Programme,1959.*

McMURRAY, Graeme: "Royals' Success Formula This Year. " *Montreal Royals Programme, 1958.*

RICHLER, Mordecai: "Up From The Minors In Montreal." The Ultimate Baseball Book. Daniel Okrent and Harris Levine. Houghton Mifflin. Boston, 1979.

SÉGUIN, Phil: "Pas de Nouveaux Records Pour Les Royaux Cette Saison." *Montreal Royals Programme, 1958.*

SOULIÈRE, Bert: "Campanella Fait Ses Eloges de Jackie Robinson, Branch Rickey et Montreal." *Montreal Royals Programme,1959.*

VERNER, Robert: "Pro Baseball in Montreal Part I—1897-1917." *Expos Baseball Magazine.* Volume One, 1975.

VERNER, Robert: "Pro Baseball in Montreal Part II—1928-1960." *Expos Baseball Magazine.* Volume Two, 1975.

NEWSPAPERS

The Gazette, Montreal (1890-1960)

The Montreal Daily Star (1890-1960)

Le Canada (1928, 1945, 1946)

The New York Times (1945, 1946)

Le Devoir (1960)

The Sherbrooke Daily Record (1928)

The Montreal Daily News (Series of articles entitled "Quebecers in the Majors" by Danny Gallagher. Sept. 6-Oct.1, 1988).

REFERENCE MATERIAL

Total Baseball:
The Ultimate Encyclopedia of Baseball. Edited by Pete Palmer and John Thorn. Harper Collins Publishers, third edition, 1993. Articles consulted:
  –"The History of Major League Baseball" by David Q. Voigt.
  –"Team Histories" by Frederick Ivor-Campbell.
  –"Jackie Robinson's Signing: The Real, Untold Story" by John Thorn and Jules Tygiel.
  –"Black Ball" by Jules Tygiel.
  –"The 100 Greatest Players" by Michael Gershman.
  –"Rival Leagues" by David Pietrusza.
  –"Night Baseball" by David Pietrusza.
  –"The Minor Leagues" by Bob Hoie.
  –"Baseball in Canada" by Bruce L. Prentice and Merritt Clifton.

The Ballplayers: Baseball's Ultimate Biographical Reference. Edited by Mike Shatzkin. Created and developed by Mike Shatzkin and Jim Charlton. Arbor House-William Morrow. New York, 1990.

Who's Who in Professional Baseball. By Martin J. Jones and Gene Karst. Arlington House. New Rochelle, New York, 1973.

Players of Cooperstown: Baseball's Hall of Fame. Publications International Limited. Lincolnwood, Illinois, 1992.

Reach's Official Base Ball Guide (1897-1900).

Reach's Official American League Guide (1901-1904).

The Reach Official American League Guide (1905-1917).

Spalding Official Base Ball Guide (1928-1936, 1938).

Reach Official American League Base Ball Guide (1937).

Spalding-Reach Official Base Ball Guide (1939, 1940).

Official Baseball Record Book (1941).

Baseball Guide and Record Book (1942-1960).

Index